DATE DUE

INTERNATIONAL CRIMINAL ACCOUNTABILITY
AND THE RIGHTS OF CHILDREN

This book is based on the annual Conference

FROM PEACE TO JUSTICE

"International Criminal Accountability and the Rights of Children"

held on 17–18 March 2005 in The Hague, The Netherlands

jointly organized by

**THE HAGUE
ACADEMIC COALITION**

and

FROM PEACE TO JUSTICE SERIES

INTERNATIONAL CRIMINAL ACCOUNTABILITY AND THE RIGHTS OF CHILDREN

Edited by

Karin Arts and Vesselin Popovski

Hague Academic Press

An Imprint of T·M·C·ASSER PRESS

Published by Hague Academic Press, an imprint of T·M·C·Asser press
P.O.Box 16163, 2500 BD The Hague, The Netherlands

<www.asserpress.nl>

T·M·C·Asser press' English language books are distributed exclusively by:

Cambridge University Press, The Edinburgh Building, Shaftesbury Road,
Cambridge CB2 2RU, UK,
or
for customers in the USA, Canada and Mexico:
Cambridge University Press, 100 Brook Hill Drive, West Nyack, NY 10994-2133, USA

<www.cambridge.org>

ISBN 10: 90-6704-227-7
ISBN 13: 978-90-6704-227-7

Cover photograph: ANP Photo © George Mollering

PRINTED IN THE NETHERLANDS

FOREWORD

Louk Box*

This book is the fruit of collaboration between the United Nations University (UNU), the Institute of Social Studies (ISS) and the Hague Academic Coalition (HAC).[1] The theme 'International Criminal Accountability and the Rights of Children', selected by the UNU and ISS, was inspired by the recent increased attention for the situation of children all over the world, combined with a deep concern about continued serious abuses of basic children's rights. International criminal law and accountability mechanisms are potentially important instruments in the fight for peace and justice. The needs and rights of children in this domain are of crucial importance, but have only recently become the subject of prominent attention.

For the UNU this theme provided a solid continuation of its earlier work in the sphere of international accountability. In November 2001 it had organised – in collaboration with the Netherlands Institute of Human Rights (SIM, Utrecht University) – an international conference under the theme 'From a Culture of Impunity to a Culture of Accountability';[2] and in July 2004 another international conference on 'Accountability for Atrocity' in Galway, Ireland at the Irish Centre for Human Rights. For the ISS the theme fitted very well with its teaching and research activities in the spheres of international law, conflict, human rights and children's rights, as profiled, among others, through its international Centre for Child and Youth Studies (iCCYS).

The HAC Annual Conference 2005 (17-18 March in The Hague) was devoted entirely to the topic of international criminal accountability and the rights of children and it provided a meeting ground for practitioners and academics involved in this domain, who otherwise only have rare opportunities to meet. It linked two conceptual and practical concerns. Firstly, the protection of children's rights, as codified in international law, against serious abuses, such as the abduction and (forced) recruitment of child soldiers, trafficking or sexual exploitation. Secondly, the development of international criminal law and other accountability mechanisms and their applicability for the protection of children's rights.

This book reflects on child rights-related aspects of international criminal accountability issues, and takes stock of relevant developments in current international human rights and humanitarian law, and in international criminal legal practice,

---

* Rector of the International Institute of Social Studies (ISS), The Hague, the Netherlands.
[1] See pp. VII–VIII for information about UNU and the HAC.
[2] See R. Thakur and P. Malcontent (eds.), *From Sovereign Impunity to International Accountability: The Search for Justice in World of States*, Tokyo, United Nations University Press 2004.

including that of the International Criminal Court and the Special Court for Sierra Leone. It is the second volume to present a comprehensive overview of relevant practice and theoretical ideas on this topic.[3] This overview is written by prominent practitioners who are shaping current practice and by academics with a special involvement in this field. The book will prove useful to a broader range of people concerned with children's rights, be they part of governmental institutions, NGOs and civil society organisations, international organisations, universities, or elsewhere.

This book would not have seen the light of day without the special efforts of persons and organisations whom I would like to thank specifically for their support. Within UNU, Hans van Ginkel, Ramesh Thakur, Vesselin Popovski and Edward Newman were instrumental. In ISS, Karin Arts and Janna van der Meulen proved to be very resourceful and creative as regards both the substantive and organisational tasks that this venture posed. Besides the UNU, ISS and HAC, the City of The Hague and the Kennisalliantie, Province of Zuid Holland, were major sponsors of the 2005 Conference. The Institut Français des Pays Bas, Agence Francophonie and the law firms Houthoff Buruma, de Brauw Blackstone Westbroek and Wladimiroff en Waling were additional sponsors. Finally, Marjolijn Bastiaans of Asser Press was a great help in producing this book.

In brief: a book that epitomizes the role of The Hague as a City of Peace and Justice. A city that brings together practitioners in international courts with academics from all over the world. May it provide the forum that a past UN Secretary-General once called The Legal Capital of the World.

---

[3] *International Criminal Justice and Children* (Rome, No Peace Without Justice and UNICEF Innocenti Research Centre 2002) probably being the first.

THE HAGUE ACADEMIC COALITION AND THE UNITED NATIONS UNIVERSITY

THE HAGUE ACADEMIC COALITION (HAC)

The Hague Academic Coaltion is a consortium of academic institutions in the fields of international relations, international law and international development. It was established to promote collaborative efforts between these six institutions. Specifically, the HAC intends to promote research, education and public debate in support of the development of international policy, law, governance and international negotiations towards justice, peace and sustainable development.

As part of this broad objective, the HAC in particular seeks to support the work of the various international courts, tribunals and other international organisations based in The Hague. Joint HAC activities in support of this mission include the organization of annual conferences and other public events in The Hague, the delivery of (postgraduate) courses, research, consultancy activities, publications and management of the Hague Justice Portal.

Within the HAC's present membership, the Carnegie Foundation, the Grotius Centre (Leiden University, Campus Den Haag), The Hague Institute for the Internationalisation of Law (HIIL) and the T.M.C. Asser Instituut work in the field of international (and European) law, whereas the Netherlands Institute for International Relations 'Clingendael' and the Institute of Social Studies (ISS) focus on international relations, international political economy and development studies. For further information, see <http://www.haguejusticeportal.net>.

UNITED NATIONS UNIVERSITY (UNU), TOKYO

United Nations University is an organ of the United Nations established by the General Assembly in 1972 to be an international community of scholars engaged in research, advanced training, and the dissemination of knowledge related to the pressing global problems of human survival, development, and welfare. Its activities focus mainly on the areas of peace and governance, environment and sustainable development, and science and technology in relation to human welfare. The University operates through a worldwide network of research and postgraduate training centres, with its planning and coordinating headquarters in Tokyo.

TABLE OF CONTENTS

LIST OF ABBREVIATIONS

AFRC	Armed Forces Revolutionary Council (Sierra Leone)
CAAC	Children and Armed Conflict
CDF	Civil Defense Forces (Sierra Leone)
CMC	Children's Municipal Council
CRC	United Nations Convention on the Rights of the Child
DDR	Disarmament, Demobilisation and Reintegration
DRC	Democratic Republic of Congo
ECHR	European Convention on Human Rights
ECOSOC	Economic and Social Council (of the United Nation)
EctHR	European Court of Human Rights
EHRR	European Human Rights Reports
EPRDF	Ethiopian Peoples' Revolutionary Democratic Front
FGM/C	Female Genital Mutilation/Cutting
HDI	Human Development Index
ICC	International Criminal Court
ICRC	International Committee of the Red Cross
ICTR	International Criminal Tribunal for Rwanda
ICTY	International Criminal Tribunal for the former Yugoslavia
IHL	International Humanitarian Law
ILO	International Labour Organization
KFOR	Kosovo Force (NATO)
LRA	Lord's Resistance Army (Uganda)
MLC	Movement for the Liberation of Congo
NATO	North Atlantic Treaty Organization
NGO	Non-Governmental Organisation
OJ	Official Journal of the European Communities
OTP	Office of the Prosecutor

POWs   Prisoners of War

RCD-N   Congolese Rally for Democracy-National
RUF   Revolutionary United Front (Sierra Leone)

SBU   Small Boys Unit
SCSL   Special Court for Sierra Leone
SGU   Small Girls Unit
SLP   Sierra Leonean Police

TRC   Truth and Reconciliation Commission

UNAMSIL   United Nations Mission in Sierra Leone
UN Doc.   United Nations Document
UNDP   United Nations Development Programme
UNGA   United Nations General Assembly
UNICEF   United Nations Children's Fund
UNITA   National Union for Total Independence of Angola
UNTS   United Nations Treaty Series
UNSC   United Nations Security Council
UPC   Union of Congolese Patriots

VWS   Victims and Witnesses Section

Part I
International Law,
Criminal Accountability
and the Rights of the Child

Chapter 1
GENERAL INTRODUCTION: A CHILD RIGHTS-BASED APPROACH TO INTERNATIONAL CRIMINAL ACCOUNTABILITY

Karin Arts*

1. INTRODUCTION

International crimes and other forms of violence against children are daily realities in today's world. It is disturbing that children and young persons are increasingly targeted deliberately and routinely for murder, rape, abduction, mutilation, recruitment as child soldiers, trafficking, sexual exploitation and many other forms of abuse. Particularly in situations of armed conflict and in complex emergencies, children prove to be vulnerable and at risk. In armed conflict, which is the main context of this book, direct and indirect risks occur for children as a result of the ongoing fighting. While some people may tend to think first of death or injury as a direct result of armed attacks (for example of civilian casualties and child soldiers), there is a host of evidence that shows that poverty, the lack of social cohesion, the lack of livelihood security, malnutrition and diseases take their toll among much larger numbers of children.[1] According to UNICEF:

> 'During emergencies, children are especially vulnerable to disease, malnutrition and violence. In the last decade, more than 2 million children have died as a direct result of armed conflict, and more than three times that number have been permanently disabled or seriously injured. An estimated 20 million children have been forced to flee their homes, and more than 1 million have been orphaned or separated from their families. Some 300,000 child soldiers – boys and girls under the age of 18 – are involved in more than 30 conflicts worldwide.'[2]

---

* Associate Professor in International Law and Development, Institute of Social Studies (ISS), The Hague, the Netherlands; staff member of the ISS/ICDI international Centre for Child and Youth Studies (iCCYS) and Convenor of the ISS MA Programme 'Human Rights, Development and Social Justice'.

[1] See, e.g., G. Machel, et al., *The Impact of War on Children : A Review of Progress since the 1996 United Nations Report on the Impact of Armed Conflict on Children* (London, Hurst 2001) p. 2; H. Cheuzeville, *Kadogo, Enfants des Guerres d'Afriques Centrale* (Paris, l'Harmattan 2003) e.g., p. 139.

[2] UNICEF, *Humanitarian Action Report 2005* (New York, UNICEF 2005) p. VII.

K. Arts & V. Popovski (eds.), International Criminal Accountability and the Rights of Children
© *2006, Hague Academic Coalition, The Hague, The Netherlands and the Authors*

In its *State of the World's Children 2006*, UNICEF presented armed conflict as dramatically escalating the risk of exclusion for children and thus seriously jeopardizing their development potential:

> 'Armed conflict causes children to miss out on their childhood in a multitude of ways. Children recruited as soldiers are denied education and protection, and are often unable to access essential health-care services. Those who are displaced, refugees or separated from their families face similar deprivations. Conflict heightens the risk of children being exposed to abuse, violence and exploitation, with sexual violence often employed as a weapon of war. Even those children who are able to remain with their families, in their own homes, may face greater risk of exclusion because of the destruction of physical infrastructure, strains on health-care and education systems, workers and supplies, and increasing personal insecurity caused by the conflict or its remnants – such as landmines and unexploded ordnance.'[3]

According to the same report, while 'firm evidence of armed conflict on children's exclusion is limited ... the available linkages are indicative of the extent of exclusion – and alarming.'[4] The examples of Darfur, the Democratic Republic of Congo, Sierra Leone, the Philippines, Nepal, Colombia, and many others tragically illustrate UNICEF's findings.

To the extent that the acts involved amount to international crimes or gross violations of human rights, the question arises whether international criminal accountability mechanisms and/or human rights-based responses meet the rights and needs of the children involved, either as victims/survivors or as perpetrators. For, simultaneously with the above-sketched increasing focus on children for abuse in times of armed conflict, international attention for the position of children and their rights has also clearly been substantially increasing in the last fifteen to twenty years. Major landmarks in this process were the adoption of the United Nations Convention on the Rights of the Child (CRC) in 1989, followed by its entry into force with record speed – within less than a year thereafter – and its near to universal ratification.[5] In the year 2000 the CRC was complemented by two Optional Protocols, addressing the involvement of children in armed conflict and the sale of children, child prostitution and child pornography, respectively.[6] In the Plan of Action in-

---

[3] UNICEF, *The State of the World's Children 2006: Excluded and Invisible* (New York, UNICEF 2005), p. 14.

[4] Ibid., p. 15. 'Of the 12 countries where 20 per cent or more of the children die before the age of five, nine have suffered a major armed conflict in the past five years ..., and 11 of the 20 countries with the most elevated rates of under-five mortality have experienced major armed conflict since 1990. Armed conflict also has devastating effects on primary school enrolment and attendance.' Ibid.

[5] The UN Convention on the Rights of the Child entered into force on 2 September 1990. As of 1 January 2006 192 states (all the states in the world, except Somalia and the United States of America) had ratified the Convention, with the large majority of ratifications having been completed in the early 1990s. However, some qualification of this successful record is required as a range of ratifications have been accompanied by rather far-reaching reservations. For details see <http://untreaty.un.org or http://www.ohchr.org/english/countries/ratification/11.htm>.

[6] The Optional Protocol on Armed Conflict entered into force on 12 February 2002, and as of 1 January 2006 it had been ratified by 105 states. The Optional Protocol on Sale of Children, Child

corporated in *A World Fit for Children*, adopted by the UN General Assembly's Special Session on Children in May 2002, the world's leaders called for the ending of 'impunity for all crimes against children by bringing perpetrators to justice and publicizing the penalties for such crimes.'[7] More precisely still, reference was made to the need to:

'Put an end to impunity, prosecute those responsible for genocide, crimes against humanity, and war crimes and exclude, where feasible, these crimes from amnesty provisions and amnesty legislation, and ensure that whenever post-conflict truth and justice-seeking mechanisms are established, serious abuses involving children are addressed and that appropriate child-sensitive procedures are provided.' [para 23.]

'[p]romote the establishment of prevention, support and caring services as well as justice systems specifically applicable to children, taking into account the principles of restorative justice and fully safeguard children's rights and provide specially trained staff that promote children's reintegration into society.'[8]

In addition to this, *A World Fit for Children* contained more specific and elaborate sections on protection from armed conflict and the elimination of trafficking and sexual exploitation of children.

Another indication of the rising international awareness of the pervasiveness of violence against children and of the need to find ways to counter this, is found in United Nations Security Council debates and resolutions on children and armed conflict. In 2000 the Council qualified 'the deliberate targeting of civilian populations or other protected persons, including children, and the committing of systematic, flagrant and widespread violations of international humanitarian and human rights law, including that relating to children', when occurring in situations of armed conflict, as possibly constituting 'a threat to international peace and security'.[9] Obviously, this classification opens the door to mandatory action under Chapter VII of the United Nations Charter. In April 2004, Security Council Resolution 1539 referred to 'the responsibilities of States to end impunity and to prosecute those responsible for genocide, crimes against humanity, war crimes and other egregious crimes perpetrated against children.'[10] In the same resolution the Security Council also strongly condemned:

'the recruitment and use of child soldiers ..., killing and maiming of children, rape and other sexual violence mostly committed against girls, abduction and forced replacement, denial of humanitarian access to children, attacks against schools and hospitals as well as trafficking, forced labour, all forms of slavery and all other violations and abuses committed against children affected by armed conflict;'[11]

Prostitution and Pornography entered into force on 18 January 2002, and as of 1 January 2006 it had been ratified by 100 states. See ibid.

[7] 'A World Fit for Children', UNGA Resolution S-27/2, 10 May 2002, para. 44(4).

[8] Ibid., para. 44(7).

[9] UN Security Council Resolution 1314, 11 August 2000, para. 9.

[10] UN Security Council Resolution 1539, 22 April 2004, fourth preambular paragraph.

[11] Ibid., para. 1.

In July 2005 the Security Council extended its commitment further still by providing for the establishment of a monitoring and reporting system on children and armed conflict, as had been proposed earlier on by Secretary-General Kofi Annan. This system is meant 'to collect and provide timely, objective, accurate and reliable information on the recruitment and use of child soldiers in violation of applicable international law and on other violations and abuses committed against children affected by armed conflict'.[12] The UN Secretary-General will report the information compiled in this way to the General Assembly and to the Security Council. A Security Council working group, composed of all Security Council members, is supposed to review all the outcomes of the system and to advise the Council on possible measures to be taken. This working group held its inaugural session in November 2005.[13]

International criminal accountability mechanisms also increasingly show child-specific features, with the currently operational Special Court for Sierra Leone (SCSL) and the International Criminal Court (ICC) clearly standing out. Here, too, the development of relevant international norms continues. While the Convention on the Rights of the Child contains a range of important provisions, among others on the recruitment of child soldiers and on various juvenile justice-related aspects, it hardly pays explicit attention to the position of child witnesses. However, both for the Special Court and for the International Criminal Court, children are possibly a crucial group of witnesses, especially in cases relating to the recruitment of child soldiers, abduction and other crimes that explicitly target children. These Courts have therefore developed certain special measures and are still elaborating further and/or fine-tuning their policies for working with child victims and witnesses. In July 2005 the Economic and Social Commission of the United Nations made an attempt to further profile the role of child witnesses by adopting a set of 'Guidelines on Justice in Matters involving Child Victims and Witnesses of Crime'. These 'set forth good practice based on the consensus of contemporary knowledge and relevant international and regional norms, standards and principles'. The Guidelines are supposed to assist in the review of domestic laws, procedures and practices; to assist in the design and implementation of relevant legislation, policy, programmes and practices; to guide persons working with child victims and witnesses at the national, regional and international levels; and 'to assist and support those caring for children in dealing sensitively with child victims and witnesses of crime.'[14]

---

[12] UN Security Council Resolution 1612, 26 July 2005, para. 2(a).

[13] 'Landmark first meeting of Security Council working group to end grave violations against children in armed conflict (16 November 2005)', <http://www.crin.org/resources/infoDetail.asp?ID-6614>, as accessed on 24 November 2005. Chapter 3 of this book by Vesselin Popovski analyses these developments in greater detail.

[14] ECOSOC Resolution 2005/20 adopted by the 36th plenary meeting on 22 July 2005, Annex, see paras. 1 and 3.

2. STRUCTURE OF THIS STUDY

This book is one of very few that explore international criminal accountability from the perspective of the rights of children.[15] It presents a range of aspects of the practice of international, regional and national judicial or quasi-judicial bodies addressing international crimes or criminal matters affecting children. The chapters involved are arranged in three Parts. After a comprehensive overview of the contents of Part I, Parts II and III will each be briefly presented in this section as well. Individual chapters that appear in these Parts will be further referred to in the remaining sections of this introduction.

Part I of this book sets out a number of general aspects relating to international law, criminal accountability and the rights of the child. This introductory chapter, in its last section, examines the implications of using the UN Convention on the Rights of the Child as a framework for analysis and intervention, as so many actors working in the realm of child rights nowadays (claim to) do and as is required if one genuinely seeks to fulfil children's rights. William Schabas, in chapter 2, clarifies the role of courts in the progressive development of relevant international law by analysing the examples of (judicial) efforts to ban the recruitment of child soldiers and to ban capital punishment for juvenile offenders. He analyses how existing customary international law provided credible legal arguments for extending legal protection against both child recruitment and the death penalty for minors. For that purpose, Schabas has reviewed the case law of the Special Court for Sierra Leone (in its path-breaking Hinga Norman Case)[16] and the Supreme Court of the United States of America (in its *Roper* v. *Simmons* Case),[17] and also relevant decisions of the Inter-American Commission on Human Rights. He concludes that, more than the human rights instruments 'proper', the 1949 Fourth Geneva Convention has played a central and crucial role in bringing about the prohibitions on recruitment and capital punishment for children. Vesselin Popovski, in chapter 3 of this book, and David Crane, in chapter 9, concur with this assessment of the significance of the Fourth Geneva Convention, but for different reasons. Respectively, they highlight the fact that the Fourth Geneva Convention was the first to establish special

---

[15] The path-breaking study by G. Machel, 'The Impact of War on Children', *UN Doc.* A/51/306 of 26 August 1996, and to a lesser extent the Machel review report of 2001 (*supra* n. 1), are cited in many publications relating to children and armed conflict, and are referred to in several chapters of this book. They mainly presented the effects of armed conflict on children. At the time they were crucial for mobilising international support for action. *International Criminal Justice and Children* (No Peace Without Justice and UNICEF Innocenti Research Centre, 2002) is the other main publication in this domain. It focussed primarily on the International Criminal Court, but also contains sections on the ICTY and ICTR, on the Special Court for Sierra Leone, on national prosecutions and on non-judicial mechanisms. However, at the time the most relevant practice was yet to be developed.

[16] Special Court for Sierra Leone, *Prosecutor* v. *Norman*, Case No. SCSL-04-14-AR72(E), Decision on Preliminary Motion Based on Lack of Jurisdiction (child recruitment), 31 May 2004.

[17] *Roper* v. *Simmons*, 543 US 551 (2005), 1 March 2005. See also A. James and J. Cecil, 'Out of Step: Juvenile Death Penalty in the United States', 11 *International Journal of Children's Rights*, No. 3 (2003), pp. 291-303.

provisions for the protection of children in times of armed conflict; and the feature of focussing on 'non-combatants', a category including prisoners of war, the ship-wrecked, and civilians (including children).

In chapter 3, after a brief presentation of the applicable international legal frame-work, Vesselin Popovski records the attempts of the UN General Assembly, the Secretary-General, his Special Representative on Children and Armed Conflict, and especially of the Security Council, to step up protection for the rights of the child in (and after) conflict situations. He concludes that the decisions taken through the years are an example of harmonious and relatively successful cooperation between these UN bodies. Chapter 4 by Saudamini Siegrist delves into the experiences with child participation in international criminal accountability mechanisms, on the ba-sis of her reading of the case of the Sierra Leone Truth and Reconciliation Commis-sion.

Children can be victims, but they can also be perpetrators of international crimes. This is taken up most explicitly in Part II, which explores various aspects of the age of criminal responsibility as seen from an international law, national law and a psychological perspective. However, all contributors to this Part of the book (and even to the study at large) share an emphasis on the duality of child violators (al-most) always and obviously being a victim of the armed conflict circumstances as well. This aspect will be taken up further when the implications of child rights-based approaches to international criminal accountability are considered, towards the end of this chapter.

Part III provides a fascinating overview of the unfolding child rights-related practice of relevant international courts. All chapters are produced by persons who themselves were recently, or still are, actively involved in the mechanism or activ-ity presented by them. They include (former) Prosecutors of the International Crimi-nal Court (Luis Moreno-Ocampo) and the Special Court for Sierra Leone (David Crane), and a Deputy Prosecutor of the International Criminal Tribunal for the former Yugoslavia (David Tolbert). A former Head of the Psychosocial Support Team of the Witnesses and Victims Unit of the Special Court for Sierra Leone (An Michels) provides an insight into the SCSL's practice in relation to 'especially vulnerable witnesses'. Jenny Kuper, who among others worked as a legal consultant for the International Committee of the Red Cross, presents her views on the importance of military training and the judicial practice thereon. Finally, Nuala Mole, on the basis of her first-hand experience gained through litigating relevant cases, explores whether the human rights approach to combating crimes against children as practised before the European Court of Human Rights in Strasbourg would provide a relevant learn-ing ground.

Hans van Ginkel, Rector of the United Nations University, ends the book with a set of concluding observations.

3. SCOPE OF THIS STUDY

So far, international criminal accountability mechanisms have mainly responded to crimes that occurred in times of armed conflict. Obviously, crimes against children also take place in post-conflict settings and in peacetime. In fact, problems of trafficking, sexual exploitation, forced labour and the like also abound in non-conflict situations. These abuses have international features, as they are often supported by transnational criminal networks. At the global level we are less equipped for tackling these problems than we perhaps now are in relation to the category of 'recognised' international crimes (genocide, war crimes and crimes against humanity). For, besides international human rights law which in itself has only limited enforcement instruments, it is primarily the national legal system of the 'sovereign' states concerned or affected that is supposed to deal with these problems.

Nevertheless, this book focuses primarily on violations of children's rights in situations of armed conflict that fall within the realm of international criminal law proper. Accordingly, the focus is mainly on war crimes, crimes against humanity and genocide. This leaves many fields of current crime against and injustice towards children uncovered, while, as just mentioned, some of these clearly have strong international features too. From this perspective, it is potentially important to compare the developments in international criminal law and accountability mechanisms with the ways in which other chapters of law, international and national, have been put into action against crimes against children and to identify lessons learned or even 'best practices'. For that reason, it would be interesting in future to engage in comparative research which considers a broader range of examples of action against crimes committed against children. The case examples of combating, through law and otherwise, Female Genital Mutilation/Cutting (FGM/C) and trafficking[18] are obvious research subjects in this regard. Another interesting comparison extends to relevant extraterritorial national legislation and related international judicial cooperation by national authorities. The problem of sex tourism provides the clearest case examples of countries of origin introducing legislation which criminalizes the sexual abuse of minors committed by their citizens abroad and allows for criminal prosecution upon their return home.[19] Some countries have also followed this approach in combating Female Genital Mutilation.[20] A comparative

---

[18] See, e.g., T. Truong and M. Belen Angeles, *Searches for Best Practices to Counter Human Trafficking in Africa: A focus on Women and Children* (Paris, Unesco 2005).

[19] See, e.g., S. Alexander, et al. (eds.), *Extraterritorial Legislation as a Tool to Combat Sexual Exploitation of Children: A Study of 15 Cases* (Amsterdam, ECPAT Europe Law Enforcement Group 1999); and J. Seabrook, *No Hiding Place: Child Sex Tourism and the Role of Extraterritorial Legislation* (London, Zed Books, 2000).

[20] See, e.g., P. Wheeler, 'Eliminating FGM: The Role of Law', 11 *The International Journal of Children's Rights* No. 3 (2003) pp. 257-271; and A. Lewnes (ed.), *Changing a Harmful Social Convention: Female Genital Mutilation/Cutting* (Florence, UNICEF Innocenti Research Centre 2005), pp. 29-30. The latter usefully sees legal responses as part of 'creating an enabling environment for change' and places strong emphasis on the need to understand the social dynamics of FGM. It presents an interesting overview of community-based actions against FGM.

assessment of the ways in which all the various bodies of law, international, regional and national, have been used to counter crimes against children that have
international dimensions, and the extent to which these have been successful, makes
for a very interesting and useful project which, however, is too broad for one book
to take up. Therefore, while here and there opening windows into other fields of
law, this book has its mainstay in international criminal and human (including
children's) rights law.

4.   THE CONVENTION ON THE RIGHTS OF THE CHILD: A FRAMEWORK FOR
     ANALYSIS AND INTERVENTION

In exploring the child rights relevance and responsiveness of international criminal
accountability mechanisms, the United Nations Convention on the Rights of the
Child (CRC) is a crucial starting point. It provides a helpful and appropriate framework for taking up the many challenges that exist in the realm of international
crimes against children. A main reason justifying this remark is the fact that the
Convention spans the various chapters in international law that may play a part in
realising the children's rights that are the subject of this book, and in establishing
international criminal accountability for violations of children's rights. These chapters are in any case: human rights law, international humanitarian law and juvenile
justice law. It is a breakthrough that the CRC unites these all too often still separate
chapters of international law in one comprehensive document. The CRC is widely
embraced as a solid and universal statement of the rights and needs of children in
all parts of the world. As pointed out earlier, the formal ratification record, with all
states except the United States and Somalia now bound by it, is maybe an indicator
of this. In practice perhaps more important is the fact that so many governmental
and non-governmental organisations have incorporated the CRC into their mission
statements and are developing child rights-based angles and approaches to their
daily work.
     The Convention on the Rights of the Child is particularly useful in supplying the
main ingredients of a child rights-based framework within which any form of concrete action or intervention should take place. The most fundamental of such ingredients are the general principles that the Convention prescribes for all action affecting
children and young persons. The main substantive objective of the Convention is to
ensure the survival and development of children. Following UNICEF, many authors and organisations categorize the 'survival and development' of children as
being also a general principle of the CRC. In this author's view, 'survival and development' make up the overall substantive objective of the Convention and are
thus of a different order than the three general CRC principles that (should) direct
the form and orientation of all implementation measures (the best interests of the
child, non-discrimination and participation).
     These three general principles provide the following operational framework. In
order to achieve the survival and development of children, a non-discriminatory
(Article 2) and participatory approach are indispensable (Article 12), and the 'best

interests of the child' (Article 3) will always have to be a primary consideration. Children and young persons exercise their rights within a context of adult guidance and/or direction. The form and nature of such guidance or direction depends on the capacities of the children concerned and on what would be consistent with the evolving capacities of children (Articles 5, 12, 14).[21] These three main general principles are in a triangular relationship with each other and jointly form the main features of child rights-based approaches. A visualization of this argument leads to the following chart:

Chart 1: CRC General Principles
A Framework for Implementing children's rights

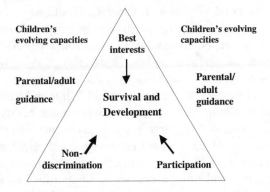

The next section will explore the concrete implications of this CRC framework for taking a child rights-based approach to international criminal accountability matters.

5. IMPLICATIONS OF THE CONVENTION ON THE RIGHTS OF THE CHILD FOR A CHILD RIGHTS-BASED APPROACH TO INTERNATIONAL CRIMINAL ACCOUNTABILITY

As pointed out above, in recent years major advances have been made in the progressive development of international criminal law and the creation of international criminal justice institutions such as the International Criminal Tribunal for the former Yugoslavia and the International Criminal Court. However, despite the overall influence and impact of the United Nations Convention on the Rights of the Child on many other legal and policy fields, for a long time the needs and rights of children in international criminal accountability mechanisms have perhaps been underex-

---

[21] For an analysis of the meaning and implications of the concept of the evolving capacities of the child, see G. Lansdown, *The Evolving Capacities of the Child* (Florence: UNICEF Innocenti Research Centre 2005).

posed. At least since only fairly recently they have been the subject of prominent attention within international criminal law and accountability mechanisms. As observed before, so far, the Special Court for Sierra Leone and the International Criminal Court clearly stand out in their efforts to give due attention to the role and rights of children. They are true pioneers in this field.

The implications of working with a child rights-based approach are manifold.[22] Going by the above framework, such an approach entails in any case that '[i]n all actions concerning children, whether undertaken by public or social welfare institutions, courts of law, administrative authorities or legislative bodies, the best interests of the child shall be a primary consideration' (Article 3 CRC). This principle should therefore play a major role in any decision-making on the choice of criminal accountability mechanisms and the extent to which child perpetrators should be exposed to them, or child victims and witnesses should be involved therein. As brought up before, besides being major victims of international crimes, children are also increasingly known to be perpetrators of such crimes, or of (other) gross violations of human rights or humanitarian law. This duality, of being both a culprit and a victim, gives rise to serious complications in deciding what in a particular situation would be in the best interest of a specific child. While children have the right to claim the exercise of criminal justice, the judicial processes, testifying as witnesses and/or being cross-examined or interrogated in courts may deepen their trauma. While there are many good reasons not to prosecute child perpetrators of crimes in international proceedings, it is also a fact that in most national legal systems that is indeed possible, and found to be necessary and opportune. However, as Claire McDiarmid has clarified in her chapter (in Part II of this book) that provides a national law perspective on the age of criminal responsibility, ideas about the desirability and required modalities of national criminal proceedings differ quite a lot. In the end, in order to determine what is in the best interests of an identified child, a careful analysis and weighing of all interests and circumstances of the particular case is required. The whole point of introducing the best interests principle in the Convention on the Rights of the Child was exactly to compel an examination of those circumstances and interests and to make sure that the child's interests proper would be given primary emphasis.

The Convention on the Rights of the Child only deals with these issues in part. Its Article 40 insists on setting a minimum age below which children shall be presumed to be incapable of infringing penal law and on the promotion of measures for dealing with children who are (allegedly) in conflict with the law 'without resorting to judicial proceedings, providing that human rights and legal safeguards are fully respected'.[23] In case criminal proceedings were found to be appropriate, CRC Articles 37 and 40 provide a clear set of requirements that such proceedings against

---

[22] See, e.g., Save the Children, *Child Rights Programming* 2nd edn. (Lima, Save the Children Sweden/Regional Programme for Latin America and the Caribbean 2005); P. Gready and J. Ensor (eds.), *Reinventing Development? Translating Rights-Based Approaches from Theory into Practice* (London, Zed Press, 2005).

[23] CRC Article 40(3b).

children should respect, be they of a national or international character. Those provisions set standards for arrest and detention, legal assistance, and fair trial conditions. Any mechanism set up by states parties to the Convention would need to hold these standards in high regard.

Part II of this book, on the criminal responsibility of minors, by Matthew Happold, Claire McDiarmid and Angela Veale, explores a range of matters in this domain – relating to the age of criminal responsibility in international and national law, the criminal capacity of minors and the role and importance of individual psychological factors in assessing capacity and responsibility. In their contributions, but also more broadly, there seems to be a fairly strong consensus that strict age limits for acquiring certain rights or privileges, or for gaining certain capacities, deny the realities of the process of the 'evolving capacities of the child', which is another major concept used in the Convention on the Rights of the Child, and deny the differences in circumstances within which children and young persons grow up. Strict age limits will often be arbitrary cut-off points. This is underlined by the lack of consensus that exists on such limits between the different national legal systems, and even within them – where often contradictory age limits are set for different purposes (e.g., the age of majority, voting, capital punishment, marriage or driving).

Both the Special Court for Sierra Leone and the International Criminal Court will not prosecute persons for crimes committed when below the age of eighteen. This stems directly from their conviction that children are victims more than perpetrators, as clearly pointed out by David Crane, An Michels and Luis Moreno-Ocampo. From the point of view of intending to focus on those who bear the greatest responsibility, that seems a defendable decision which serves, or at least need not be in contradiction with, the best interests of the child. While there may well be situations where it is in the interest of children to be held accountable, international criminal court proceedings will only rarely, if ever at all, be the most appropriate form for doing so. Still, the dilemmas involved here only gain in intensity if one considers as another side of the coin that usually child soldiers commit, or are made to commit, serious crimes alongside adult soldiers. Often this will be the result of force and/or extreme pressure put upon them. However, according to Amnesty International there are apparently also cases 'in which the child soldier concerned was clearly in control of his or her actions, and not coerced, drugged or forced into committing atrocities. Some have become child soldiers voluntarily and committed atrocities voluntarily.'[24] What in the end would then justify the non-prosecution of the children involved, whereas the adults would be exposed to criminal proceedings, regardless of the level? Angela Veale, in chapter 7, has presented a related argument, pointing out that child 'soldierism' may also have a positive impact on the children involved, by boosting their self-confidence, certain skills and leadership experience. While she would like this positive impact to be seen as a resource

---

[24] Amnesty International, 'Child Soldiers: Criminals or Victims?', <http://web.amnesty.org/library/print/ ENGIOR500022000>, accessed in March 2005.

for peace building, she signals that this would go against the main rationale for exempting children from criminal responsibility.

One may argue that child recruitment into armed forces is in itself a war crime; or that in the end child soldiers are overridingly victims rather than perpetrators and should therefore not be prosecuted. Yet such impunity may encourage military commanders to assign the 'dirtiest' orders to child soldiers. In that way, a decision not to prosecute would indirectly expose child soldiers to more risks rather than protecting them. The likely key to solutions, as Part II of this book advocates, nevertheless seems to lie in taking seriously the idea that accountability does not necessarily involve criminal responsibility, holding children accountable therefore does not necessarily require criminal proceedings, and that usually a large range of other options would exist, including a broad range of alternative procedures and/or rehabilitation programmes.

Another key element of taking a child rights-based approach to criminal accountability matters that has a straightforward connection with issues of agency and capacities of children is that of participation. According to CRC Article 12, 'State parties shall assure to the child who is capable of forming his or her own views the right to express those views freely in all matters affecting the child, the views of the child being given due weight in accordance with the age and maturity of the child.' This implies in particular that the child shall be provided with 'the opportunity to be heard in any judicial and administrative proceedings affecting the child, either directly, or through a representative or an appropriate body.' Implementing the participation requirements of the CRC is a major challenge for many actors claiming to work under a child rights-based mandate and, for most, requires fundamental changes in attitudes towards children. In this book, the element of participation is most straightforwardly (although indirectly) represented by the chapter by Saudamini Siegrist of the UNICEF Innocenti Centre in Florence, who has been involved in various child participation exercises in the sphere of criminal justice, including the preparation of the child-friendly version of the report of the Sierra Leone Truth and Reconciliation Commission, the first ever of its kind and therefore rightly qualified as 'unprecedented' by the Commission itself.[25] The report was produced 'so that the children of Sierra Leone would be able to read and understand it, and others outside Sierra Leone might better comprehend what the children of Sierra Leone had experienced during the war.'[26] Children were involved throughout. More specifically, according to the report:

'Over 100 children were involved in the drafting, of whom 15 worked closely with the Commission. Discussions of the child-friendly report, led by children, were also aired on the Voice of Children Radio. During the first-ever Children's National Assembly,

[25] Truth and Reconciliation Commission for Sierra Leone, *Truth and Reconciliation Commission Report for the Children of Sierra Leone: Child-Friendly Version* (Accra, Graphic Packaging September 2004), <http://www.unicef.org/infobycountry/sierraleone_23937>, first paragraph of 'Acknowledgements'
[26] Ibid., second paragraph of 'Acknowledgements'.

held in Freetown in December 2003, meetings were convened to discuss the child-friendly report, which brought children together from all districts around the country. Excerpts from the discussions on the child-friendly report that took place at the Children's National Assembly were broadcast on national television and radio.

…

The child-friendly version of the Commission's report is therefore a culmination of children's involvement and perspective throughout the process, from initial preparation to background research to the preparation of the final text. In addition, the last chapter of the child-friendly version is a menu of activities, created by the children, to outline their role in disseminating the findings and recommendations of the Commission.'[27]

Other important perspectives on participation by children in criminal accountability mechanisms arise from the role of children as witnesses in international criminal procedures. In the view of An Michels, in her chapter on child witnesses at the Special Court for Sierra Leone, child testimonies are of enormous significance, as they will often bring exclusive evidence about international crimes committed against children. At the same time, apart from the opportunity to be heard and to participate in the proceedings, the SCSL has relatively little to offer the child as its possibilities to support witnesses or to provide reparation are, respectively, limited or non-existent. This may sometimes pose serious (ethical) dilemmas or problems. The International Criminal Court will have more options in this respect. David Tolbert, in chapter 11 about the ICTY, notes a debatable feature of ICTY procedures in relation to child witnesses. For, in case a child does not make the solemn declaration that is expected from all witnesses before testifying, her or his testimony will need corroboration. According to Tolbert this is arguable, if not wrong, especially as in the case of testimonies by victims of a sexual assault, corroboration is not required. From a perspective of child participation as advocated in the CRC, this is indeed a flaw. Again, the International Criminal Court has the space to deal with this matter more flexibly as it has the power to accept the relevant child's testimony as it stands (that is without corroboration) if the ICC judges are convinced of its reliability.

The third and last general principle of the Convention on the Rights of the Child that should be part of child rights-based approaches is that of non-discrimination. According to Article 2, states shall ensure the CRC 'to each child within their jurisdiction without discrimination of any kind, irrespective of the child's or his or her parent's or legal guardian's race, colour, sex, language, religion, political or other opinion, national, ethnic or social origin, property, disability, birth or other status.' This means that states 'shall take all appropriate measures to ensure that the child is protected against all forms of discrimination or punishment on the basis of the status, activities, expressed opinions, or beliefs of the child's parents, legal guardians, or family members.' The non-discrimination principle among others prescribes gender sensitivity. In relation to child soldiers, for example, this is still a major challenge in many settings. Up to 40 per cent of the estimated 300,000 children

---

[27] Ibid., 'Methodology', paras. 7 and 9.

associated with armed groups are girls (i.e., 120,000).[28] Nevertheless, they remain largely invisible and most people see the image of a boy when being confronted with the term 'child soldier'. According to Save the Children, however, research from the Democratic Republic of Congo shows that 'it is a misconception that girls do not take part in combat. In 2002, nearly half the girls associated with armed groups described their primary role as 'fighting'.'[29] The large majority of girl soldiers are exposed to severe sexual violence. The trauma and stigma attached to such violence often makes it very difficult for them to come out in the open with their experiences once the conflict has calmed down or is over. For, '[g]irls returning home are often marginalised and excluded from their communities. They are viewed as violent, unruly, dirty, or as promiscuous troublemakers.'[30] If post-conflict measures, such as Disarmament, Demobilisation and Reintegration (DDR) or educational programmes, or refugee camp management, fail to recognise these realities of girls' lives, the result will be that the girls involved will be discriminated against as the programmes or facilities offered will, in practice, not, or hardly, be accessible and/or relevant for them. In practice girls do not indeed manage to use DDR programmes in numbers which are proportionate to their association with armed groups. In the case of Save the Children reintegration programmes, for example, less than 2 per cent of the children participating in the DRC programme were girls. And, 'just 4.2 per cent of girls known to have been in fighting forces went through the formal DDR process.'[31] In this book, gender justice and the importance of equal treatment is an important feature of the chapter by An Michels.

The combination of the three basic elements of a child rights-based approach, that is putting the best interests of the child first, participation and non-discrimination, jointly construct a framework for quality intervention. This provides a formidable challenge for all possible criminal accountability mechanisms, international and domestic.

6.   CONCLUDING OBSERVATION: PREVENTION REQUIRED

This book provides a great deal of material on efforts to make international criminal accountability mechanisms more child-friendly and improving their respect for children's rights. As one of the few attempts to gather such material so far, the book inevitably inventorizes the problems in this area, and *ad hoc* solutions found to them, more than that it goes into structural solutions and preventive action on the core problem of international crimes and gross human rights violations committed

---

[28] *Forgotten Casualties of War: Girls in Armed Conflict* (London, The Save the Children Fund, 2005) p. 1.

[29] Ibid., p. 11.

[30] Ibid., p. 2.

[31] Ibid., p. 1. See also *'Don't Forget US': The Education and Gender-Based Violence Protection Needs of Adolescent Girls from Darfur in Chad* (New York, Women's Commission for Refugee Women and Children July 2005).

against children. Nevertheless, as one attempt to work towards the latter, Jenny Kuper explores the prospects of military training as a concrete tool to prevent child recruitment and other crimes against children committed by the military. The adoption of Codes of Conduct for UN personnel serving on peace-keeping missions provides another interesting concrete example.[32]

More broadly, further campaigns to bring home the main messages of the UN Convention on the Rights of the Child to all children and adults in this world, and to help to point out how concretely children's rights can be respected and promoted on the ground, will unfortunately remain a sheer necessity for a long time to come. Likewise, responses that hold the perpetrators of international crimes against children accountable for their deeds will remain necessary as well. Much of the work required will have to be determined and carried out in the national, if not local setting. In relation to this, Luis Moreno-Ocampo, in his chapter 8 on the International Criminal Court, has pointed out that national and international criminal justice responses possibly go hand in hand and reinforce each other. At least minimally he has made the point that the ICC project can only become a success if it is actively supported from the grass-roots level and if it is transposed into national legal systems. That will require the joining of forces by all interested governmental, non-governmental and civil society organisations.

Overall, in order to lessen the negative burden of conflict on children, most governments – both of states that are directly experiencing armed conflict and states in peace, in North and South, East and West – need to engage in much more comprehensive and active policies in this regard. In parallel with, for example, developments relating to domestic violence, the obligations to respect, fulfil and protect children's rights in times of armed conflict are increasingly seen as encompassing an emphasis on positive (active and proactive) children's/human rights obligations,[33] including the duty to prevent gross violations of children's rights by non-state actors as in the case of child soldier recruitment. In this regard the UN Convention on the Rights of the Child presents an unequivocal agenda for implementation.

---

[32] See, e.g., United Nations Organization Mission in the Democratic Republic of Congo, *Information on Conduct in the Democratic Republic of Congo regarding the Prohibition of Sexual Abuse and/ or Exploitation by all members of the Civilian and Military components of MONUC*, <http://www.monuc.org/downloads/Code_of_conduct_MONUC.pdf>.

[33] See, e.g., P. Alston, *Non-State Actors and Human Rights*, Collected Course of the Academy of European Law (Oxford, Oxford University Press, 2005); M. Nowak, *Introduction to the International Human Rights Regime* (Leiden, Nijhoff 2003) e.g., p. 50; I. Westendorp and R. Wolleswinkel, *Violence in the Domestic Sphere* (Oxford, Intersentia 2005); CEDAW complaint 2003, *Ms. A.T.* v. *Hungary* <http://www.un.org/womenwatch/daw/cedaw/protocol/decisions-views/A.T.-v-Hungary-2-2003.pdf>.

Chapter 2
THE RIGHTS OF THE CHILD, LAW OF ARMED CONFLICT AND CUSTOMARY INTERNATIONAL LAW: A TALE OF TWO CASES

William A. Schabas*

1. INTRODUCTION: THE EVOLUTION OF THE RIGHTS OF THE CHILD

Two judicial decisions issued in 2004 and 2005 signal major advances in the protection of the rights of the child, in particular from the standpoint of customary international law. On 1 March 2005, the Supreme Court of the United States held that imposition of the death penalty for crimes committed by children was 'cruel and unusual punishment' and, therefore, unconstitutional.[1] The decision confirms the virtual universal abolition of this practice and, thereby, the indubitable entry of the norm into the category of customary international law. Nine months earlier, on 31 May 2004, the Special Court for Sierra Leone stated that the recruitment of children under fifteen into armed forces or using them to participate actively in hostilities was not only prohibited by customary international law but also subject to individual criminal responsibility, and that this had been the state of the law since at least 30 November 1996, the date from which the Court may exercise jurisdiction.[2]

These two judgments, one by the third *ad hoc* international criminal tribunal established by the United Nations and the other by one of the world's most important national constitutional courts, represent very significant developments in the law concerning the protection of the rights of the child in a general sense. They also confirm the importance of customary international law in this area. For both reasons they merit more detailed consideration.

Perhaps no body of international law has shown more dynamism in recent years than the rights of the child. The expression 'rights of the child' was first used in the 1924 Declaration of the Rights of the Child, adopted by the League of Nations

---

* Professor of Human Rights Law, National University of Ireland, Galway and Director, Irish Centre for Human Rights.

[1] *Roper* v. *Simmons*, 543 US 551 (2005).

[2] *Prosecutor* v. *Norman*, Case No. SCSL-04-14-AR72(E), Decision on Preliminary Motion Based on Lack of Jurisdiction (Child Recruitment), 31 May 2004.

K. Arts & V. Popovski (eds.), International Criminal Accountability and the Rights of Children
© *2006, Hague Academic Coalition, The Hague, The Netherlands and the Authors*

General Assembly.[3] There are references involving the protection of children in the 1948 Universal Declaration of Human Rights, in the 1949 Fourth Geneva Convention and in the Declaration of the Rights of the Child that was adopted by the United Nations General Assembly on 20 November 1959.[4] Yet, as Judge Geoffrey Robertson noted in his dissenting opinion in *Prosecutor* v. *Norman*:

> 'Children are a very recent subject of human rights law, omitted from the 18th Century declarations on the Rights of Man because they were then regarded as the property of their parents. The League of Nations, moved by the numbers of children orphaned in the First World War, issued a declaration in 1924 about the duties of governments to provide food, shelter and medical attention for poor children. The Universal Declaration of Human Rights says no more than that "motherhood and childhood are entitled to special care and assistance". The International Covenant on Civil and Political Rights vaguely gives protection to children as part of "the family" and affords them just one right – to acquire a nationality.'[5]

It was not until the 1980s that a comprehensive body of international law concerning the rights of the child began to emerge. This was marked primarily by the adoption, in December 1989, of the Convention on the Rights of the Child.[6] At about the same time, international lawyers began to unleash the protective potential of customary international law in this area. In 1987, the Inter-American Commission on Human Rights considered whether the prohibition of juvenile executions, by then well established as a norm of treaty law,[7] was also recognised under customary international law. The Commission said that the norm was 'emerging'. It concluded that there was a prohibition on juvenile executions, with an age cut-off somewhat less than eighteen, but declined to say what the age actually was.[8] The Inter-American Commission reversed this decision in 2002, ruling that execution for crimes

---

[3] Declaration on the Rights of the Child, 1924, reprinted in S. Detrick (ed.), *The United Nations Convention on the Rights of the Child: A Guide to the Travaux Préparatoires* (Dordrecht, Martinus Nijhoff Publishers, 1992) p. 712.

[4] Universal Declaration of Human Rights, UNGA Res. 217 A (III), *UN Doc.* A/810 (1948), Article 25(2); Geneva Convention of 12 August 1949 Relative to the Protection of Civilians, (1950) 75 *UNTS* 287, Articles 14, 17, 23, 24, 38, 50, 68, 82; Declaration of the Rights of the Child, UNGA Res. 1386(XIV), *UN Doc.* A/4354 (1959).

[5] *Prosecutor* v. *Norman*, Case No. SCSL-2000-14-AR72(E), Dissenting Opinion of Justice Robertson, 31 May 2004, para. 24.

[6] Convention on the Rights of the Child, UNGA Res. 44/25, annex.

[7] Geneva Convention of 12 August 1949 Relative to the Protection of Civilians, (1950) 75 *UNTS* 287, Article 68(4); International Covenant on Civil and Political Rights, (1976) 999 *UNTS* 171, Article 6(5); Protocol Additional to the 1949 Geneva Conventions and Relating to The Protection of Victims of International Armed Conflicts, (1979) 1125 *UNTS* 3, Article 77(5); Protocol Additional to the 1949 Geneva Conventions and Relating to The Protection of Victims of Non-International Armed Conflicts, (1979) 1125 *UNTS* 609, Article 6(4); American Convention on Human Rights, (1978) 1144 *UNTS* 123, Article 5(5).

[8] *Roach & Pinkerton* v. *United States* (Case No. 9647), Resolution No. 3/87, reported in: *OAS Doc.* OEA/Ser.L/V/II.71 doc. 9 rev. 1, p. 147; *Inter-American Yearbook on Human Rights 1987* (Dordrecht, Martinus Nijhoff 1990) p. 328; 8 *Human Rights Law Journal* (1988) p. 345, para. 60.

committed under the age of eighteen was forbidden by customary international law.[9]

2. BANNING CAPITAL PUNISHMENT OF CHILDREN

The 1 March 2005 ruling by the Supreme Court in *Roper* v. *Simmons* is a defining moment not only within the constitutional jurisprudence of the United States but also in the development of customary international law concerning the rights of children. By a five-four majority, one of the world's eminent constitutional courts has prohibited the imposition of capital punishment for crimes committed while under the age of eighteen. The Supreme Court applied the eighth amendment to the United States Constitution, which forbids 'cruel and unusual punishment', thereby overturning a judgment it had issued, by another slender five-four majority, in 1989.[10] According to the Court:

> 'A majority of States have rejected the imposition of the death penalty on juvenile of-
> fenders under 18, and we now hold this is required by the Eighth Amendment [...]Our
> determination that the death penalty is disproportionate punishment for offenders un-
> der 18 finds confirmation in the stark reality that the US is the only country in the
> world that continues to give official sanction to the juvenile death penalty. This reality
> does not become controlling, for the task of interpreting the Eighth Amendment re-
> mains our responsibility. Yet at least from the time of the Court's decision in *Trop*, the
> Court has referred to the laws of other countries and to international authorities as in-
> structive for its interpretation of the Eighth Amendment's prohibition of cruel and un-
> usual punishments.'[11]

After recalling its earlier holdings that the death penalty could only be imposed for 'the worst offenders', the Supreme Court referred to three general differences between juveniles under eighteen and adults that meant they could not reliably be classified in such a category. It explained:

> 'First, as any parent knows and as the scientific and sociological studies respondent
> and his *amici* cite tend to confirm, lack of maturity and an underdeveloped sense of
> responsibility are found in youth more often than in adults and are more understand-
> able among the young. These qualities often result in impetuous and ill-considered ac-
> tions and decisions.[...]The second area of difference is that juveniles are more
> vulnerable or susceptible to negative influences and outside pressures, including peer
> pressure.[...]The third broad difference is that the character of a juvenile is not as well
> formed as that of an adult. The personality traits of juveniles are more transitory, less
> fixed.[...]These differences render suspect any conclusion that a juvenile falls among

---

[9] *Domingues* v. *United States of America* (Case No. 12.285), Merits, Report No. 62/02, 22 October 2002, para. 85.

[10] *Stanford* v. *Kentucky*, 492 US 361 (1989).

[11] *Roper* v. *Simmons*, 543 US 551 (2005), pp. 14, 21.

the worst offenders. The susceptibility of juveniles to immature and irresponsible behaviour means their irresponsible conduct is not as morally reprehensible as that of an adult.'[12]

The Court then reasoned that once the diminished culpability of juveniles was recognised, the two main penological justifications for the death penalty, retribution and deterrence, necessarily applied with lesser force to juveniles than to adults:

'As for retribution, we remarked in *Atkins* that "[i]f the culpability of the average murderer is insufficient to justify the most extreme sanction available to the State, the lesser culpability of the mentally retarded offender surely does not merit that form of retribution". The same conclusions follow from the lesser culpability of the juvenile offender. Whether viewed as an attempt to express the community's moral outrage or as an attempt to right the balance for the wrong to the victim, the case for retribution is not as strong with a minor as with an adult. Retribution is not proportional if the law's most severe penalty is imposed on one whose culpability or blameworthiness is diminished, to a substantial degree, by reason of youth and immaturity. As for deterrence, it is unclear whether the death penalty has a significant or even measurable deterrent effect on juveniles, as counsel for the petitioner acknowledged at oral argument.[13]

The judgment attests to a remarkable dynamism in the Court, and shows the growing influence of international legal developments on the more progressive of the judges. It also amounts to a roadmap for human rights lawyers in the United States, setting out arguments that can be crafted into a case for total abolition. If the overall perspective of a majority of the judges of the Court does not change dramatically in the years to come, judicial prohibition of capital punishment in the United States would seem to have a place on the judicial agenda within a reasonable period of time.

This exciting precedent of the United States Supreme Court has consequences well beyond the borders of that country. The Court's reliance on the eighth amendment to the Constitution, prohibiting cruel and unusual punishment, means that the judgment is also relevant to the application of the spectrum of national and international human rights instruments that prohibit torture or cruel, inhuman and degrading treatment or punishment, using a variety of formulations that are similar in substance if slightly different in terminology.[14]

The United States is probably the last country in the world to have retained the practice of executing persons for juvenile offences. In 1990, when the Convention on the Rights of the Child entered into force, there were about ten countries that still indulged in this barbarous practice. Steadily, over the ensuing years, in initiatives

---

[12] Ibid., pp. 15-17.

[13] Ibid., p. 17.

[14] Among them: Universal Declaration of Human Rights, UNGA Res. 217 A (III), *UN Doc.* A/810 (1948), Article 5; International Covenant on Civil and Political Rights, (1976) 999 *UNTS* 171, Article 7; Convention Against Torture and Other Cruel, Inhuman or Degrading Treatment or Punishment, UNGA Res. 39/46, annex.

that were driven largely by the international obligations they had assumed under the Convention (Article 37(a) states: 'No child shall be subjected to torture or other cruel, inhuman or degrading treatment or punishment. Neither capital punishment nor life imprisonment without possibility of release shall be imposed for offences committed by persons below eighteen years of age...'), this small number shrank gradually until only the United States remained. With its rejection of the practice, it is safe to say that the norm prohibiting executions for crimes committed under the age of eighteen now belongs indubitably to the corpus of customary international law. Although there may still be isolated examples, as Roger Hood's recent study confirms,[15] the abandonment of juvenile executions in the United States brings an end to the list of states that attempt to defend or justify the practice. Like other barbarous acts that were once widely practiced and are now universally condemned – slavery and torture, for example – juvenile executions are now part of the dustbin of history.

The beginnings of the international condemnation of juvenile executions can be traced to 1949. The Fourth Geneva Convention, adopted on 12 August 1949, prohibits the execution of persons for crimes committed while under the age of eighteen, to the extent that the offender is a 'protected person', that is, a civilian in an occupied territory during an international armed conflict. The measure resulted from a proposal at the Seventeenth International Conference of the Red Cross by the International Union for the Protection of Children and recognises the principle that children are not fully responsible for their actions, either because of immaturity or coercion.[16] The addition of the provision created no real difficulty for the delegates at the Geneva Diplomatic Conference where the Conventions were adopted, and was barely discussed.[17] The Drafting Committee of Committee III changed the wording to provide that the death penalty could not be applied for an individual under eighteen at the time of the offence,[18] thereby preventing the execution of eighteen year olds for crimes committed during their minority. The authoritative Commentary on Article 68(4) states: 'The clause corresponds to similar provisions in the penal codes of many countries, and is based on the idea that a person who has not reached the age of eighteen years is not fully capable of sound judgment, does not always realize the significance of his actions and often acts under the influence of others, if not under constraint.'[19]

---

[15] 'Capital Punishment and Implementation of the Safeguards Guaranteeing Protection of the Rights of those Facing the Death Penalty, Report of the Secretary-General', *UN Doc.* E/2005/3, paras. 76-82.

[16] O.M. Uhler, et al., *Commentary, IV, Geneva Convention Relative to the Protection of Civilian Persons in Time of War* (Geneva, International Committee of the Red Cross 1958) pp. 371-372.

[17] The United States delegate, during first reading of the provision in Committee III, said: 'The abolition of the death penalty in the case of protected persons under eighteen years of age (last paragraph) was a matter which called for very careful consideration before such a sweeping provision was adopted.' Summary record of nineteenth meeting of Committee III, in *Final Record of the Diplomatic Conference of Geneva of 1949*, Vol. IIA (Berne, Federal Political Department 1950), p. 673.

[18] Annex 299, in *Final Record of the Diplomatic Conference of Geneva of 1949, Vol. III* (Berne, Federal Political Department, 1950) p. 141. See also: Letter of the International Union for Child Welfare, Annex 272, p. 131.

[19] See Uhler, et al., *supra* n. 16, pp. 346-347.

The prohibition of juvenile executions by international humanitarian law was broadened considerably with the adoption of the Additional Protocols to the Geneva Conventions in 1977. Article 77(5) of Additional Protocol I states that the death penalty for an offence related to the armed conflict shall not be executed on persons who had not attained the age of eighteen years at the time the offence was committed.[20] The provisions are found in the human rights section of the Additional Protocol, under the sub-heading 'Measures in Favour of Women and Children'. The provision applies to all persons 'in the power of a party to the conflict', that is, not only to 'protected persons'. It was first proposed in the International Committee of the Red Cross draft for the 1972 Conference of Government Experts[21] and submitted without any substantive change at the outset of the 1974 Diplomatic Conference.[22] The representative of the International Committee of the Red Cross explained that it was a repetition of Article 68(4) of the Fourth Geneva Convention but that inclusion in the draft protocol would extend the prohibition because the category of protected persons was larger.[23] The provision was studied by a Working Group of Committee III, which settled on the age of eighteen because this was also used in a corresponding provision of the draft second protocol.[24] The original text had specified that the death penalty could not be 'pronounced', but this was changed to 'executed' upon the request of one delegate who indicated that his country's legislation did not prohibit 'pronouncement' but did prohibit 'execution'.[25] The provision was adopted by consensus in Committee III and in the plenary Conference.[26] According to the authoritative Commentary on Article 77(5), '... it can be said that the death penalty for persons under eighteen years of age is ruled out completely.'[27]

---

[20] Protocol Additional to the 1949 Geneva Conventions and Relating to The Protection of Victims of International Armed Conflicts, (1979) 1125 *UNTS* 3.

[21] *Conference of Government Experts on the Reaffirmation and Development of International Humanitarian Law Applicable in Armed Conflicts, Geneva, 3 May-3 June 1972 (second session), Basic Texts I* (Geneva, International Committee of the Red Cross 1972) p. 21; *Conference of Government Experts on the Reaffirmation and Development of International Humanitarian Law Applicable in Armed Conflicts, Geneva, 3 May-3 June 1972 (second session), Report on the Work of the Conference, II (Annexes)* (Geneva, International Committee of the Red Cross 1972) p. 9: '*Article 60 – Death penalty* In no case shall the death penalty be pronounced on civilians who are under eighteen years at the time of the offence ...' The United States experts wanted the age limit changed to fifteen. See *ICRC Doc.* CE/COM III/PC 14.

[22] International Committee of the Red Cross, *Documents of the Diplomatic Conference*, Vol. I, Part III, p. 22: '*Article 68. – Protection of children* [...] 3. The death penalty for an offence related to a situation referred to in Article 2 common to the Convention shall not be pronounced on persons who were under eighteen years at the time the offence was committed.' The reference to 'Conventions' was meant to indicate the four 1949 Geneva Conventions.

[23] *ICRC Doc.* CDDH/III/SR.45, para. 8.

[24] *ICRC Doc.* CDDH/407/Rev.1, para. 64.

[25] Ibid.; *ICRC Doc.* CDDH/III/SR.59, paras. 7-18.

[26] *ICRC Doc.* CDDH/III/SR.59, para. 18, and *ICRC Doc.* CDDH/SR.43, para. 55.

[27] C. Pilloud and J. Pictet, 'Article 77 – Protection of Children', in Y. Sandoz, et al., *Commentary on the Additional Protocols of 8 June 1977 to the Geneva Conventions of 12 August 1949* (Geneva, Martinus Nijhoff 1987) pp. 897-905, at p. 904.

Even more far-reaching is the corresponding provision in Additional Protocol II, because it applies to non-international armed conflict. At the 1972 Conference of Government Experts, draft Article 6 dealing with children was submitted in two versions, one stating 'fifteen' and the other stating 'eighteen',[28] and the age cut-off was in effect the only point in dispute in the Drafting Committee. The experts in the Drafting Committee, with the exception of the United States,[29] seemed virtually unanimous on the fact that eighteen should be the age.[30] The proposal submitted to the Diplomatic Conference set the age at eighteen.[31] The representative of the International Committee explained that the experts consulted had been in general agreement that it was possible to prohibit or postpone the death penalty in these circumstances.[32] Sweden, unhappy with the limitations of this position, announced that it would submit an amendment calling for total abolition of the death penalty.[33] Pakistan provided one of the few opposition voices, arguing that a stipulation that the death penalty could not be pronounced on persons under eighteen would encourage rebels to force juveniles to participate in armed conflicts.[34]

The prohibition on juvenile executions has also become a central element in international human rights law concerning the death penalty. The principal treaty in this respect is the International Covenant on Civil and Political Rights. Article 6(5) of the Covenant states that '[s]entence of death shall not be imposed for crimes committed by persons below eighteen years of age'. The problem with this norm is its lack of universal application. Several of the countries where the practice persisted until quite recently were either not parties to the Covenant or else – this was the case with the United States – had ratified the Covenant with a reservation to Article 6(5) with respect to juvenile offenders. In comments addressed to the United Nations Special Rapporteur on Summary and Arbitrary Executions: 'the [United States] Government's view was that general international law did not prohibit the execution of those committing capital crimes under age 18, provided that adequate due process guarantees were provided and that, although a number of nations prohibited the execution of such offenders, the practice of these States lacked the uniformity and *opinio juris* necessary to create a norm of customary international law.'[35]

---

[28] *Conference of Government Experts on the Reaffirmation and Development of International Humanitarian Law Applicable in Armed Conflicts, Geneva, 3 May-3 June 1972 (second session), Report on the Work of the Conference, I* (Geneva, International Committee of the Red Cross 1972) p. 77, para. 2.153.

[29] Ibid., p. 76, para. 2.149.

[30] Ibid., paras. 2.155-2.156.

[31] International Committee of the Red Cross, *supra* n. 22, p. 36: '*Article 10. – Penal prosecutions.* 4. The death penalty shall not be pronounced for an offence in relation to the armed conflict committed by persons below eighteen years of age and shall not be carried out on pregnant women.' An amendment submitted by Canada renewed the option between eighteen and fifteen years of age: *ICRC Doc.* CDDH/I/259, Article 5.

[32] *ICRC Doc.* CDDH/I/SR.34, para. 4.

[33] Ibid., para. 15; *ICRC Doc.* CDDH/I/261.

[34] *ICRC Doc.* CDDH/I/SR.34, para. 19. This view was endorsed by Nigeria, which suggested the age limit be reduced to sixteen.

[35] *UN Doc.* E/CN.4/1990/22, para. 431.

The prohibition on juvenile executions in international human rights law first appears in an Egyptian proposal submitted to the Commission on Human Rights in 1950 for one of the early drafts of the Covenant. It proposed to prohibit execution of offenders under the age of seventeen, but was never voted upon.[36] The draft adopted by the Commission contained a prohibition on the execution of pregnant women, but said nothing about young offenders.[37] The idea was revived several years later when the draft Covenant was being debated by the Third Committee of the General Assembly. Japan submitted an amendment by which the Covenant would prohibit sentence of death 'on minors',[38] saying it was aimed at protecting the lives of children and young persons, who already enjoyed special protection pursuant to the draft Covenant on economic, social, and cultural rights.[39] Japan criticized a companion amendment on the subject, advanced by Guatemala,[40] that suggested the death penalty could be imposed after a young offender had attained the age of majority.[41] Finland was apparently the first to suggest that the provision make specific reference to persons under eighteen, arguing that this was also the age used in the Fourth Geneva Convention.[42] A Working Party of the Committee attempted to reach a compromise. There was no agreement on the proper formulation, and three alternatives were considered: 'minors', 'persons below eighteen years of age', and 'juveniles'. For no apparent reason, the chair suggested that the Committee vote first on the phrase 'persons below eighteen years of age',[43] which was then adopted in a very close vote[44] with the result that the alternatives were never considered. It is surely of interest that the prohibition of juvenile executions was not even included in the Commission on Human Rights draft of the Covenant, and that the age threshold in the final version of the treaty was determined in this almost accidental manner. But whatever the uncertainty surrounding formulation of the norm, by 1985 when Canada proposed that it be incorporated in the draft of the Convention on the Rights of the Child,[45] there was no controversy or debate whatsoever on the point. This is a good example of the progressive development of international human rights law.

---

[36] *UN Doc*. E/CN.4/384: 'Offenders under the age of 17 years shall not be sentenced to death or to imprisonment with hard labour for life.' Also: *UN Doc*. E/CN.4/SR.139, para. 28; *UN Doc*. E/CN.4/384.

[37] *UN Doc*. E/2256, *UN Doc*. E/2447, *UN Doc*. A/2929. Suggestions that such a prohibition might be included had been made on occasion in the Commission, but never crystallized into a proposed amendment: *UN Doc*. E/CN.4/SR.139, para. 28; *UN Doc*. E/CN.4/384.

[38] *UN Doc*. A/C.3/L.655 and Corr. 1: 'Sentence of death shall not be imposed for crimes committed by minors, and shall not be carried out on children and young persons or on a pregnant woman.'

[39] *UN Doc*. A/C.3/SR.814, para. 19.

[40] *UN Doc*. A/C.3/L.647: 'Sentence of death shall not be carried out on minors or on a pregnant woman.' This amendment was later withdrawn: *UN Doc*. A/C.3/SR.816, para. 19.

[41] Ibid.

[42] *UN Doc*. A/C.3/SR.819, para. 10.

[43] Ibid., para. 19.

[44] Ibid., para. 21, by twenty one votes to nineteen, with twenty eight abstentions.

[45] *UN Doc*. E/CN.4/1985/64, Annex II, p. 4.

The text of Article 6(5) of the International Covenant on Civil and Political Rights reappears in Article 4(5) of the American Convention on Human Rights, but there is no reference whatsoever to the death penalty in the African Charter on Human and Peoples' Rights. The omission is corrected in Article 5(3) of the African Charter on the Rights and Welfare of the Child, which says that the '[d]eath sentence shall not be pronounced for crimes committed by children'. As for the Arab Charter, it prohibits imposing the death penalty on persons under the age of eighteen,[46] which is a somewhat different norm than what is expressed elsewhere. The norm can also be found in such 'soft law' instruments as the Safeguards Guaranteeing the Rights of those Facing the Death Penalty[47] and the Standard Minimum Rules for the Administration of Juvenile Justice (the 'Beijing Rules').[48]

The European Convention on Human Rights, adopted in 1950, imposes no such restriction on the death penalty in Article 2(1). This is explained by the relatively primitive formulations then prevailing in international human rights law with respect to the death penalty, although the model used in the Fourth Geneva Convention was well known to the drafters of the European Convention. It is not apparent that juvenile executions were ever carried out in states parties to the European Convention before the death penalty became thoroughly abolished within Council of Europe member states, in the mid-1990s.[49] The 1953 British Royal Commission on Capital Punishment reported that it was possible to impose a death sentence on persons as young as twelve (India and Pakistan), fourteen (Canada) and sixteen (South Africa), but that the United Kingdom, France and Belgium all set an age limit of eighteen.[50] The European Union's Minimum Standards Paper on capital punishment issued in 1998, which is used by the Union in its diplomatic initiatives with third states, declares: 'Capital punishment may not be imposed on: ... persons below 18 years of age at the time of the commission of their crime.'[51]

The prohibition of execution of juvenile offenders is really nothing more than a specific manifestation of the general rule establishing a threshold for criminal responsibility. The difficulty with the norm is that the age limit for execution varies, and historically, in some jurisdictions, it has been very low indeed. To take an example that today seems anomalous, as recently as the early 1960s Canadian courts sentenced to death a young offender who was fourteen at the time of the crime, and

---

[46] Arab Charter on Human Rights, 18 *Human Rights Law Journal* (1997), p. 151, Article 12.

[47] ESC Res. 1984/50, annex, *UN Doc.* E/1984/84.

[48] UNGA Res. 40/33 (1985), annex, para. 17.2.

[49] See H.G. Frank, *The Barbaric Punishment: Abolishing the Death Penalty* (The Hague, Martinus Nijhoff Publishers 2003).

[50] Royal Commission on Capital Punishment 1949-1953, *Report* (London, HMSO 1953) Cmd. 8932, pp. 452-453.

[51] 'Guidelines for EU Policy Towards Third Countries on the Death Penalty', in Council of the EU, *European Union Annual Report on Human Rights 1998/1999* (Brussels, General Secretariat of the Council, 2000) Annex 7, pp. 64-66, <http:ue.eu.int/uedocs/cmsUpload/HR1999EN.pdf>. Note that Article 2(2) of the European Union Charter of Fundamental Rights, *OJ* C 364/1, 18 December 2000, prohibits the death penalty under all circumstances.

he was only saved from the noose as a result of executive clemency.[52] And in 1989, when Ireland finally ratified the International Covenant on Civil and Political Rights, it formulated a reservation to Article 6(5), acknowledging that its legislation still allowed for execution of persons under the age of eighteen, although in the event of a death sentence imposed by a court, the executive would commute the sentence.

In recent years, there has been growing acceptance of the proposition that the prohibition on executions for crimes committed under the age of eighteen is a norm of customary international law. Momentum for this derived from the virtually universal ratification of the Convention on the Rights of the Child, without reservation to Article 37(a). The exception, of course, was the United States, which has signed but not ratified the Convention. This left a rather big hole in arguments that there was a universal prohibition on juvenile executions.

In 2000, a resolution adopted by the United Nations Sub-Commission on the Protection and Promotion of Human Rights stated that 'international law concerning the imposition of the death penalty in relation to juveniles clearly establishes that the imposition of the death penalty on persons aged under 18 years at the time of the offence is in contravention of customary international law.'[53] In 2002, in a petition directed against the United States, the Inter-American Commission on Human Rights confirmed the customary nature of the prohibition on juvenile executions:

'[T]he Commission is satisfied, based upon the information before it, that this rule has been recognized as being of a sufficiently indelible nature to now constitute a norm of *jus cogens*, a development anticipated by the Commission in its Roach and Pinkerton decision. As noted above, nearly every nation state has rejected the imposition of capital punishment to individuals under the age of 18. They have done so through ratification of the ICCPR, UN Convention on the Rights of the Child, and the American Convention on Human Rights, treaties in which this proscription is recognized as non-derogable, as well as through corresponding amendments to their domestic laws. The acceptance of this norm crosses political and ideological boundaries and efforts to detract from this standard have been vigorously condemned by members of the international community as impermissible under contemporary human rights standards. Indeed, it may be said that the United States itself, rather than persistently objecting to the standard, has in several significant respects recognized the propriety of this norm by, for example, prescribing the age of 18 as the federal standard for the application of capital punishment and by ratifying the Fourth Geneva Convention without reservation to this standard. On this basis, the Commission considers that the United States is bound by a norm of *jus cogens* not to impose capital punishment on individuals who committed their crimes when they had not yet reached 18 years of age. As a *jus cogens* norm, this proscription binds the community of States, including the United States.

---

[52] J. Sher, *'Until You are Dead': Steven Truscott's Long Ride into History* (Toronto, Vintage Canada 2002).
[53] 'The Death Penalty in Relation to Juvenile Offenders', *UN Doc.* E/CN.4/Sub.2/RES/2000/17, para. 6.

The norm cannot be validly derogated from, whether by treaty or by the objection of a state, persistent or otherwise.'[54]

Roper v. *Simmons* does not refer to customary international law and it is only influenced in the most general sense by international developments. Yet the virtually universal abolition of the practice, to which the Supreme Court makes reference in the judgment, is undoubtedly the product of the progress in international law concerning the rights of the child. It is a process that began with the Fourth Geneva Convention of 1949, and that evolved in a variety of instruments until being confirmed in the 1989 Convention on the Rights of the Child. Thus, *Roper* v. *Simmons* is the final piece in the puzzle, eliminating the last exception to practice of juvenile executions.

3. EFFORTS TO OUTLAW THE RECRUITMENT OF CHILD SOLDIERS

On 31 May 2005, the Appeals Chamber of the Special Court for Sierra Leone (SCSL) ruled that the recruitment of children under fifteen into armed forces or using them to participate actively in hostilities was prohibited by customary international law and, moreover, subject to individual criminal responsibility. The Chamber was addressing a challenge to the indictment of Sam Hinga Norman, who had participated in the civil war in Sierra Leone as the national coordinator of a pro-government paramilitary group called the Civil Defense Forces. The *Norman* indictment included the following:

'24. At all times relevant to this Indictment, The Civil Defense Forces did, in the Republic of Sierra Leone, conscript or enlist children under the age of 15 years into armed forces or groups, and in addition, or in the alternative, use them to participate actively in hostilities.

By his acts of omissions in relation, but not limited to, these events, Sam Hinga Norman pursuant to Article 6.1 and, or alternatively Article 6.3 of the Statute, is individually criminally responsible for the crime alleged below:

Count 8: Conscripting or enlisting children under the age of 15 years into armed forces or groups or using them to participate actively in hostilities, an Other Serious Violation of International Humanitarian Law, punishable under Article 4.c of the Statute.'[55]

In effect, Article 4 of the Statute of the Special Court for Sierra Leone, which is entitled 'Other Serious Violations of International Humanitarian Law', says that '[t]he Special Court shall have the power to prosecute persons who committed the

---

[54] *Domingues* v. *United States of America*, Case 12.285, Merits, Report No. 62/02, 22 October 2002, para. 85 (references omitted).

[55] *Prosecutor* v. *Norman*, Case No. SCSL 2003-08-I, Indictment, 7 March 2003.

following serious violations of international humanitarian law: [...] (c) Conscripting or enlisting children under the age of 15 years into armed forces or groups or using them to participate actively in hostilities.'[56]

As the Sierra Leone Truth and Reconciliation Commission pointed out in its October 2004 Report, the use of child soldiers by all of the armed factions, including the pro-government forces, was a unique feature of the Sierra Leone conflict. The Commission noted that the rebel Revolutionary United Front (RUF) was the first to abduct and forcibly recruit child soldiers, and that with the passage of time, the RUF established a separate children's unit known as the Small Boys Unit (SBU) and Small Girls Unit (SGU). The government soon followed suit during the military regime of Captain Valentine Strasser (1992-1996), significantly expanding the army by bringing in children as recruits. The SBU terminology had long been familiar to Sierra Leoneans. SBUs were part of the British colonial army, and several of the military leaders in the Sierra Leone civil war of the 1990s had begun their careers at the age of thirteen or fourteen, back in the 1950s, in British uniform.

Most of the recruitment into the rebel units was a result of abduction. But the Truth Commission found that with the pro-government Civil Defense Forces (CDF), of which Hinga Norman was the commander, many children became soldiers 'voluntarily', on the basis of patriotism. Parents volunteered and paid for the initiation of their children into the CDF. The Commission noted that parents were told that initiation would confer upon their children mystical powers which would make them impervious to bullets and would protect them.

The Truth Commission explained that child soldiers lived in a hostile and extremely violent environment. They became socialized by the violence and committed heinous crimes, often under the influence of drugs and alcohol. According to the Commission:

'Child soldiers were often forced by their captors to commit heinous atrocities in order to demonstrate loyalty to them and their cause. Atrocities often included carrying out killings, amputations and the rape of loved ones, community members, relatives and peers. Atrocities against family and community made it extremely difficult for child-soldiers to escape and return home. Unsuccessful escapes met with swift and violent reprisal intended to ensure that no child combatant attempted it. Some of the child witnesses testified to the commission of their experiences.'[57]

Norman's lawyers argued that prosecution for recruitment violated the rule against retroactive criminal prosecution (*nullum crimen sine lege*), which is set out in such international instruments as the Universal Declaration of Human Rights[58] and the

---

[56] For a further account of the use of child soldiers in Sierra Leone and the work of the Special Court for Sierra Leone, see Part III of this book, chapters 9 and 10 by David Crane and An Michels.

[57] *Witness to Truth: Report of the Sierra Leone Truth and Reconciliation Commission* (Freetown, SLTRC, 2004) Vol. 3B, chapter 4.

[58] Universal Declaration of Human Rights, UNGA Res. 217 A (III), *UN Doc.* A/810 (1948), Article 11(2).

International Covenant on Civil and Political Rights.[59] There was apparently nothing illegal about the practice under the national law in force in Sierra Leone at the relevant time. The Military Forces Act 1961 prohibited the recruitment of a child below the age of seventeen and a half unless the person's parents or guardian or other competent authority gave consent.[60] As noted above, prominent military leaders in the conflict had themselves joined the SBUs of the British colonial army, and may well have viewed the recruitment of children as a career opportunity, not a human rights violation.

The Appeals Chamber of the Special Court considered that it was competent to consider the legality of the provision in question. There is nothing in its Statute suggesting that the Court has the authority to refuse to apply a provision that it considers to conflict with the *nullum crimen* principle. Judge Robertson, dissenting, was actually prepared to 'grant a declaration to the effect that [the accused] must not be prosecuted for an offence of enlistment [...] alleged to have been committed before the end of July 1998.'[61] Judge Robertson did not explain the legal basis of his authority to make such a declaration, except to affirm, with reference to a textbook of Professor Antonio Cassese, that 'the principle of non-retroactivity of criminal rules is now solidly embodied in international law. It follows that courts may only apply substantive criminal rules that existed at the time of commission of the alleged crime.'[62] While disagreeing with Judge Robertson on the merits of the issue, his colleagues on the SCSL Appeals Chamber implicitly agreed that they were empowered to, in effect, disregard provisions of the Statute that they felt to be contrary to the *nullum crimen* maxim: 'It is the duty of this Chamber to ensure that the principle of non-retroactivity is not breached. As essential elements of all legal systems, the fundamental principle *nullum crimen sine lege* and the ancient principle *nulla poena sine lege*, need to be considered.'[63] In another case, the SCSL Appeals Chamber said: 'The Special Court cannot ignore whatever the Statute directs or permits or empowers it to do unless such provisions are void as being in conflict with a peremptory norm of general international law.'[64]

Its sister institution, the International Criminal Tribunal for the former Yugoslavia (ICTY), has taken the view that it had the authority to pronounce itself on the legality of its actual creation, under the *competence de la competence* maxim.[65]

---

[59] International Covenant on Civil and Political Rights, (1976) 999 *UNTS* 171, Article 15.

[60] Section 16(2) of the Sierra Leone Military Forces Act No. 34 of 1961.

[61] *Prosecutor* v. *Norman*, Case No. SCSL-2000-14-AR72(E), Dissenting Opinion of Justice Robertson, 31 May 2004, para. 47.

[62] Ibid., para. 16, citing A. Cassese, *International Criminal Law* (Oxford, Oxford University Press 2003) p. 153.

[63] *Prosecutor* v. *Norman*, Case No. SCSL-2000-14-AR72(E), Decision on Preliminary Motion Based on Lack of Jurisdiction (Child Recruitment), 31 May 2004, para. 25. See also: *Prosecutor* v. *Kallon* et al., Case No. SCSL-2004-15-AR72(E), Decision on Constitutionality and Lack of Jurisdiction, 13 March 2004, paras. 80-82.

[64] *Prosecutor* v. *Taylor*, Case No. SCSL-2003-01-I, Decision on Immunity from Jurisdiction, 31 May 2004, para. 43.

[65] *Prosecutor* v. *Tadić*, Case No. IT-94-1-AR72, Decision on the Defence Motion for Interlocutory Appeal on Jurisdiction, 2 October 1995.

Moreover, the ICTY has applied the *nullum crimen* norm as a rule of interpretation in effect ruling that the Security Council, when adopting the ICTY Statute, did not intend to go beyond existing customary international law, and that the subject-matter provisions of the Statute ought therefore to be construed in a manner consistent with customary international law. But it is quite another thing to contemplate declaring a provision of a statute invalid because it conflicts with customary international law. Indeed, the ICTY Appeals Chamber has affirmed that 'it is open to the Security Council – subject to respect for peremptory norms of international law (*jus cogens*) – to adopt definitions of crimes in the Statute which deviate from customary international law.'[66] Possibly the SCSL Appeals Chamber considered *nullum crimen* to be such a *jus cogens* norm.

The test, then, for the Special Court, was whether Article 4(c) of the SCSL Statute was compatible with customary international law in effect at the relevant time of the indictment. Article 4(c) of the SCSL Statute is in fact identical to Article 8(b)(xxvi) of the Rome Statute of the International Criminal Court, which is applicable to international armed conflict, and it is virtually identical to Article 8(e)(vii), which is applicable to non-international armed conflict (the Rome Statute provision refers to 'the national armed forces' rather than 'armed forces or groups'). The Rome Statute was adopted on 17 July 1998, by a vote of 120 in favour to 7 opposed, with 21 abstentions. But according to the Secretary-General of the United Nations, in his report on the draft SCSL Statute, the Rome Statute provision had a 'doubtful customary nature',[67] and it was preferable to explicitly criminalise the acts of '[a]bduction and forced recruitment of children under the age of 15 years ...'.[68] According to the Secretary-General:

> 'While the definition of the crime as "conscripting" or "enlisting" connotes an administrative act of putting one's name on a list and formal entry into the armed forces, the elements of the crime under the proposed Statute of the Special Court are: (a) abduction, which in the case of the children of Sierra Leone was the original crime and is in itself a crime under common article 3 of the Geneva Conventions; (b) forced recruitment in the most general sense – administrative formalities, obviously, notwithstanding; and (c) transformation of the child into, and its use as, among other degrading uses, a "child-combatant".'[69]

The Security Council disagreed, and proposed that Article 4(c) of the SCSL Statute be modified 'so as to conform it to the statement of the law existing in 1996 and as currently accepted by the international community',[70] in other words, to the text found in the Rome Statute. The Security Council made no claim that the provisions

---

[66] *Prosecutor* v. *Tadić*, Case No. IT-94-1-A, Judgment, 15 July 1999, para. 296.

[67] 'Report of the Secretary-General on the Establishment of a Special Court for Sierra Leone', *UN Doc.* S/2000/915, para. 18.

[68] Ibid., p. 22.

[69] Ibid., para. 18.

[70] 'Letter dated 22 December 2000 from the President of the Security Council addressed to the Secretary-General', *UN Doc.* S/2000/1234, p. 2.

was a norm of customary international law in 1996. The proposal was then accepted by the Secretary-General without comment.[71]

After canvassing a range of authorities supporting the criminalisation of recruitment of child soldiers, a majority of the Appeals Chamber dismissed the motion.[72] Judge Geoffrey Robertson's dissenting opinion reflected on the position taken by the Secretary-General at the time the Statute was drafted:

'It might strike some as odd that the state of international law in 1996 in respect to criminalisation of child soldiers was doubtful to the UN Secretary-General but very clear to the President of the Security Council only two months later. If it was not clear to the Secretary-General and his legal advisors that international law had by 1996 criminalised the enlistment of child soldiers, could it really have been any clearer to Chief Hinga Norman or any other defendant at that time, embattled in Sierra Leone?'[73]

The majority pointed to several authorities indicating the progressive establishment of a norm prohibiting the conscripting and enlistment of child soldiers, beginning with Article 14 of the Fourth Geneva Convention of 1949, which authorises the establishment of hospital and safety zones and localities for the protection of 'children under fifteen' from 'the effects of war'. But the Fourth Geneva Convention applies to protected persons, and is only authority for a general proposition that international humanitarian law encourages favourable treatment for children, which is an uncontroversial suggestion. The 1977 Additional Protocols go much further, of course. Article 77(2) of Additional Protocol I requires parties to an international armed conflict to 'take all feasible measures in order that children who have not attained the age of fifteen do not take a direct part in hostilities' and to 'refrain from recruiting them into their armed forces'. In an unfortunate sign of equivocation on this point, Article 77(3) contemplates the possibility of children under fifteen participating in armed conflict 'in exceptional cases'. Article 4(3)(c) of Additional Protocol II, which applies to non-international armed conflict, is more certain: 'Children who have not attained the age of fifteen years shall neither be recruited in the armed forces or groups nor allowed to take part in hostilities.'

The norms established in the Additional Protocols are reflected in the humanitarian law provision of the Convention on the Rights of the Child (CRC), which was adopted in 1989 and entered into force the following year. As the SCSL Appeals Chamber noted, by 30 November 1996 all but six states in the world had ratified the Convention. CRC Article 38 stipulates that states parties are to 'take all feasible measures to ensure that persons who have not attained the age of fifteen

---

[71] 'Letter dated 12 January 2001 from the Secretary-General addressed to the President of the Security Council', *UN Doc.* S/2001/40, p. 1.

[72] *Prosecutor* v. *Norman*, Case No. SCSL-2000-14-AR72(E), Decision on Preliminary Motion Based on Lack of Jurisdiction (Child Recruitment), 31 May 2004.

[73] *Prosecutor* v. *Norman*, Case No. SCSL-2000-14-AR72(E), Dissenting Opinion of Justice Robertson, 31 May 2004, para. 6.

years do not take a direct part in hostilities' and that they 'shall refrain from recruiting any person who has not attained the age of fifteen years into their armed forces'. On the basis of these provisions, and their wide acceptance by states, the SCSL Appeals Chamber concluded that '[p]rior to November 1996, the prohibition on child recruitment had also crystallised as customary international law.'[74] Moreover, as a 'rule protecting fundamental values', the SCSL Appeals Chamber concluded that violation of the prohibition on child recruitment constituted a criminal offence leading to individual responsibility under international law.[75]

Judge Robertson's dissenting opinion concerns only the date at which the norm became part of customary international law. For Judge Robertson, it could not be said that child recruitment was a crime under international criminal law prior to 17 July 1998, when the Rome Statute was adopted.[76] While relevant to the SCSL prosecutions for events between 30 November 1996 and 17 July 1998, as far as subsequent acts are concerned, Judge Robertson only confirms the customary legal nature of the offence of child recruitment as things now stand.

Treaties do not always codify customary international law, even in the spheres of international humanitarian law and international criminal law, and the SCSL Appeals Chamber may be a bit too overconfident in its reliance on the incorporation of child recruitment in the Rome Statute. Treaties are the fruit of diplomatic compromise, and may sometimes exceed and often fall short of customary law. For example, the Rome Statute appears to deviate from custom in a number of areas, including its inadequate codification of prohibited weapons[77] and its failure to incorporate the prohibition on conspiracy to commit genocide, set out in Article III of the 1948 Genocide Convention. Some have charged that the recognition of a defence of property in the case of war crimes, in Article 31(1)(c) of the Rome Statute, is a violation of *jus cogens*, and consequently null and void, pursuant to the Vienna Convention on the Law of Treaties.[78] When Belgium ratified the Rome Statute, it appended a declaration stating that it considered that Article 31(1)(c) could only be applied and interpreted 'having regard to the rules of international humanitarian law which may not be derogated from.'[79]

There cannot be much doubt that the drafters of the Rome Statute believed that by adding child recruitment to the list of war crimes in Article 8, they were making new law and not codifying existing law.[80] Nor is the fact that the Security Council chose to include child recruitment in the SCSL Statute proof that it constitutes cus-

---

[74] Ibid., para. 17.

[75] Ibid., paras. 28-53.

[76] *Prosecutor* v. *Norman* (Case No. SCSL-2000-14-AR72(E)), Dissenting Opinion of Justice Robertson, 31 May 2004, para. 24.

[77] Rome Statute of the International Criminal Court, *UN Doc.* A/CONF.183/9, Article 8(2)(b)(xx).

[78] E. David, *Principes de Droit des Conflits Armés*, 2nd edn. (Brussels, Bruylant 1999) p. 693.

[79] *Multilateral Treaties Deposited with the Secretary-General*, chapter XVIII, available through <http://untreaty.un.org>.

[80] As noted by Judge Robertson: *Prosecutor* v. *Norman*, Case No. SCSL-2000-14-AR72(E), Dissenting Opinion of Justice Robertson, 31 May 2004, para. 32.

tomary law. In 1994, when the Security Council adopted the Statute of the International Criminal Tribunal for Rwanda, it included crimes that were based upon humanitarian treaty law provisions, notably those in Additional Protocol II, and appeared to understand that it was in fact going beyond customary international law.[81] The SCSL Appeals Chamber ruling is therefore not without imperfections. Still, this seems to be inherent in the process of development of international custom in the areas of human rights and humanitarian law. The Commission of Inquiry set up by the United Nations Security Council with respect to Darfur suggested, in its January 2005 Report, that states should formally object if they contest pronouncements by international criminal tribunals concerning the state of customary international law.[82] And there have been no such challenges to the *Norman* ruling.

4. CONCLUSION

In different ways, these two cases – *Roper* v. *Simmons* and *Prosecutor* v. *Norman* – mark important progress in the judicial protection of the rights of children. Interestingly, from the perspective of international law the departure point in analysing the issues raised in each of the two cases is the Fourth Geneva Convention of 1949, and not the human rights instruments. In different ways, the Fourth Convention set in motion a process by which the protection of specific rights of the child has entered the corpus of customary international law. While limited in scope, the two precedents may well mark the beginning of a more widespread and robust process by which the human rights of the child, essentially as codified by the Convention on the Rights of the Child, are regarded as being customary in nature and enforceable by both national and international courts.

---

[81] 'Report of the Secretary-General Pursuant to Paragraph 5 of Security Council Resolution 955 (1994)', *UN Doc.* S/1995/134, para. 12.

[82] 'Report of the International Commission of Inquiry on Violations of International Humanitarian Law and Human Rights Law in Darfur', *UN Doc.* S/2005/60, para. 501.

Chapter 3
CHILDREN IN ARMED CONFLICT: LAW AND PRACTICE OF THE UNITED NATIONS

Vesselin Popovski*

1. INTRODUCTION

As substantiated in chapter 1, children are vulnerable in armed conflicts and are harshly affected by them. They suffer both directly – as the victims of hostilities – and indirectly, as wars destroy their childhood, family, education and life expectations. This chapter analyses the developing law and practice of the United Nations regarding children's rights in situations of armed conflict. Following a sketch of the relevant international legal framework, the contributions of the General Assembly, the Secretary-General, his Special Representative on Children and Armed Conflict, and, in particular, the UN Security Council (UNSC) are analysed. The importance of the involvement of the Security Council in the issue of children and armed conflict has been widely recognised and lies, for example, in the fact that the Council can determine a 'threat to the peace, breach of the peace or act of aggression' and, in response, can adopt decisions binding on all UN member states.[1] For example, in 1993-1994, in the face of genocide, mass murder and ethnic cleansing, the Security Council established the International Criminal Tribunals for the Former Yugoslavia (ICTY) and Rwanda (ICTR) in order to make the prosecution of international crimes possible, the victims of which were many children as well as adults. For the first time in the history of international tribunals, aggravated sentences were handed down as a result of the fact that the crimes had targeted children.[2] Over time the UNSC resolutions that specifically concern children, including the landmark Reso-

---

* Director of Studies at the International Order and Justice, Peace and Governance Programme at the United Nations University, Tokyo, Japan. All the opinions expressed are personal and do not involve any institution.

[1] See chapter VII of the UN Charter; the Reports of the UN Secretary-General to the UNSC on the issue, e.g., 'Children and Armed Conflict: Report of the Secretary-General', *UN Doc.* A/59/695–S/2005/72, 9 February 2005; G. Machel, 'The Impact of War on Children', *UN Doc.* A/51/306 of 26 August 1996, chapter 15, 'A Children's agenda for peace and security', available through <www.unicef.org/graca>; and *International Criminal Justice and Children* (No Peace Without Justice and UNICEF Innocenti Research Centre, 2002) pp. 46-48.

[2] See, e.g., ICTY, *Prosecutor* v. *Kunarac and others* and chapter 11 of this book by David Tolbert.

K. Arts & V. Popovski (eds.), International Criminal Accountability and the Rights of Children
© *2006, Hague Academic Coalition, The Hague, The Netherlands and the Authors*

lution 1612 (2005) which established a monitoring and reporting mechanism to collect information on child soldiers with the aim of stopping this exploitative criminal practice, have increased in number and have gained impact.

2. THE INTERNATIONAL LEGAL FRAMEWORK

The international criminalisation of offences against children dates back to the 1949 Geneva Conventions, which first established special provisions for the protection of children in times of war. Articles 24 and 50 of the Fourth Geneva Convention (1949) extend special protection measures to children, making them effective and independent subjects of international humanitarian law. The universal and compulsory character of the Geneva Conventions[3] implies that, at least theoretically, military commanders could face prosecution for a failure to ensure that children, orphaned as a result of war, 'are not left to their own resources, and that their maintenance, the exercise of their religion and their education are facilitated in all circumstances.'[4] Furthermore, Article 77 of Additional Protocol I (on international armed conflict) and Article 4 of Additional Protocol II (on non-international armed conflict) have codified the protection of children in situations of armed conflict. These articles oblige the states parties to refrain from recruiting persons under the age of fifteen.[5]

In parallel with the process of the criminalisation of abuses of children in time of war (by international humanitarian law), the accountability for violations of children's rights in time of peace (human rights law) has also been advanced, mostly through the adoption of the landmark 1989 UN Convention on the Rights of the Child (CRC).[6] Article 38 of the CRC deals with the age limit for the recruitment of soldiers: 'States Parties shall refrain from recruiting any person who has not attained the age of fifteen years into their armed forces'.[7] This age limit was a result of difficult political compromise and was already considered too low by many at the time of the adoption of the CRC. A few months later, the 1990 African Charter on the Rights and Welfare of the Child was signed, which prohibited the recruitment or direct participation in hostilities or internal strife of anyone under the age of eighteen.[8]

---

[3] The most universal regime in international humanitarian law with 192 states parties (see <www.icrc.org>), more than the UN Charter. Only two states in the world – Nauru (a UN member) and Niue (a non-member of the UN) – have not yet ratified the Geneva Conventions.

[4] Article 24 of the Fourth Geneva Convention, <http://www.unhchr.ch/html/menu3/b/91.htm>.

[5] Additional Protocol to the Geneva Conventions, <http://www.unhchr.ch/html/menu3/b/93.htm>.

[6] The ratification record of the CRC is extraordinary for such a new international regime, with 192 states parties (all states except Somalia and the USA). See also chapter 1 by Karin Arts.

[7] UNGA Resolution 44/25, December 1989. The full text of the CRC is available at <http://www.unicef.org/crc/crc.htm>.

[8] *OAU Doc.* CAB/LEG/24.9/49 (1990) available at <http://www.africa-union.org>. It entered into force in 1999. On the African Charter, see, e.g., K. Arts, 'The International Protection of Children's Rights in Africa: the 1990 OAU Charter on the Rights and Welfare of the Child', in 5 *African Journal of International and Comparative Law* (1993) pp. 139-162, and articles by D. Chirwa, A. Lloyd and D. Olowu in 10 *International Journal of Children's Rights* (2002), pp. 127-198.

The 26th International Conference of the Red Cross and Red Crescent in December 1995 recommended the age of eighteen as a limit for participation in armed forces. In June 1999 International Labour Organization (ILO) Convention No. 182 (Prohibition and Immediate Action for the Elimination of the Worst Forms of Child Labour) defined the compulsory recruitment of children for use in armed conflict as one of the 'worst forms' of child labour and prohibited it.

The African Charter and the ILO Convention were instrumental in raising the minimum age for recruitment into armed forces from 15 to 18 in the CRC Optional Protocol on the Involvement of Children in Armed Conflict which entered into force in 2002. This Protocol requires the states parties to:

- 'ensure that members of their armed forces who have not attained the age of 18 years do not take a direct part in hostilities' (Article 1);
- 'ensure that persons who have not attained the age of 18 years are not compulsorily recruited' (Article 2);
- 'raise the minimum age for the voluntary recruitment ... recognizing that under the Convention persons under the age of 18 years are entitled to special protection' (Article 3).

The Protocol also addressed non-state armed groups, making it illegal under any circumstances 'to recruit or use in hostilities persons under the age of 18'.[9]

In July 1998 the Rome Statute of the International Criminal Court was opened for signature and ratification. It entered into force on 1 July 2002. Article 8(2)(xxvi) classifies 'conscripting or enlisting children under the age of fifteen into the national armed forces or using them to participate actively in hostilities'[10] as a war crime both in international and internal armed conflict. The establishment of the International Criminal Court (ICC) provided an independent judicial mechanism of international accountability for this crime. In January 2002 a Special Court for Sierra Leone (SCSL) was established by an agreement between the United Nations and the government of Sierra Leone. Article 4(c) of the Special Court's Statute[11] literally incorporates the above language of the ICC Statute. In an extraordinary advancement of the criminalisation of the use of children in armed forces, on 31 May 2004, in the case of *Prosecutor* v. *Norman*, the SCSL stated that the enlistment of child soldiers has been prohibited in customary international law and was the subject of international criminal responsibility even before the adoption of the ICC Statute – effectively from the beginning of the SCSL jurisdiction in November 1996. More details on this case and its implications are presented in the chapters by Schabas and Crane in this book.

---

[9] See Article 4, <http://www.unhchr.ch/html/menu2/6/protocolchild.htm>.

[10] The Rome Statute is available at <http://www.un.org/law/icc/statute/romefra.htm>.

[11] <http://www.sierra leone.org/specialcourtstatute.html>.

3. CONTRIBUTIONS OF THE UNITED NATIONS GENERAL ASSEMBLY

In November 1959 the United Nations General Assembly (UNGA) adopted a Declaration of the Rights of the Child.[12] It recalled the (very short) Geneva Declaration passed by the League of Nations in 1924, and expressed some basic concerns, such as that 'the child must be among the first to receive protection and relief' and 'shall be protected against all forms of neglect, cruelty and exploitation.'[13] The 1959 Declaration consisted of 10 general principles and paid specific attention to the child as a vulnerable person who 'by reason of his physical and mental immaturity needs special safeguards and care, including legal protection'. The Declaration was the first to establish the principle of the 'best interests of the child', in principles 2 and 7. It spelled out the right of the child from birth to have a name and a nationality (principle 3) and the entitlement to free and compulsory elementary education (principle 7). Principle 9 requires the establishment of a minimum age (though not specified) for employment and prohibits the engagement of a child 'in any occupation or employment which would prejudice his health or education, or interfere with his physical, mental or moral development.' This text, although not binding law, could be regarded as an early expression of the United Nations' concern about the use of children in armed forces.

In 1974 the United Nations General Assembly adopted the Declaration on the Protection of Women and Children in Emergency and Armed Conflict[14] – which took a gender-based approach to the suffering of 'the most vulnerable members of the population'. This Declaration, typical for the time of its adoption, deplores the colonial and racist foreign domination 'cruelly suppressing the national liberation movements and inflicting heavy losses and incalculable suffering on the population under their domination, including women and children.' The Declaration demanded that 'all forms of repression and cruel and inhuman treatment of women and children, including imprisonment, torture, shooting, mass arrests, collective punishment, destruction of dwellings and forcible eviction, committed by belligerents in the course of military operations or in occupied territories shall be considered criminal.' This amounts to a good example of the expression of *opinio juris* on the prohibition and prosecution of gender crimes, as later codified in the UN Convention Against Torture, the Convention on the Rights of the Child and the expanding international criminal jurisdiction ultimately leading to the Statute of the International Criminal Court.

The 1974 UNGA Declaration does not specify children in armed conflict as a vulnerable group, distinct from adults. It rather expresses a consciousness 'for the destiny of mothers, who play an important role in society, in the family and particularly in the upbringing of children.' Understandably, this was in line with the more

---

[12] UNGA Resolution 1386 (XIV), 20 November 1959.
[13] <http://www1.umn.edu/humanrts/instree/k1drc.htm>, principles 8 and 9 respectively. For the text of the Geneva Declaration, see <http://www1.umn.edu/humanrts/instree/childrights.html>.
[14] UNGA Resolution 3318 (XXIX), 14 December 1974.

general attention, characteristic of that time, paid by the United Nations Economic and Social Council to civilians in armed conflict and also to women as a discriminated group (and not only in colonial or occupied territories).

With the end of the Cold War and the adoption of the Convention on the Rights of the Child, the human rights agenda has come to devote much greater attention to the rights of children than before. In 1990 the UN World Summit on Children adopted an ambitious World Declaration on the Survival, Protection and Development of Children in the 1990s and a Plan of Action.[15] These two documents, however, have limited relevance for children in armed conflict, as they mention only a general need for protection and make no specific recommendations. The 1993 World Conference on Human Rights in Vienna came up with a more solid initiative. It recommended, among other things, a particular study on the impact of armed conflict on children. Article 50 of the World Conference's final document (the Vienna Declaration) proposed to the UN Secretary-General that he should:

'initiate a study into means of improving the protection of children in armed conflicts. Humanitarian norms should be implemented and measures taken in order to protect and facilitate assistance to children in war zones. Measures should include protection for children against indiscriminate use of all weapons of war, especially anti-personnel mines. The need for aftercare and rehabilitation of children traumatized by war must be addressed urgently.'[16]

The UNGA adopted this proposal and included the protection of children in armed conflict as a separate item on its annual agenda. In March 1994 the General Assembly adopted Resolution A/48/157 which requested the Secretary-General to undertake a comprehensive expert study on the participation of children in armed conflict. The world waited for a long time to see the results of the Vienna initiative. In 1996, the comprehensive Report entitled 'Impact of Armed Conflict on Children', presented a shocking revelation of abduction and forcible recruitment of child soldiers, as well as horrific sexual and other exploitation of children in tens of countries in many continents.[17] One momentous contribution of this Report was that it did not spare the names of countries where these notorious practices occurred. In addition, the Report made far-reaching recommendations and underlined the need for creating implementation mechanisms that involve various actors – governments, regional organisations, UN bodies, the World Health Organisation, the Bretton Woods institutions, the International Committee of the Red Cross, inter-institutional mechanisms, and civil society. As a first step it suggested the establishment of a Special Representative of the Secretary-General on Children and Armed Conflict. In September 1997, Mr. Olara Otunnu – the enthusiastic and committed former Ambassador to the UN and Foreign Minister of Uganda – was appointed. His Office engaged in efforts to implement various tasks voicing children's rights and to advocate con-

---

[15] <http://www.unicef.org/wsc/plan.htm#Protection>.
[16] <http://www.unhchr.ch/huridocda/huridoca.nsf/(Symbol)/A.CONF.157.23.En?OpenDocument>.
[17] G. Machel, *supra* n. 1.

crete steps to stop their violation in armed conflicts. The Office has cooperated with many organs within and outside the United Nations in its attempts to contribute to: reducing the abuse of children; the release and rehabilitation of child soldiers; achieving a complete end to the recruitment and use of children in conflict situations.[18]

In October 2002 the General Assembly adopted the document entitled 'A World Fit for Children' (A/S-27/2) summarizing most of the achievements during the decade since the first World Summit for Children. In the Outcome Document of the 60th Session in September 2005 the General Assembly reaffirmed its commitment to the promotion and protection of the rights and welfare of children. It called upon states to take effective measures to prevent the recruitment and use of children in armed conflict by armed forces and groups and to prohibit and criminalise such practices.

4.   UN SECURITY COUNCIL RESOLUTIONS, SECRETARY-GENERAL REPORTS
     AND EFFORTS BY THE SPECIAL REPRESENTATIVE ON CHILDREN AND
     ARMED CONFLICT

Graca Machel wrote in her book that the UN Security Council had discussed the issue of children in armed conflict for the first time in an informal meeting in 1996, when it 'recognized that more and more children caught in situations of armed conflict were being left in a vast security void'.[19] On 29 June 1998 the Security Council convened its first formal meeting (No. 3897) on the particular harmful impact of armed conflict on children. After the meeting, a Presidential Statement strongly condemned 'the targeting of children in armed conflict, including their humiliation, brutalization, sexual abuse, abduction and forced displacement, as well as their recruitment and use in hostilities in violation of international law.' It called upon states 'to comply strictly with their obligations under international law' and 'to prosecute those responsible for grave breaches of international humanitarian law'.[20] Not coincidentally, this happened exactly on the eve of the adoption of the Rome Statute of the International Criminal Court.

The first Security Council resolution dealing entirely with children in armed conflict was Resolution 1261 (1999). It repeated the condemnation of the targeting of children in armed conflict and the obligation of states to prosecute the violations from the earlier Presidential statement and urged all partied to armed conflicts to:

---

[18] For full information and reports of Otunnu's Office see <http://www.un.org/special-rep/children-armed-conflict/English/index.html>. In February 2006 Ms. Radhika Coomarsaswamy succeeded Otunnu.

[19] G. Machel, et al., *The Impact of War on Children: A Review of Progress since the 1996 United Nations Report on the Impact of Armed Conflict on Children* (London, Hurst 2001) p. 173.

[20] 'Statement by the President of the Security Council', *UN Doc.* S/PRST/1998/18, 29 June 1998, available through <http://documents.un.org>.

- ensure that the protection and welfare of children is taken into account during peace negotiations and throughout the peace process (para. 7);
- undertake feasible measures during armed conflicts to minimize the harm suffered by children, such as 'days of tranquility' (para. 8);
- abide by concrete commitments made to ensure the protection of children (para. 9);
- take special measures to protect children, in particular girls, from rape and sexual abuse and take into account the special needs of the girl child in armed conflict and its aftermath, including the delivery of humanitarian assistance (para. 10);
- ensure full safe and unhindered access of humanitarian personnel and the delivery of humanitarian assistance to all children affected by armed conflict (para. 11);

The resolution demanded that, through political and other efforts, states and all parts of the UN system ensure an end to the recruitment and use of children in armed conflict in violation of international law (para. 13). This first resolution thus did not make an attempt to link the violations of children's rights with the more robust enforcement mechanisms of the Security Council. It requested the UN Secretary-General to ensure that peacekeeping personnel have appropriate training in the protection of children (para. 19) and asked him to submit a report on the implementation of the resolution (para. 20). The Secretary-General's first report on children and armed conflict to the Security Council was submitted on 19 July 2000 (S/2000/712) and presented a truly detailed account of the existing situation and problems. The report made 55 recommendations and paved the way for further actions.

Less than a month after the Secretary-General's first report, the Security Council adopted a new Resolution 1314 (of 11 August 2000) which now linked the issue of children in armed conflict with the Council's mandatory power under the UN Charter. The preamble to the resolution reiterated 'the purposes and principles of the Charter of the UN and the primary responsibility of the Security Council for the maintenance of international peace and security.' Its paragraph 9 determined that 'the deliberate targeting of civilian populations ... including children, and the committing of systematic ... violations of international humanitarian and human rights law, including that relating to children, in situations of armed conflict may constitute a threat to international peace and security.' This unambiguously expressed the readiness of the Council, where necessary, to activate enforcement measures under Chapter VII. Connected with the opportunity provided by Article 13(b) of the ICC Statute for the Security Council to refer violations of international humanitarian law to the Prosecutor of the ICC, this text could be read as anticipating the emergence of a framework, both legal and political, to end impunity for crimes against children, including the forceful recruitment of child soldiers. An important opportunity in this regard was taken in 2005 by Security Council Resolution 1593, which referred the situation in Darfur, Sudan, to the ICC Prosecutor. The text of Resolution 1593 is short and does not contain a specific child-related context. However, the text of a previous and more detailed Resolution 1591 on Darfur mentions, among other violations, sexual violence against girls and makes a direct reference to the previous entirely child-oriented Resolution 1460.

It is essential that modern international law encompasses the notion of universal jurisdiction and requires that all courts can prosecute persons suspected of serious international crimes, regardless of where those crimes were committed and irrespective of the nationality of the accused or the nationality of the victims. Crimes for which universal jurisdiction can be applied include grave breaches of the Geneva Conventions and violations of the Convention Against Torture. The full list of serious crimes under international law that can be dealt with by national judicial organs under universal jurisdiction, as suggested by the Princeton Project on Universal Jurisdiction, includes: (1) piracy, (2) slavery, (3) war crimes, (4) crimes against peace, (5) crimes against humanity, (6) genocide, and (7) torture.[21]

An important practical result of the involvement of the Security Council in issues concerning children in armed conflict was the inclusion of child protection advisers in United Nations peacekeeping operations. Resolution 1314 urged regional organisations to establish, within their secretariats, child protection units. It encouraged states to obtain the release of children abducted during armed conflicts and to reunite them with their families, and to strengthen the capacity of national institutions and local civil society for ensuring the sustainability of child protection.[22]

The orientation towards a more robust approach in Security Council Resolution 1314 was not just an empty threat. Very soon after the adoption of this resolution, the Security Council applied its authority in practice by demanding the release of child soldiers in the Democratic Republic of Congo (DRC). Apart from adopting general child-thematic resolutions only, the Security Council then started more broadly to address country-specific concerns and to take particular actions, often using mandatory decisions under Chapter VII of the UN Charter. In this way, the broad determination in UNSC Resolution 1314 that violations of international humanitarian law (such as recruiting child soldiers) constitute a 'threat to the peace', led to practical achievements. For example, Security Council Resolution 1332 (2000) which addressed the civil war in the DRC called on 'all armed forces and groups immediately to cease all campaigns for the recruitment, abduction, cross-border deportation and use of children.' At the same time, in its paragraph 14, it demanded 'immediate steps for the demobilization, disarmament, return and rehabilitation of all such children'. Even though Resolution 1332 was not strictly a Chapter VII resolution, this courageous step in fact led to the return of 165 Congolese children to UNICEF from a training camp in Uganda.[23] The next Security Council resolu-

---

[21] *The Princeton Principles on Universal Jurisdiction* (Princeton, Program in Law and Public Affairs 2001) p. 29.

[22] See paras. 16, 17 and 18 respectively.

[23] Later reported in 'Children and Armed Conflict: Report of the Secretary-General', *UN Doc.* A/56/342–S/2001/852, 7 September 2001.

tion on the DRC, Resolution 1341 (2001), determined the situation as a threat to international peace and security. Acting under Chapter VII, and in much stronger language than in Resolution 1332, the Security Council demanded, in paragraph 10, 'an effective end to the recruitment, training and use of children' in armed forces and requested the Secretary-General to entrust his Special Representative with pursuing these objectives on a priority basis.

The above-mentioned measures regarding children in the Democratic Republic of Congo were further extended by Resolution 1355 (2001), which repeated the demand to end the use of child soldiers, but importantly added 'adequate and sustained resources for long-term reintegration'.[24] The resolution also called 'on all relevant parties to ensure that urgent child protection concerns, the plight of girls affected by the conflict, the protection and safe return of refugee and internally displaced children ... are addressed in all national, bilateral and regional dialogues.'[25] The resolution was the first to develop the idea of constant monitoring and reporting of the implementation of child protection obligations under humanitarian and human rights law.[26]

In his 2001 Report to the Security Council, the Secretary-General emphasized some concrete achievements on children in armed conflicts resulting from the robust approach of Resolution 1314.[27] Olara Otunnu visited the DRC to meet President Kabila and other political and military leaders. Together, they elaborated and adopted a five-point plan to end child soldiering.[28] The government of Rwanda enacted legislation allowing girls – the heads of households after the 1994 genocide – to inherit farms and other properties. Colombia raised the minimum age for recruitment into the armed forces to eighteen years. The Government of Sierra Leone established a National Commission for War-Affected Children. In Angola in May 2001, 60 children were abducted by the National Union for Total Independence of Angola (UNITA), but an international publicity campaign led by UNICEF prompted UNITA to release them after 20 days. These are some examples of the crucial role that monitoring and reporting can play in child protection.

In a separate chapter of his report, the Secretary-General also addressed issues of impunity and redressing abuse. The growing attention to children's involvement in justice and truth-seeking processes contributed to the establishment of two significant accountability mechanisms in Sierra Leone. Firstly, the Special Court for Sierra Leone (SCSL) was empowered to prosecute, among other crimes, the recruitment of child soldiers. Secondly, the Truth and Reconciliation Commission (TRC) was charged with devoting attention to the full range of children's war-time experiences in a systematic manner. The work of both organs is discussed further in

---

[24] Ibid., para. 18.
[25] Ibid., para. 14.
[26] Ibid., para. 35.
[27] Ibid., paras 11-14.
[28] On these and other concrete achievements, see further Olara Otunnu Report, *UN Doc.* A/56/453, 9 October 2001.

chapters 4, 9 and 10 of this book. The Office of the Special Representative of the Secretary-General on Children and Armed Conflict contributed to the efforts to provide concrete child-centred guidance during the development of the SCSL and the Sierra Leone TRC. The Office issued guidelines regarding the participation of and/or impact on children in different capacities – as participants, victims, witnesses or perpetrators of grave abuses during armed conflict – to be conveyed to the SCSL prosecutor and judges, and to the Truth and Reconciliation Commissioners.

Another result was that the mandates of UN transitional administrations and field missions were reformulated to ensure that truth-seeking processes address war crimes against children. In East Timor, during the visit of the International Commission of Inquiry on East Timor, UNICEF organised a special session to draw attention to the violations inflicted upon children, and to raise awareness among NGOs and the local population. The Historical Clarification Commission in Guatemala noted the large extent to which children suffered, their social disintegration caused by the conflict, the stigmatization of the victims and the widespread forceful enlisting of young men between fifteen and eighteen in the civil patrols. It called on the United Nations to assist in the implementation of its recommendations, including the child-specific ones.

On 20 November 2001 the Security Council adopted Resolution 1379, and further extended the framework of child protection. It decided to include explicit provisions for child protection in all its future peacekeeping operations (para. 2), and demanded that the parties to a conflict must respect and promote 'days of immunization' and other opportunities for the safe delivery of necessary services to children in affected areas (para. 4). The Council put the protection of children in a larger context, linking armed conflict with terrorism, illicit trade in minerals, trafficking in small arms and other criminal activities (para. 6). It addressed various actors with specific requests and demands: the parties in conflict (para. 8), the UN member states (para. 9), the Secretary-General (para. 10), UN agencies and funds (para. 11), the international financial institutions (para. 12), and regional organisations (para. 13). It is important to emphasize paragraph 9 of UNSC Resolution 1379, which could be seen as a trigger of Charter Chapter VII, as it explicitly authorises sanctions. The Security Council urged member states to 'consider appropriate legal, political, diplomatic, financial and material measures, in accordance with the Charter of the UN, in order to ensure that parties to armed conflict respect international norms for the protection of children.' This text, connected with the determination in the previous Resolution 1314 that situations where children are not protected can amount to 'threats to the peace', opens the road to sanctions, although not for the use of force. The most important measure, spelled out in Resolution 1379, is the request that, when preparing the next report, the Secretary-General attaches a list of parties to armed conflicts that recruit or use children in violation of their international obligations in situations that threaten the maintenance of international peace and security. This was the end of tactful diplomacy – the time had now come to name and shame the recruiters and users of child soldiers, including governments!

Following UNSC Resolution 1379, the Secretary-General issued his next report which marked the movement from codification towards implementation.[29] He reported that two essential legal instruments had entered into force – the Optional Protocol to the CRC on the involvement of children in armed conflict and the Rome Statute of the International Criminal Court. The report welcomed the commitments to the protection of children made in countries such as Colombia, Congo, Rwanda, Sierra Leone, Sri Lanka and Sudan, and the efforts of the UN Special Representative Olara Otunnu and his visits to Ethiopia, Eritrea, Angola, Afghanistan, and Guatemala. According to the Secretary-General, the United Nations was continuing its practice to appoint Child Protection Advisers in its peacekeeping missions. The missions in the DRC and Sierra Leone were strengthened with 8 and 2 persons respectively. Such an adviser was also appointed in Angola: UNSC Resolution 1433 charged the United Nations Mission in Angola with the task of assisting the Government's coordination of humanitarian assistance to vulnerable groups with special concern for children, and specifically charged a Child Protection Adviser with that undertaking.[30] Another example of child-related texts in a country-specific UNSC resolution was Resolution 1436 in which the Council encouraged the government of Sierra Leone to continue to pay special attention to the needs of women and children, and welcomed the steps taken by the United Nations Mission in Sierra Leone (UNAMSIL) to prevent the sexual abuse and exploitation of women and children.[31] The Secretary-General reported progress in other areas of concern addressed by Security Council resolutions: impunity, landmines, small arms, sexual exploitation, displaced persons, disarmament, the special needs of young people, and others.

Following the request made in UNSC Resolution 1379, for the first time this Secretary-General report listed in an annex all the parties to armed conflict (23 altogether) that recruit or use children in situations determined as 'threats to the peace'. Among them were the governments of and military groups in Afghanistan, Burundi, DRC, Liberia and Somalia. The report also acknowledged the existence of other groups recruiting children, in countries which are not listed on the Security Council agenda as 'threats to the peace' such as Colombia, Northern Ireland, Chechnya, Myanmar, Nepal, the Philippines, Sudan, Uganda and Sri Lanka. On the positive side, the Secretary-General report mentioned countries where conflicts have recently ended and where the governments are committed to demobilizing child soldiers and not to recruit them again: Angola (with between 6,000 and 8,000 demobilized), Guinea-Bissau, Kosovo and Sierra Leone (with 6,850 demobilized). Similarly, it mentioned countries where conflicts have been over for some time, but with some legacy of child soldiers: Cambodia, El Salvador, Guatemala, Honduras, Mozambique and Nicaragua. Another element of positive news was that in the on-

---

[29] 'Children and Armed Conflict: Report of the Secretary-General', *UN Doc.* S/2002/1299, 26 November 2002.
[30] Ibid., para. 3.
[31] Ibid., paras 14 and 15.

going conflict between Ethiopia and Eritrea there had been no recruitment or use of child soldiers.

At the next meeting on children and armed conflict, on 30 January 2003, the Security Council adopted Resolution 1460 (2003). It further focused attention on the list of parties that violated the obligations not to recruit and use children in armed conflict, and expressed an intention to develop clear and time-bound action-plans to end this practice.[32] It demanded that the parties listed in the Secretary-General's annex, including governments, must provide information to Olara Otunnu concerning the ending of recruitment and the use of child soldiers and reiterated the sanctions implied in paragraph 9 of UNSC Resolution 1379. In a further warning the Council expressed the 'intention to consider taking appropriate steps to further address this issue in accordance with the Charter of the UN and its resolution 1379, if it deems that insufficient progress is made.'[33] This is a clear indicator that the Security Council is serious about possible sanctions for a failure to implement the requirements to stop the recruitment and use of children in armed conflict.

Resolution 1460 also addressed an entirely new concern, by requesting the protection of children from deployed United Nations personnel itself. Paragraph 10 noted 'cases of sexual exploitation and abuse of women and children, especially girls, in humanitarian crisis, including those cases involving humanitarian workers and peacekeepers' and requested the contributing countries 'to develop appropriate disciplinary and accountability mechanisms'. Resolution 1460 also gave concrete guidance as to what the Security Council would expect from the next Secretary-General Report, including information on the progress made by the parties listed in the Annex, and further specific proposals on ways to ensure monitoring and reporting in a more effective and efficient way within the existing UN system.[34]

In November 2003 the next Secretary-General Report came out.[35] It warned that, despite some progress, children 'continue to be the main victims of conflicts'. For example, in Mambasa in the Democratic Republic of Congo at the end of 2002, 24 children were summarily executed by soldiers of the Movement for the Liberation of Congo (MLC) and of the Congolese Rally for Democracy – National (RCD-N). Nine other children were executed by another warring faction, the Union of Congolese Patriots (UPC). In Colombia many children have become victims of arbitrary killing, notoriously known as 'social cleansing'. Following the request of the Security Council, the Secretary-General Report added Annex II which included 18 parties that recruited children in conflicts that were not on the agenda of the Security Council: Chechnya, Colombia, Myanmar, Nepal, Northern Ireland, the Philippines, Sri Lanka, Sudan and Uganda. Moreover, the Ivory Coast was added to Annex I, which then contained 27 parties. The 2003 Report referred to some progress

[32] Ibid., para. 4.

[33] Ibid., para.6.

[34] Ibid., para. 16.

[35] 'Children and Armed Conflict: Report of the Secretary-General', *UN Doc.* A/58/546–S/2003/1053, 10 November 2003.

as well. However, although some facts are encouraging, in general the reader is left with mixed impressions at best. Improvements in some parts were accompanied by a continuation of the recruitment of children in other parts. Some released child soldiers had been re-recruited into armed forces.

One important innovation of the 2003 Report is that it seeks more actively to develop a philosophy for more comprehensive and systematic monitoring, reporting and action – what in the earlier Report was referred to as an 'era of application'. The Secretary-General made three proposals to facilitate monitoring and reporting. Firstly, specific standards should be set for action in the form of clear laws and procedures. Secondly, attention should be devoted to the most egregious violations, such as the recruitment of child soldiers. And thirdly, the work should be shared among a network of various bodies, each of which brings value-added benefits of jurisdiction, competence and/or expertise.

In April 2004 the Security Council responded through Resolution 1539. It fully supported the Secretary-General's concept for monitoring and reporting practices of recruitment and the use of child soldiers and gave him the green light for devising a systematic and comprehensive plan of action.[36] The resolution gave the parties listed in the Secretary-General's report a three-month deadline to prepare concrete and time-bound plans of action to halt the recruitment and use of child soldiers. Resolution 1539 further hardened its tone in relation to the possible application of sanctions against non-cooperative parties, that is those who 'refuse to enter into dialogue, fail to develop an action plan or fail to meet the commitments included in their action plan'. It even went as far as to list the options of possible 'targeted and graduated measures', such as a 'small arms embargo'.[37]

On 9 February 2005 the Secretary-General issued his next Report which, as of the date of submitting this chapter, contains the most comprehensive account of compliance efforts and progress in ending the recruitment and use of children in armed conflict.[38] The list of 'named and shamed' parties had slightly changed. Afghanistan and Liberia had been dropped from the list, as they now have cooperative governments which are committed to ending the recruitment of children into the armed forces. However, Somalia's list had expanded from 4 to 10 parties, and Sudan's from 2 to 5 parties. The Report moves from country to country and presents in details the successes and the remaining concerns regarding children in armed conflict. It not only attends to the recruitment (or demobilization) of child soldiers, but also names and shames those parties that target, kill, maim, rape, or terrorize children – with the Beslan school tragedy (Russia) as a clear and notorious example of the last-mentioned. The sexual exploitation and abuse of children, unfortunately also by UN personnel, for example in the Democratic Republic of Congo, is also given prominent attention. In view of the continuing and widespread and unaccept-

---

[36] Ibid., para. 2.
[37] Ibid., para. 5(c).
[38] 'Children and Armed Conflict: Report of the Secretary-General', *UN Doc.* A/59/695–S/2005/72, 9 February 2005.

able patterns of violations, in an excellent re-emphasis of the Security Council's enforcement role, the Secretary-General in his 2005 Report strongly recommended that the Council should take 'targeted and concrete measures … [which] should include the imposition of travel restrictions on leaders and their exclusion from any governance structures and amnesty provisions, the imposition of arms embargoes, a ban on military assistance and restrictions on the flow of financial resources to the parties concerned'.[39]

Most importantly, the 2005 Report presents a comprehensive, standardized, clearly mandated and authoritative 'Action Plan for the Establishment of a Monitoring, Reporting and Compliance Mechanism'.[40] One may only welcome such a step, which is further proof that the 'era of implementation' has started. The Action Plan identifies six grave violations that should be monitored: killing and maiming of children; recruiting or using child soldiers; attacks against schools or hospitals; rape and sexual violence; abduction and denial of humanitarian access. The mechanism created by the Action Plan involves all possible actors – governments and UN bodies, the International Criminal Court, regional organisations, NGOs and civil society – in a cooperative mosaic (presented in a clear and comprehensive vertical chart) linked by the Task Force on Children and Armed Conflict (CAAC) at Headquarters level and the Task Force on Monitoring and Reporting at country-level.

A week after the 2005 Secretary-General Report had appeared, the UN Commission on Human Rights issued a Report by Special Representative Olara Otunnu, which further detailed the role to be played by actors external to the United Nations.[41] On 23 February 2005 Otunnu addressed the Security Council with the statement 'Era of Application: Instituting Compliance and Enforcement for CAAC'. In an emotional ending, recalling the famous song by Bob Marley: 'Hear the children cryin', Otunnu asked the Council not to let down the expectations of children for 'redemption songs'. The Security Council did not let children down. On 26 July 2005 it adopted Resolution 1612, the most comprehensive so far on children and armed conflict. It signalled its approval of the proposed Action Plan for the global protection of children in armed conflict. Olara Otunnu called the resolution 'groundbreaking in several respects'.[42] With 2 million children killed and 6 million injured in conflicts over the past decade, the Security Council unanimously condemned the continued recruitment of child soldiers, and approved the mechanism for monitoring, reporting on and punishing those responsible.[43] For the first time the United Nations established a formal, structured and detailed compliance re-

---

[39] Ibid., p. 13.

[40] Ibid., pp. 14 et seq.

[41] Commission on Human Rights, 'Establishing a Monitoring, Reporting and Compliance Mechanism for the Protection of Children Exposed to Armed Conflict: Report of the Special Representative of the Secretary-General for Children and Armed Conflict, Olara A. Otunnu', *UN Doc*. E/CN.4/2005/77, 15 February 2005.

[42] Olara Otunnu, 'Ending Wars Against Children', *International Herald Tribune*, 6-7 August 2005, p. 4.

[43] Paras. 1-3.

gime, bringing together all key elements to ensure compliance and accountability. The mechanism will monitor grave violations by both states and non-state actors, focusing especially on the six most egregious crimes, as identified in previous resolutions and reports, and setting time-bound national and rebel action plans to comply with international law. Especially created task forces at country level would gather evidence and forward it to the Secretary-General, who would then report to the Security Council and the General Assembly. The Council established its own working group to review these reports and to make recommendations on possible measures to promote the protection of children affected by armed conflict.[44]

The Security Council also expressed concern about the lack of progress by offending parties on developing and implementing the action plans for ending violations[45] and urged them to undertake efforts in close collaboration with UN peacekeeping missions and UN country teams. It repeated verbatim the possibility of applying Chapter VII measures,[46] but unfortunately fell short of a more serious threat at this stage. The Council did not even match the sanctions suggested by the Secretary-General in his Report. It limited the language to an arms embargo only and did not mention a travel ban or the freezing of funds as other possible measures.

Resolution 1612 welcomed recent initiatives by some regional and sub-regional organisations to: mainstream child protection into their advocacy, policies and programmes; develop peer review programmes and monitoring and reporting mechanisms; and include child-protection training in their peace and field operations.[47] It also urged member states, the UN system and other multilateral organisations 'to take appropriate measures to control illicit sub-regional and cross-border activities harmful to children, including illicit exploitation of natural resources, illicit trade in small arms, abduction of children.'[48]

The future of the monitoring and reporting on CAAC is now back in the hands of the Secretary-General and his Special Representative who should follow up and urge states, non-state actors, UN bodies and others to implement the Action Plan, now with further backing by the Security Council, if and where necessary.

5. CONCLUSION

In summary, in the last decade the main political UN bodies have acted in harmony and with a sense of commitment regarding the protection of children in armed conflict. This is an example of fruitful cooperation between principal UN organs with regard to a serious and evolving global problem concerning the core of the organisation: the maintenance of international peace and security. The authority of

---

[44] Para. 8.
[45] Para. 7.
[46] Para. 9.
[47] Para. 13.
[48] Para. 16.

the Security Council to impose, if and where necessary, enforcement measures under Chapter VII, was gradually clarified and joined by the commitment and resources of the Secretary-General. This helped to create a strong and comprehensive
monitoring and reporting mechanism with the intertwined aims of ending the notorious and criminal practices of recruiting and abusing children in armed conflict,
and the promotion and provision of further protection measures to that especially
vulnerable group of people in armed conflict: the children.

Chapter 4
CHILD PARTICIPATION IN INTERNATIONAL CRIMINAL ACCOUNTABILITY MECHANISMS: THE CASE OF THE SIERRA LEONE TRUTH AND RECONCILIATION COMMISSION

Saudamini Siegrist*

1. INTRODUCTION: INTERNATIONAL CRIMINAL ACCOUNTABILITY AND CHILDREN

Modern warfare has exposed children to the worst possible violence and abuse. An increasing number of 'internal wars', fought within national boundaries, have destabilized communities and destroyed families, and have often left children unprotected. The statistics on the impact of war on children are well known and often quoted. For example:

- 90 per cent of wartime causalities are civilians – half are children;
- wars have caused more than 2 million child deaths since 1990;
- wars have caused serious injuries to more than 6 million children since 1990;
- 20 million children have been forced to flee their homes due to war;
- 300,000 child soldiers have been active in 30 conflicts;
- 1 million children have been orphaned or separated from relatives due to war;
- landmines kill or maim 8,000 to 10,000 children each year.[1]

The statistics are estimates and, most likely, underestimates. As pointed out above, what is known with certainty is that today's conflicts have brutally targeted children for mass killings, deliberate and systematic rape, and abduction into armed groups where they may be forced to commit atrocities against their own families, friends and communities. Most of these violations and crimes are committed with impunity.

---

* Project Office, Child Protection, UNICEF Innocenti Research Centre, Florence, Italy.
[1] G. Machel, *The Impact of War on Children: A Review of Progress Since the 1996 United Nations Report on the Impact of Armed Conflict on Children* (London, Hurst 2001); *UNICEF Humanitarian Action Report 2003*, UNICEF, New York, 2003.

K. Arts & V. Popovski (eds.), International Criminal Accountability and the Rights of Children
© 2006, Hague Academic Coalition, The Hague, The Netherlands and the Authors

As sketched in chapters 1 and 3 of this book, by Karin Arts and Vesselin Popovski, the shared responsibility of the international community in ending impunity for crimes against children has become clearly accepted over time, for example under the influence of the pivotal Graça Machel *Report on the Impact of Armed Conflict on Children*, submitted in November 1996 to the United Nations General Assembly.[2] That Report also called for accountability, and for improved monitoring and reporting of crimes against children in armed conflicts to support the accountability mechanisms.

The formal commitment is clear. But exactly how can we end impunity, how can we achieve accountability and hold the perpetrators responsible for grave violations, for genocide, crimes against humanity and war crimes? Prevention is obviously the best response. But when prevention fails and violations occur, the comprehensive and systematic monitoring and reporting of violations is necessary. The United Nations Children's Fund (UNICEF) is working closely with the Office of the Special Representative of the UN Secretary-General for Children and Armed Conflict, and other UN and NGO partners committed to improving accountability for serious crimes against children. Efforts are currently underway to develop a mechanism for the monitoring and reporting of serious violations against children in armed conflict, as called for by Security Council Resolution 1612.[3] At the same time, more reliable mechanisms for truth, reconciliation and justice seeking are needed to address human rights violations committed during armed conflict, to create processes for reconciliation, and to re-establish confidence in the rule of law. Much of the work in this area is unprecedented, and so collaboration among a wide range of partners is needed in order to determine the best way forward.

2.   THE PROLIFERATION OF INTERNATIONAL CRIMINAL ACCOUNTABILITY MECHANISMS AND CHILD PARTICIPATION

In recent years, the international focus on accountability has led to the establishment of transitional justice mechanisms in a number of post-conflict situations, including the *ad hoc* International Criminal Tribunals for the former Yugoslavia (ICTY) and for Rwanda (ICTR), the Special Court for Sierra Leone (SCSL), national justice systems and numerous truth commissions, as well as the establishment of the International Criminal Court (ICC). Accountability for crimes against children is included as a focus of transitional justice and, as a result, children have become participants as victims and witnesses, both in judicial and in non-judicial post-conflict truth and justice-seeking processes. The Special Court for Sierra Leone

---

[2] G. Machel, *The Impact of War on Children*, *UN Doc*. A/51/306 of 26 August 1996, available at <www.unicef.org/graca>.

[3] *UN Doc*. S/RES/1612 (2005), 26 July 2005. See also, 'Report of the Secretary-General to the Security Council on Children and Armed Conflict', *UN Doc*. A/59/695-S/2005/72, 9 February 2005, discussed in the previous chapter.

marks the first time that children have been actively involved as witnesses in an international tribunal. While the SCSL Statute allows for the prosecution of children who were above the age of fifteen at the time of the alleged commission of the crime, it was decided that children below eighteen would not meet the requirements of the competence to prosecute 'those who bear the greatest responsibility' for crimes within the Court's jurisdiction. In fact, at the time of writing no international court or tribunal has indicted a child. This policy is also reflected in the Rome Statute, which limits the jurisdiction of the International Criminal Court to persons over the age of eighteen.[4]

Truth commissions offer another approach, a non-judicial alternative to pursue accountability for serious human rights abuses committed during armed conflicts. Whereas legal proceedings are likely to involve only a few perpetrators of wartime atrocities, truth commissions are able to involve the public more broadly and to engage directly with communities, including children. Children have participated in various capacities in the work of recent truth commissions. The Truth and Reconciliation Commission in Sierra Leone, in particular, has sought to involve children and to adopt child-friendly measures to protect children's rights throughout the process. In doing so it created a new precedent for engaging children more systematically in truth-seeking and reconciliation processes at the community level.

In order to advance accountability for crimes against children it is essential that transitional justice mechanisms address violations against children through investigation, the prosecution of the perpetrators and redress for the victims. In doing so, child-friendly procedures should protect children's involvement in transitional truth and justice-seeking mechanisms.[5] It is also important to recall that children's involvement in post-conflict justice processes is not an isolated activity, but is part of a larger process of transition and reconciliation, rooted in the human rights-based approach. This approach seeks to realise children's rights within the broader cultural, social, economic and political context and to address the root causes of violations. Instead of focusing on specific problems and symptoms within a limited context, the human rights-based approach builds holistic, long-term solutions, laying the foundation for a fair, stable and just society. This implies, for example, the need to work towards strengthening the capacity of children to participate as active citizens and to contribute to decision-making processes that affect their lives. This means involving children in all aspects of family, school and community life, including reconciliation, justice and peace-building processes during post-conflict transition.[6]

The fundamental principle guiding efforts to improve accountability for serious crimes against children, and for children's involvement in transitional justice pro-

---

[4] See, e.g., *International Criminal Justice and Children* (Rome, No Peace Without Justice and UNICEF Innocenti Research Centre 2002) p. 109.

[5] Ibid., p. 13.

[6] UNICEF, *Adolescent Programming in Conflict and Post-Conflict Situations* (New York, UNICEF August 2004).

cesses, is the best interests of the child. As pointed out in chapter 1 by Karin Arts, this is one of the founding principles of the Convention on the Rights of the Child (CRC) and lies at the heart of child rights-based approaches. While there is international consensus supporting the principle of the best interests of the child, its practical application may vary according to local capacity and cultural norms. In situations where extensive war crimes have been committed against children, brutally violating all norms and standards, legal experts may seek to involve children as witnesses in order to prosecute the perpetrators of war crimes. The involvement of children in such processes can help to achieve accountability and also to build up children's capacity and self-esteem. However, the impact and risks must be carefully weighed and special protection (including child-friendly procedures) must be developed so as to ensure that children are not exposed to further harm as a result of their involvement.[7] The best interests of the child must certainly come first.

Another principle that is fundamental to the CRC and to child rights-based approaches is the principle of participation, that is, children's right to express their views in matters affecting their lives.[8] For, the human rights-based approach is participatory, and seeks to create the capacity and context for democratic citizenship. Children have demonstrated, again and again, that they want to play an active role and that they are powerful motivators, innovative thinkers, strategists and idealists. But child participation is not a 'quick fix'. In order for children to become genuine participants and partners in such a process they need guidance and support, and there must be long-term commitment to help young people achieve realistic and sustainable goals.

Establishing a positive role for children is important at all times, but under the extreme conditions of war it is even more crucial. If young people face the injustices of war without the possibility to envision a better future, then youthful optimism may be frustrated. Without hope in the future, young people are more easily provoked to act in rash ways or to resort to destructive behaviour. Addressing their rights to participate and guiding their efforts to achieve realistic goals is therefore an urgent priority.[9]

While children can contribute to improved accountability for serious violations during wartime, it is important to emphasize that the burden of responsibility for truth, reconciliation and peace-building must not, under any condition, be shifted onto their shoulders. It is one thing to invite children's participation in processes of truth and justice-seeking, but it is another matter altogether to suggest that they can somehow solve the problems of society. In communities torn apart by war it is

---

[7] Humanitarian principles and standards of conduct for humanitarian workers have been developed by various actors over the past several years, based largely on international humanitarian law and the work of the International Committee of the Red Cross. UNICEF's humanitarian principles, first developed in 1997-1998, include the 'do no harm' principle. In 2003, UNICEF's humanitarian principles were revised and now also include the principle of accountability, which has come to be recognized as a critical part of codes of conduct in humanitarian action.

[8] Convention on the Rights of the Child, Article 12.

[9] UNICEF, *supra* n. 6.

essential that both the principles and the limits of participation are well understood. Great care is needed because children's active participation in community development and peace-building may be at odds with their protection and serious risks may be involved. Children's successful participation in the Colombia Children's Peace Movement helps to illustrate this point. The Children's Peace Movement, which began in 1996, resulted in a massive mobilization of young people throughout Colombia. Almost 3 million children came out to vote for peace in a national referendum that they organised. Their efforts inspired the country and a year after the children's referendum more than 10 million adults went to the polls – which was twice the turnout during previous elections – and voted in favour of the Mandate for Peace, Life and Liberty, calling for an end to hostilities.[10] The success of the Colombian Children's Peace Movement was widely acclaimed and the children were twice nominated for the Nobel Peace Prize, but they did not bring an end to the war and it is important to remember that. In addition, some of the children who became leaders in the Peace Movement were threatened by rebel and paramilitary forces due to their role in peace-building. Children can play a crucial role and their efforts should be encouraged, but risks must be anticipated and protection measures must be put in place so that children's involvement in peace-building does not undermine their right to protection.[11] These are sobering thoughts which underline the careful consideration that is necessary to ensure that children's involvement in truth, reconciliation and justice-seeking processes does not put them at risk or expose them to further harm, and that their best interests are served at all times. The challenge is how best to provide children and adolescents with opportunities, guidance, support and protection in order to participate in a meaningful way.

Another example of children's successful participation in community development and peace-building is the creation of Children's Municipal Councils (CMCs) in the occupied Palestinian territory, where hundreds of children are working in partnership with mayors, city officials, parents, teachers and local leaders to take positive action in their communities. These children, aged twelve to fifteen, campaign in school-based elections to represent their classmates in collaboration with local municipal government. By encouraging participation in community activities CMCs develop children's potential and, at the same time, increase their protection, demonstrating that with proper guidance and support young people can become catalysts for positive change in their communities. The children who serve on CMCs in the occupied Palestinian territory receive training in human rights and develop their agenda based on the Convention on the Rights of the Child. Many of them can quote the Convention by heart. When the Children's Municipal Council of Gaza City presented its agenda in 2004, one of its priorities was the need for safe play areas, referring to Article 31 of the Convention, which requires states parties to recognise the child's right to play. Another priority, with reference to Article 23 of the CRC specifying the rights of children with disabilities, was to build a ramp in

---

[10] UNICEF, *The State of the World's Children 2000* (New York, UNICEF 2000) pp. 41-43.
[11] UNICEF, *supra* n. 6, p. 5.

the building where they hold meetings so that one of the children, who is confined to a wheelchair, would have access. Although the boy was able to enter the building with the help of the other children, he wanted to enter on his own and the children wanted to help in order to make that possible. The top priority on the agenda of the CMC was the right to protection during armed conflict, as stated in Articles 38 and 39 of the CRC.

Children's grasp of the Convention on the Rights of the Child was also evident during the preparation of the child-friendly Truth and Reconciliation Commission (TRC) report for Sierra Leone. A 10-year old girl, who was among the Children's Forum Network members participating in the preparation of the TRC report, was outspoken and confident in articulating actions for the implementation of the recommendations of the TRC based on the Convention on the Rights of the Child. She argued her position from a human rights perspective and made it clear that children can engage proactively in actions in support of human rights within their communities.

These examples – from Colombia, the occupied Palestinian territory and Sierra Leone – illustrate that Children understand that the Convention on the Rights of the Child is their ticket to the future. But they cannot get there alone, they are counting on the guidance and support of their families, teachers, mentors, friends and community leaders.

3.   CHILDREN'S PARTICIPATION IN THE SIERRA LEONE TRUTH AND
      RECONCILIATION COMMISSION: SOME BACKGROUND INFORMATION

Truth commissions can play a key role in addressing the past and in re-establishing the rule of law in post-conflict situations.[12] By providing a forum for victims, witnesses and perpetrators to recall their experiences, and by documenting the crimes committed during the war, TRCs can serve as an important tool to build stability in societies where entire populations have been traumatized. Truth-seeking mechanisms have the potential to engage communities in accountability processes and are a potentially effective and safe mechanism for children's involvement.

The Truth and Reconciliation Commission for Sierra Leone originates from the Lomé Peace Agreement and was established by an Act of the Sierra Leone Parliament in February 2000. As with many other truth commissions, the key objectives of Sierra Leone's TRC were to create an impartial record of human rights violations that occurred during the war, to provide a public forum for accountability, to help initiate the process of healing and reconciliation for victims, witnesses, perpetrators and families, to help restore a sense of justice in the social and political order, and to make recommendations to the Government to prevent future conflicts.

---

[12] 'The Rule of Law and Transitional Justice in Conflict and Post-Conflict Societies: Report of the Secretary-General', *UN Doc.* S/2004/616, 23 August 2004.

Over 25 truth commissions have been convened in various countries over the last decades and several have addressed the experiences of children, but the TRC for Sierra Leone was the first to specifically focus on children as victims and witnesses, and to profile their role as actors in the reconciliation process. It was also the first truth commission to prepare a children's version of the report.[13] The participation of children in the Sierra Leone TRC process was anticipated from the beginning of the Commission's work. Section 7(3) of the Sierra Leone TRC Act called for the Commission to 'implement special procedures to address the needs of such particular victims as children or those who have suffered sexual abuses as well as in working with child perpetrators of abuses or violations.' This was in recognition of the fact that children had been deliberately, systematically and routinely targeted for the worst possible abuses during the 10-year civil war in Sierra Leone. As many as 10,000 children were abducted or forcibly recruited into armed forces and groups. Many were taken from their homes, drugged, threatened with death and forced to kill. Thousands were abducted for sexual slavery. Thousands of children were massacred, raped and mutilated. It was therefore essential that children should become involved in the process of truth, reconciliation and justice-seeking. As stated in the report: 'We, who survived the war, are determined to go forward. We will look to a new future and help build the road to peace.'[14]

In June 2001, a year after the establishment of the TRC, UNICEF convened a planning meeting in Freetown, in collaboration with the National Forum for Human Rights and UNAMSIL (the United Nations Mission in Sierra Leone) and including national and international child rights experts and a group of Sierra Leonean children. The purpose of the meeting was to recommend policies and procedures for involving children in the TRC process. Children participated in that meeting, and prepared their own report and recommendations. Based on the key findings of the planning meeting, it was determined that a special effort would be made to involve children in the TRC process. It was further decided that all aspects of their participation would be consistent with a child rights-based approach, and thus rooted in the Convention on the Rights of the Child. The children who participated in that first Freetown planning meeting were accompanied by social workers who provided support throughout the meeting. Together, the children presented their expectations of the TRC to the experts. They gave particular emphasis to the voluntary nature of children's participation, and to the need to protect the confidentiality of children's statements and children's anonymity. It was also noted that all children involved in the TRC should be recognised primarily as victims of the war that targeted them and exploited their vulnerability. These priorities and concerns were further developed and expressed by child participants throughout the process.

---

[13] Truth and Reconciliation Commission for Sierra Leone, *Truth and Reconciliation Commission Report for the Children of Sierra Leone: Child-Friendly Version* (Accra, Graphic Packaging September 2004) p. 8, <http://www.unicef.org/infobycountry/sierraleone_23937>.
[14] Ibid., p. 3.

4.   PROCEDURES TO PROTECT CHILDREN INVOLVED IN THE TRC PROCESS

The involvement of children in truth, reconciliation and justice processes must be safeguarded through special protection and child-friendly procedures that, at all times, serve the child's best interests. It should be clearly stated that the right to participation and the right to protection go hand-in-hand. The best interests of the child have to guide all policies and practices and must be given priority over all other concerns.

To protect children's involvement in the Truth and Reconciliation Commission in Sierra Leone, UNICEF, together with other UN agencies and the Child Protection Network – national and international NGOs and government counterparts – developed special procedures including, for example, special hearings for children, closed sessions, a safe and comfortable environment for interviews, protecting the identity of child witnesses, and staff trained in psychosocial support for children. Through the Framework for Cooperation, the Sierra Leone TRC and child protection agencies formally agreed to work together on these measures and procedures, in line with their respective mandates and roles. As stated in the Framework for Cooperation, the TRC's policy was to treat all children coming before the Commission as witnesses. Child protection agencies agreed to assist TRC statement takers through overall guidance and advice on involving children. Specifically this entailed: identifying child statement givers, facilitating access to child statement givers; and providing psychosocial support for child statement givers.

It was decided from the beginning that all participation by children in the TRC must be voluntary. This means that children should agree to participate, understand the purpose of giving a statement before the Commission and that they, together with their guardians, come to an informed decision. It also means that a child can change his or her mind and decide to freely withdraw from the process at any time, with the knowledge that a decision not to participate is also participation.

Eight principles for protection were included in the Framework for Cooperation:

i)   The participation of children in the TRC process shall be guided by the best interests of the child. The children will be treated with dignity and respect.

ii)   Any participation of children shall be voluntary on the basis of informed consent by the child and her/his guardian.

iii) The safety and security of all child statement givers is paramount. Statements can only be obtained in places considered safe and friendly to the child.

iv)   Children must be in an appropriate psychosocial state to give statements. The taking of statements from children must ensure the protection of their physical, spiritual and psychological well-being.

v)   The confidentiality and anonymity of the child shall be guaranteed at all stages of the TRC's work. All statements given by children shall be confidential, and there shall be no sharing of information obtained by the TRC with any outside body, including the Special Court.

vi) In principle, statements shall be obtained on a one-on-one basis, with only the statement taker and the child present, except when the child wishes the presence of a social worker and/or guardian. Girls shall be interviewed by female TRC statement takers only.

vii) Psychosocial and other appropriate support services shall be available for child statement givers.

viii) All statement takers and designated social workers shall receive further training in taking statements from children.

Two questions were deemed essential to help to identify possible child participants: whether the child was able to give a statement and whether the child would be willing to give a statement. A vulnerability assessment and safety checklist were developed as part of the Framework for Cooperation to help to determine whether a child would be secure and confident enough to proceed with the TRC process. While the procedures agreed upon in the Framework for Cooperation were not closely adhered to in all instances and many inconsistencies occurred in the process of statement-taking, the Framework was ground-breaking in establishing norms for the involvement of children in the process and the experience and lessons learned have created a valuable precedent.

5. THE ROLE OF CHILDREN IN THE WORK OF THE SIERRA LEONE TRC

A key activity involving children in the Sierra Leone Truth and Reconciliation Commission was statement-taking at the community level. Child participants were interviewed by a statement taker, with the support of a child protection worker, to ensure that children were not adversely affected and that proper follow-up measures would take place. Most children who were interviewed by the TRC were identified through the child protection and reintegration programme. This also helped to ensure that their involvement was safe and that follow-up measures took place. Nearly 200 children participated across the 13 districts and this had a significant impact on the overall process.

Many children also participated in the thematic hearings on children, which took place on 16 and 17 June 2003, coinciding with the 'Day of the African Child'. The purpose of these hearings was to raise awareness and to provide visibility for children's issues, as well as to recommend actions for improving the situation of young people in post-war Sierra Leone. Recorded children's testimonies were shown at the hearings, without revealing the identity of the children involved. Other children, representing youth clubs, appeared in person at the hearings. Clips from the more general statements were broadcast live on Radio UNAMSIL and on television. The Children's Forum Network also prepared a formal submission to the Commission, documenting the impact of the war on children. Based on the children's statements and testimonies specific recommendations were made for each district.

In the beginning, there was confusion regarding the relationship between the TRC and the Special Court and some children were afraid that their statements to the TRC might be shared with the Special Court. Once it was explained that there would be no sharing of information outside the Truth Commission and that all children would be considered only as victims of the war, more children came forward to give statements. Girls were more reluctant to participate in the TRC process, in particular those who had been sexually exploited, because they were afraid and did not want their story to be told to others.

There were challenges in coordinating the efforts between the TRC and child protection agencies. The success of the collaboration varied from district to district. In some cases, the TRC took statements from children directly without the support of child protection agencies. In most cases, children had a good understanding of the purpose of the TRC and why their statement was important, but some children were not well informed and thought that the TRC could provide financial support or send them to school. This demonstrated the importance of working closely with children to ensure that they are well informed and prepared, in advance. It also demonstrated that sensitization and awareness-raising campaigns at the community level are critical in explaining the purpose of the Commission's work and in promoting the participation of children, and that collaboration and coordination with child protection organisations is essential from the very beginning of the process.

6.   THE LESSONS LEARNT FROM CHILD PARTICIPATION IN THE SIERRA LEONE TRC

Initially, there were concerns about the possible negative impacts on children of having to remember the horrors of the war but, in the end, such impacts were not discerned. Instead, children's participation in the TRC helped them to come to terms with their experiences. After the hearings most children expressed a sense of relief and pride in their contribution. As a result of the involvement of children in the Sierra Leone TRC, a number of key 'lessons learnt' can be identified. More attention should be given to collaboration and coordination with child protection organisations from the very beginning of the process. Timely sensitization and awareness-raising campaigns at the community level – aimed at both adults and children and formulated according to the needs of the community – are critical to explain the purpose and to promote the participation of children. Children's participation in a truth and reconciliation process should be entirely voluntary and there should be no pressure to participate. In addition, children should retain the right to withdraw their participation at any time. This needs to be explained explicitly so that it is well understood by children and their parents or guardians.

Statements from children should be taken by staff with a background in human rights and child protection. More broadly, child-friendly procedures should be used in all cases when interviewing children. Parents, guardians or social workers should be present when requested by the child. Special procedures are needed so that the involvement of children in truth and justice-seeking mechanisms is confidential. These procedures include, for example, conducting interviews in a secure environment and organising closed hearings for children. Girls should be interviewed by female staff, unless male staff are requested, and measures should be taken to ensure gender sensitivity. It is essential that statement-takers, Commissioners and TRC staff speak and understand the language of the child. Psychosocial support for children should be provided throughout all stages of the process: prior to and during the statement-taking, as well as after the hearings.

Traditional ceremonies and forgiveness rituals can help to support the work of a TRC, but these practices should be in accordance with international child rights standards, for example by protecting the identity of the child and ensuring that all participation is entirely voluntary.

Children can continue to play an important role after the conclusion of the work of a TRC by helping to raise awareness about the Commission in their schools and communities and by lobbying for the implementation of the TRC recommendations. While an evaluation is needed to assess the overall impact of children's involvement in the TRC on the community, as well as the impact on children themselves, the Sierra Leone example clearly shows that children, as active partners, can help to break the cycle of violence and re-establish confidence in the rule of law.

7.   THE CHILD-FRIENDLY TRUTH AND RECONCILIATION COMMISSION REPORT

The preparation of a child-friendly version of the final report of the Truth and Reconciliation Commission provided another opportunity to involve children in the Commission's work. The child-friendly version is a much shorter and simpler version of the full report that children can read and understand. It is the first of its kind anywhere in the world. The preparation of a child-friendly TRC report was first discussed when experts and children met in Freetown, in June 2001, to plan how children would take part in the Truth and Reconciliation Commission. The submission to the Truth and Reconciliation Commission by the Children's Forum Network made a similar recommendation, calling for a child-friendly version of the report that children could read and understand, 'as a measure to prevent recurrence of what happened'. The production of the child-friendly report was undertaken by UNICEF, in collaboration with the United Nations Mission in Sierra Leone (UNAMSIL) and the Truth and Reconciliation Commission, and, of course, working together with children in Sierra Leone. The child-friendly text is based on the official report, on information in the TRC database (including statements by children), on testimony given by children in closed and public hearings, and on presentations delivered during the thematic hearings on children conducted on 16 and 17 June 2003 on the occasion of the 'Day of the African Child'. Formal submissions to the Commission by child protection agencies and others, in particular the submission prepared by the Children's Forum Network, proved a valuable source of information. Children's voices are included in all these resources.

The most concrete participation in the drafting of the report came from three national children's networks – the Children's Forum Network, the Voice of Children Radio, and the Children's National Assembly. Over 100 children participated, with a team of 15 closely involved, meeting with the writer on a daily basis. Discussions of the child-friendly report, led by children, were aired on the Voice of Children Radio in Freetown. During the first-ever Children's National Assembly, held in Freetown in December 2003, meetings were convened to discuss the child-friendly report, which brought together children from all districts around the country. Excerpts from the discussions on the child-friendly report that took place at the Children's National Assembly were broadcast on national television and radio. The children concerned were eager to play a role and to give shape to a report that would bring about positive action for and by children.

The child-friendly Truth and Reconciliation Commission report is thus a culmination of children's involvement and perspectives throughout the process, from initial preparation, to background research, to the preparation of the final report. The Children's Forum Network continued to assist with input in the design process, working in close collaboration with the Truth and Reconciliation Commission, and with UNICEF and UNAMSIL. In addition, the last chapter of the child-friendly version is a menu of activities, created by children, to outline their role in disseminating the findings and recommendations of the Truth and Reconciliation Commission.

In October 2004 when the child-friendly TRC report was presented to the President of the country, the Children's Forum Network, a national child-led organisation that gives voice to children throughout all the districts of Sierra Leone, prepared the following statement:

> 'We, the children of Sierra Leone, were the most vulnerable group during the decade-long civil war. We want to be the first priority on the Government's agenda ... We want to see the needs of children addressed in a pragmatic way ... including improved access to education, health care and nutrition, and the elimination of child labour and sexual exploitation ... we want recreational spaces.'

In their presentation, the Children's Forum Network also recommended that children should be given a stronger voice in the democratic decision-making process. They asked for the adoption of a Children Act by Parliament, as a way to give national weight to the rights of children outlined in the Convention on the Rights of the Child. They asked for special attention to be given to those children most affected by the war, especially girls who did not benefit from the demobilization programme. And they requested that the child-friendly version of the TRC report be incorporated in the school curriculum.

On 28 October 2004, the Government of Sierra Leone presented the child-friendly Truth and Reconciliation Report for Sierra Leone to a joint session of the General

Assembly, the Security Council and the ECOSOC at the UN Headquarters in New York.

8. CONCLUSION: CHILD PARTICIPATION IS ESSENTIAL FOR POST-WAR RECONCILIATION

Post-war reconciliation and the return to civilian life is a long process. In Sierra Leone the Truth and Reconciliation Commission was part of this process, helping families and communities to find ways to forgive and rebuild, and to look towards the future. For the children of Sierra Leone reconciliation means reuniting with families, attending school and finding a place in the community. From the children's point of view, education and vocational training are essential for regaining a sense of normality and hope for the future. In the statements given to the TRC children identified returning to school as their number one priority.

Reconciliation also means accountability. By gathering testimonies and creating an accurate record that acknowledges the crimes committed, the TRC gave survivors a public forum to voice the wrongs which they had suffered. At the same time, it provided a basis for social and political reform to prevent further abuse. Children's participation – and children's voice and agency – in this process demonstrated how children can be active partners, helping to break the cycle of violence and to re-establish confidence in the rule of law. However, their participation must be guided, supported and protected every step of the way.

Child rights advocates and humanitarian workers operating in different countries and contexts can play a key role in facilitating the participation of young people in post-conflict peace-building and reconciliation. Much more effort is urgently needed to create opportunities for children's peaceful participation. The voice of the children who took part in the preparation of the Sierra Leone child-friendly TRC report expresses both the challenges and the possibilities they face:

'We have inherited the history of war, and those scars do not disappear all at once ... We need help and advice to protect ourselves from further exploitation. We need to know how to earn a living and how to create new opportunities in our lives. We need to recover our dignity and our pride... How can we build a bridge to the future? But, if not us, then who else can do it? The future is our challenge, and we cannot refuse. That is not all. We want our vision to go beyond the borders of our country. We are children and citizens of Sierra Leone, and we are also children and citizens of the world. We want to share our ideas with children in other countries, to tell our story and bring the hope and dream of peace to children everywhere.'[15]

---

[15] Ibid., p. 42.

Chapter 5
THE AGE OF CRIMINAL RESPONSIBILITY FOR INTERNATIONAL CRIMES UNDER INTERNATIONAL LAW

Matthew Happold*

1. INTRODUCTION

The May 2004 decision of the Appeals Chamber of the Special Court for Sierra Leone in *Prosecutor* v. *Samuel Hinga Norman*[1] makes it clear that the recruitment or use of children under fifteen years of age to participate actively in hostilities is a crime under international law. However, although recent international efforts have focused on holding accountable those who recruit child soldiers, the issue of the criminal responsibility of child soldiers themselves has also arisen, in Sierra Leone and elsewhere. On a number of occasions efforts have been made to prosecute former child soldiers. In 2001, Human Rights Watch intervened with the government of the Democratic Republic of Congo to urge that death sentences imposed on four child soldiers should not be carried out.[2] The four were aged between fourteen and sixteen years old at the time they were arrested, and had been tried, convicted and sentenced by the Court of Military Order. In the event, the four were not executed but it appears that earlier, in 2000, the Congolese government did execute a fourteen-year-old child soldier.[3] In another example, in 2002 the Ugandan authorities brought treason charges against two former Lord's Resistance Army (LRA) fighters – two boys aged fourteen and sixteen – although following lobbying by Human Rights Watch, the charges were withdrawn. According to Human Rights

---

* Matthew Happold is Lecturer in Law, University of Nottingham, United Kingdom.
[1] *Prosecutor* v. *Samuel Hinga Norman*, Case No. SCSL-2004-14-AR729E, Appeals Chamber, Special Court for Sierra Leone, Decision on preliminary motion based on lack of jurisdiction (child recruitment), 31 May 2004. For commentary on the decision, see A. Smith, 'Child Recruitment and the Special Court for Sierra Leone', 2 *Journal of International Criminal Justice* No. 4 (2004) p. 1141; and M. Happold, 'International Humanitarian Law, War Criminality and Child Recruitment: The Special Court for Sierra Leone's Decision in *Prosecutor* v. *Samuel Hinga Norman*', 18 *Leiden Journal of International Law* No. 2 (2005), p. 283.
[2] Human Rights Watch, *Letter to Foreign Minister of Democratic Republic of Congo*, 2 May 2001.
[3] Human Rights Watch monthly e-mail update, *Congo Spares Child Soldiers*, June 2001; and Human Rights Watch press release, *Congo: Don't Execute Child Soldiers: Four Children to be Put to Death*, 2 May 2001.

K. Arts & V. Popovski (eds.), International Criminal Accountability and the Rights of Children
© *2006, Hague Academic Coalition, The Hague, The Netherlands and the Authors*

Watch, the boys had been kidnapped and forcibly inducted into the rebel Lord's Resistance Army and had voluntarily surrendered to the Ugandan army.[4]

In these cases, the crimes charged were crimes under domestic law. However, child soldiers have frequently committed acts amounting to international crimes as well.[5] All persons have a duty to comply with international humanitarian law and failure to do so can give rise to criminal sanctions. Indeed, there is most often a considerable overlap between domestic criminal law and international criminal law, with certain types of behaviour being criminal in both domestic legal systems and international law.

One of the reasons why armed forces and groups recruit child soldiers is that they are more easily led and more suggestible than are adults.[6] Children are less socialised, and more docile and malleable than adults, and hence are more easily persuaded or coerced into committing atrocities. Even if not specifically recruited for such purposes, children's evolving mental and moral development may mean that they are more prone to behaving badly than adult troops are. However, in a number of recent conflicts child soldiers have also been used deliberately for committing atrocities. This, in turn, has led to debate concerning the extent to which these children should be held responsible for their actions or simply seen as innocent tools of their superiors.[7] Accordingly, this chapter will consider the consequences of children's mental and moral immaturity for their criminal responsibility for their actions.

As Chapter 6 by Claire McDiarmid will show in more detail, national approaches to the age of criminal responsibility vary widely. However, there are a number of good reasons for regulating the issue at the international level, at least as regards children's responsibility for international crimes. In the first instance, international crimes are often distinguished from crimes under national law because they tran-

---

[4] See Human Rights Watch, *Uganda: Letter to Minister of Justice*, 19 February 2003; Human Rights Watch press release, *Uganda: Drop Treason Charges Against Child Abductees*, 4 March 2003; John Eremu, 'Treason Suspects Apply for Amnesty', *New Vision*, 5 April 2003; and Human Rights Watch monthly e-mail update, *Treason Charges Against Child Soldiers Dropped*, April 2003.

[5] For examples of such behaviour, see R. Brett and M. McCallin, *Children: The Invisible Soldiers* rev. edn. (Stockholm, Rädda Barnen 1998) pp. 92-93. In this chapter, the term 'international crimes' will be used to refer to behaviour which gives rise to individual criminal responsibility as a matter of international law and not to conduct which international law requires states to criminalise in their own domestic law. Discussion will concentrate on crimes within the jurisdiction of the various international criminal tribunals: genocide, crimes against humanity and war crimes.

[6] Ibid., pp. 153-154. See also the comments in C.P. Dodge, 'Child Soldiers of Uganda and Mozambique', in C.P. Dodge and M. Raundalen (eds.), *Reaching Children in War: Sudan, Uganda and Mozambique* (Bergen, Sigma Forlag 1991); I. Cohn and G.S. Goodwin-Gill, *Child Soldiers: The Role of Children in Armed Conflicts* (Oxford, Oxford University Press 1994) p. 26; Human Rights Watch, *Easy Prey: Child Soldiers in Liberia*, 1994, p. 57; Amnesty International, *Sierra Leone: Childhood – A Casualty of Conflict*, 2000, p. 4; and Human Rights Watch, *Stolen Children: Abduction and Recruitment in Northern Uganda*, 2003, p. 9.

[7] In this chapter the term 'child' means a person under eighteen years of age. CRC Article 1 provides that: 'For the purposes of the present Convention a child means every human being below the age of eighteen unless, under the law applicable to the child, majority is attained earlier.'

scend national boundaries and are of concern to the international community. If this is correct, it should follow that states' responses to such international crimes should be the same, or at least substantially similar, as those to national crimes as in prosecuting international crimes states are acting not only on their own behalf but also as agents of the international community. Secondly, from the perspective of the potential defendant, it would seem wrong for an individual's liability under international law to depend upon the place of prosecution. Thirdly and finally, with regard to at least some international crimes, such as genocide and grave breaches of the 1949 Geneva Conventions, states are obliged to prosecute and punish offenders. Permitting states to decide their own age of criminal responsibility would allow them to determine the scope of their international obligations.

2. INFANCY AND INDIVIDUAL CRIMINAL RESPONSIBILITY

Most systems of criminal law take the view that before a person can be held blameworthy and, hence, punishable, his behaviour must have contained an element of fault. To be guilty of a crime, particularly with regard to serious offences, it is not enough simply to have done a particular prohibited act; there must be the requisite *mens rea* (guilty mind) as well as the *actus reus* (wrongful act).[8] Consequently, it is possible to escape criminal liability by showing that one was lacking a guilty mind, for example that the act was committed accidentally rather than intentionally, or whilst in a state of automatism.

In respect of one class of person, however, a lack of *mens rea* is presumed. As Simester and Sullivan write in relation to the defence of infancy:

'Although it is a defence of status (no-one under 10 years of age [the minimum age of criminal responsibility in England and Wales] can commit a crime), the status is predicated on assumptions concerning a person's mental development and consequent moral irresponsibility for her actions.'[9]

By virtue of this presumption, children (or at least some of them) escape criminal liability for their acts.[10]

It has been argued that international crimes have such onerous *mens rea* requirements that children will always lack capacity to commit them. Genocide, for example, requires a special genocidal intent in that: 'The perpetrator intended to destroy, in whole or in part, ... [a] national, ethnical, racial or religious group, as such.'[11] However, most international crimes do not require proof of any special intent. They

---

[8] See A. Ashworth, *Principles of Criminal Law* 3rd edn. (Oxford, Oxford University Press 1999) pp. 87-88.

[9] A. Simester and R. Sullivan, *Criminal Law: Theory and Doctrine* 1st edn. (Oxford, Hart Publishing 2000) p. 541.

[10] Ibid., pp. 644-645.

[11] See the ICC Elements of Crimes, Article 6: Genocide.

merely require knowledge of the existence of particular circumstances. Crimes against humanity have a contextual element, requiring proof that they were 'committed as part of a widespread or systematic attack directed against the civilian population', but it needs only to be shown that '[t]he perpetrator knew that the conduct was part of' such an attack.[12] War crimes require that the prohibited conduct 'took place in the context of and was associated with' an armed conflict but only require proof that '[t]he perpetrator was aware of factual circumstances that established the existence' of the conflict.[13] In most cases, the problem would seem to be one of proof rather than of principle. Indeed, one might go further and say that there is no principled difference between the issues arising from attempts to hold children responsible for complex domestic and complex international crimes. At best, the argument is over-inclusive. In each case the difficulties will be the same and, as a result, the argument cannot be used to distinguish children's legal responsibility for international crimes from their criminal responsibility in domestic law.

However, with regard to the criminal responsibility of children for international crimes, a particular problem exists. It is unclear what the minimum age of criminal responsibility in respect of international crimes actually is. Indeed, it is unclear whether international law fixes a minimum age of criminal responsibility at all. Although it is clear that too low a national minimum age of criminal responsibility will breach international law, where the line is to be drawn has not been specified.

Additional Protocol I

During the negotiations of Additional Protocol I to the Geneva Conventions, the representative of Brazil proposed that what is now Article 77(5) of the Protocol[14] be amended to add the sentence: 'Penal proceedings shall not be taken against, and sentence not pronounced on, persons who were under sixteen years at the time the offence was committed.'[15] The proposed amendment was not accepted. However, the Italian representative, without objecting to the article as it was adopted, stated that he would have wished that it included an additional paragraph prohibiting any criminal prosecution and conviction of children for offences of which at the time of commission they were too young to understand the consequences.[16] Committee III, to whom the draft article had been assigned, agreed that there was a general principle that a person cannot be convicted of an offence if, at the time (s)he committed it, (s)he was unable to understand the consequences of her or his act. The Commit-

---

[12] Ibid., Article 7: Crimes Against Humanity.

[13] Ibid., Article 8: War Crimes.

[14] Article 77(5) prohibits the execution of the death penalty for offences related to an international armed conflict on persons who had not attained the age of eighteen years at the time when the crime was committed.

[15] Official Records of the Diplomatic Conference on the Reaffirmation and Development of International Humanitarian law Applicable in Armed Conflicts (1974-1777: Geneva, Switzerland), O.R. III, p. 307; CDDH/III/325.

[16] Ibid., O.R. XV, p. 219; CDDH/II/SR.59.

tee decided, however, to leave the issue to national regulation. One might consider such a rule a general principle of law and, as such, a rule of international law.[17] However, the rule would seem to permit states either to fix a minimum age below which children are presumed not to be criminally responsible or to determine culpability on an individual basis, by applying a test of whether an accused understood the consequences of his or her acts at the time (s)he committed them.

It has occasionally been argued that Additional Protocol Article 77(2) itself fixes the minimum age of criminal responsibility for war crimes at fifteen. Such a reading of the provision is based on the idea that if a child under fifteen is too young to fight (s)he should also be considered to be too young to be held criminally responsible for his or her actions. Such a reading of Article 77(2) is, however, unwarranted. It is unsupported by the text itself, which makes no reference to child soldiers' criminal responsibility. And, as we have seen, the negotiators specifically decided to include no such provision in the final text of Article 77. The ideas standing behind such a reading of Article 77(2), however, have been influential in debates about what should be the minimum age of criminal responsibility for international crimes.

The United Nations Convention on the Rights of the Child

The Convention on the Rights of the Child (CRC) takes matters a little further. Article 40(3a) provides that state parties to the Convention shall seek to establish a minimum age below which children shall be presumed not to have the capacity to infringe the criminal law. However, no minimum age of criminal responsibility is stipulated. All that the Convention requires of states is that they establish a minimum age of criminal responsibility. It is left to each state to decide what that age should be.

The relevant provisions of the United Nations Standard Minimum Rules on the Administration of Juvenile Justice ('the Beijing Rules') and their commentary[18] are, however, more enlightening. CRC Article 40 was drafted so as to reflect the approaches to juvenile justice taken in the Beijing Rules,[19] and although these Rules and their commentary are not in themselves binding, they do provide an indication of the shared thinking of states on the issue. Rule 4, on the age of criminal responsibility, is not particularly helpful, merely stating that:

'In those legal systems recognising the concept of the age of criminal responsibility for juveniles, the beginning of that age shall not be fixed at too low an age limit, bearing in mind the facts of emotional, mental and intellectual maturity.'

---

[17] See also G. Van Bueren, *The International Law on the Rights of the Child* (Dordrecht, Martinus Nijhoff 1995) p. 173.

[18] UNGA Resolution 40/33, annex; *UN Doc.* A/40/53 (1985).

[19] See S. Detrick, *A Commentary on the United Nations Convention on the Rights of the Child* (Dordrecht, Martinus Nijhoff 1999) p. 700.

This seems to require even less than the CRC, as there is no obligation to establish a minimum age of criminal responsibility. However, the commentary to the rule is more interesting. It sees disparities in national minimum ages of criminal responsibility as the product of historical and cultural differences. It goes on to say that:

> 'The modern approach would be to consider whether a child can live up to the moral and psychological components of criminal responsibility; that is, whether a child, by virtue of his or her individual discernment and understanding, can be held responsible for antisocial behaviour. If the age of criminal responsibility is fixed too low or if there is no lower age limit at all, the notion of responsibility would become meaningless.'

In other words, criminal responsibility should only be imposed when there is some element of fault, that is, sufficient mental and moral awareness on the part of the individual committing the prohibited act of the consequences or potential consequences of his or her actions. The commentary also links the imposition of criminal responsibility to the granting of civil rights, such as the right to marry and the right to vote. Such rights, of course, are frequently only granted from age sixteen, seventeen or eighteen. The commentary ends by stating that efforts should be made to agree an international standard minimum age of criminal responsibility. Unfortunately, no such agreement has yet been possible.

Elucidation of the requirements of Article 40(3a) of the Convention on the Rights of the Child has been given by the Committee on the Rights of the Child, established under Article 43 of the Convention to monitor states' compliance with its provisions. On a number of occasions in its comments on states' periodic reports, the Committee has expressed concern when it appeared that no minimum age of criminal responsibility had been fixed.[20] In a general discussion on the administration of juvenile justice, the Committee considered that criminal responsibility should not be determined by reference to subjective factors, such as 'the attainment of puberty, the age of discernment or the personality of the child',[21] as doing so led to invidious discrimination. The implication is that only objective factors, such as age, are appropriate criteria. The reason for this was given during discussion of Senegal's initial report to the Committee. There, a Committee member stated that:

> 'She was concerned that children's judges were given the possibility of considering that a child could be criminally responsible on the basis of his personality. However, if there was a minimum age below which the law recognized that no child could infringe the criminal law, then there could be no possibility for differences of interpretation.'[22]

However, the Committee has been less definite about the minimum age at which criminal responsibility can be fixed. The Committee has frequently expressed con-

---

[20] See the instances listed in R. Hodgkin and P. Newell, *Implementation Handbook for the Convention on the Rights of the Child* fully rev. edn. (New York, UNICEF 2002) pp. 602-603.

[21] See Committee on the Rights of the Child, 'Report on the tenth session' (Geneva, 30 October-17 November 1995), *UN Doc.* CRC/C/46 (1995), paras. 203-238, in para. 218.

[22] *UN Doc.* CRC/C/SR/248, para. 26.

cern that the minimum age set by states has been too low, but, apart from welcoming a Nigerian proposal to set the age limit for criminal responsibility at eighteen in its national legislation, has not expressed a view on what it should be.[23]

The European Court of Human Rights

Discussion of this issue did take place in the judgments of the European Court of Human Rights in *T.* v. *United Kingdom* and *V.* v. *United Kingdom*.[24] Both T. and V. were ten years old when they abducted and killed a two-year old boy. Aged eleven, they were tried in public in an adult court before a judge and jury (although some allowances were made for their age), convicted of murder and abduction, and sentenced to an indefinite period of detention. They applied to the European Court of Human Rights on the ground, amongst others, that their treatment had violated Article 3 of the European Convention on Human Rights, which prohibits torture and other inhuman or degrading treatment or punishment.

The Court concluded that the attribution to the applicants of criminal responsibility for their acts did not violate Article 3. It found Article 4 of the Beijing Rules and CRC Article 40(3a) of little help, even though the Committee on the Rights of the Child had recommended that the United Kingdom give serious consideration to raising its minimum age of criminal responsibility.[25] Nor did it consider that there was any common standard amongst the member states of the Council of Europe as to the minimum age of criminal responsibility.[26] Consequently, the Court held that:

'Even if England and Wales is among the few European jurisdictions to retain a low age of criminal responsibility, the age of ten cannot be said to be so young as to differ disproportionately from the age-limit followed by other European States. The Court concludes that the attribution of criminal responsibility does not in itself give rise to a breach of Article 3 of the Convention.'[27]

One might consider that the fact that a practice is not unusual is not, of itself, enough to legitimise it. A number of common practices breach the human rights of those subjected to them. In addition, in basing its conclusions on the lack of consensus amongst the contracting states, the Court granted states a wide margin of appreciation in respect of an issue within the scope of Article 3, which is an absolute, non-

---

[23] See Hodgkin and Newell, *supra* n. 20, p. 603.

[24] *T.* v. *United Kingdom* and *V.* v. *United Kingdom* (2000) 30 *European Human Rights Law Reports* 121. The two cases were heard together. See also chapter 13 of this book, by Nuala Mole.

[25] 'Concluding Observations on the United Kingdom's Initial Report', *UN Doc*. CRC/15/Add.34 (1995), para. 34.

[26] *T.* v. *United Kingdom* and *V.* v. *United Kingdom supra* n. 24, p. 146. At the time, the age of criminal responsibility was seven in Cyprus, Ireland, Liechtenstein and Switzerland; eight in Scotland; thirteen in France; fourteen in Austria, Germany, Italy and many eastern European States; fifteen in the Scandinavian States; sixteen in Andorra, Portugal and Poland; and eighteen in Belgium, Luxembourg and Spain.

[27] Ibid., p. 176.

derogable right. In a joint partly dissenting opinion, five judges[28] took issue with the majority's assessment. Standards could be ascertained from the relevant international instruments and the practice of the member states of the Council of Europe. In the dissenting judges' view:

> 'Only four Contracting States out of forty-one are prepared to find criminal responsibility at an age as low as, or lower than, that applicable in England and Wales. We have no doubt that there is a general standard among the member States of the Council of Europe under which there is a system of relative criminal responsibility beginning at the age of thirteen or fourteen – with special court procedures for juveniles – and providing for full criminal responsibility at the age of eighteen or above. ... Even if Rule 4 of the Beijing Rules does not specify a minimum age of criminal responsibility, the very warning that the age should not be fixed too low indicates that criminal responsibility and maturity are related concepts. It is clearly the view of the vast majority of Contracting States that this kind of maturity is not present in children below the age of thirteen of fourteen.'[29]

Taking the age of criminal responsibility together with the trial procedure and sentencing, they considered that there had been a breach of European Convention Article 3.[30] The minority stated that: 'Bringing the whole weight of the adult criminal process to bear on children as young as eleven is, in our view, a relic of times where the effect of the trial process and sentencing on a child's physical and psychological conditions and development as a human being was scarcely considered, if at all.'[31] At least with regard to whether there are any emerging standards as to the minimum age of criminal responsibility, it is submitted that the reasoning of the minority of the Court is to be preferred.

The Statute of the Special Court for Sierra Leone

Consideration of the minimum age of criminal responsibility also took place during the drafting of the Statute of the Special Court for Sierra Leone. The statutes of international criminal tribunals drafted previously had ignored or avoided the issue. The statutes of the International Criminal Tribunals for Former Yugoslavia and Rwanda did not include any provisions governing the age of criminal responsibility[32] and neither tribunal has indicted any person below the age of eighteen.[33] The

---

[28] Judges Pastor Ridruejo, Ress, Makarcyzk, Tulkens and Butkevych.

[29] *T.* v. *United Kingdom* and *V.* v. *United Kingdom supra* n. 24, p. 203.

[30] Ibid., p. 202.

[31] Ibid.

[32] See the 'Report of the Secretary-General pursuant to para. 2 of Security Council Resolution No. 808 (1993)', *UN Doc.* S/25704, reprinted in 32 *International Legal Materials* 1170, para. 58 (1993): 'The international tribunal [for the former Yugoslavia] will have to decide on various personal defences which may relieve a person of individual criminal responsibility, such as minimum age or mental incapacity, drawing upon the general principles of law recognised by all nations.'

[33] It has been argued that the lack of such a provision marked a tacit understanding that eighteen was the minimum age of criminal responsibility for the purposes of the two statutes.

issue was addressed in the Rome Statute of the International Criminal Court, but not in any enlightening manner. Article 26 of the Statute provides that: 'The Court shall have no jurisdiction over any person who was under the age of 18 at the time of the alleged commission of the offence.' Both the language of the article and its drafting history show that the provision is procedural rather than substantive in nature. It is simply the jurisdiction of the International Criminal Court that is excluded, leaving the treatment of child war criminals to national courts.[34] Indeed, it appears that one of the reasons for this exclusion of jurisdiction was to avoid arguments as to what the minimum age of responsibility for international crimes should be.[35] The NGO Caucus on Children's Rights in the ICC had called for the Statute to specify a minimum age at which individuals could be held criminally responsible for crimes within the Court's jurisdiction, which they argued should be eighteen.[36] During the negotiations, however, suggestions as to where the minimum age of criminal responsibility should be fixed varied between twelve to eighteen years of age.[37] A jurisdictional solution was then adopted to sidestep these disagreements.[38]

With regard to the Statute of the Special Court for Sierra Leone, however, the issue could not be avoided. In the conflict there, child soldiers tortured, maimed, raped and killed. Those same children, however, had frequently been abducted and forcibly recruited into armed groups, and subjected to sustained abuse by their comrades. In his report on the establishment of a Special Court, the United Nations Secretary-General acknowledged the difficulty of prosecuting child soldiers for war crimes and crimes against humanity, given their dual status as both victims and perpetrators.[39] His report described considerable disagreement as to how juvenile offenders should be dealt with. According to the Secretary-General:

'The question of child prosecution was discussed at length with the Government of Sierra Leone both in New York and in Freetown. It was raised with all the interlocutors of the United Nations team; the members of the judiciary, members of the legal profession and the Ombudsman, and was vigorously debated with members of civil society, non-governmental organizations and institutions actively engaged in child-care and rehabilitation programmes.

The Government of Sierra Leone and representatives of Sierra Leone civil society clearly wish to see a process of judicial accountability for child combatants presumed

---

[34] See R.S. Clark and O. Triffterer, 'Article 26: exclusion of jurisdiction over persons under eighteen', in O. Triffterer (ed.), *Commentary on the Rome Statute of the International Criminal Court: Observers' Notes, Article by Article* (Baden-Baden, Nomos Verlag 1999) p. 499.

[35] Ibid., p. 497.

[36] Caucus on Children's Rights in the ICC, 'Recommendations and Commentary for the December 1997 Preparatory Committee Meeting on the Establishment of an International Criminal Court', on file with the author.

[37] Clark and Triffterer, *supra* n. 34, p. 495.

[38] Although it has been argued that the provision cannot be said to be totally neutral, as its adoption was also about avoiding having to establish a special system of juvenile justice for the ICC.

[39] 'Report of the Secretary-General on the establishment of a Special Court for Sierra Leone', *UN Doc.* S/2000/915, 4 October 2000.

responsible for the crimes falling within the jurisdiction of the Court. It is said that the people of Sierra Leone would not look kindly upon a court which failed to bring to justice children who committed crimes of that nature and spared them the judicial process of accountability. The international non-governmental organizations responsible for child-care and rehabilitation programmes, together with some of their national counterparts, however, were unanimous in their objections to any kind of judicial accountability for children below 18 years of age for fear that such a process would place at risk the entire rehabilitation programme so painstakingly achieved.'[40]

Similarly, when in October 2000 eleven members of the Security Council visited Sierra Leone, they reported that:

'The possibility that children should be prosecuted by the Special Court was the subject of animated debate in Sierra Leone and there appeared to be no prevailing view. In the view of the Government of Sierra Leone, the Court should prosecute those child combatants who freely and willingly committed indictable crimes. On the other hand, non-governmental and United Nations agencies, especially those engaged in the protection of children, favoured excluding those under the age of 18 years.'[41]

In the end, the mission made no recommendations in relation to the establishment of the Special Court, stating that the issues required further discussion by the Security Council.[42]

Article 7(1) of the Secretary-General's draft Statute provided that: 'The Special Court shall have jurisdiction over persons who were 15 years of age at the time of the alleged commission of the crime.' Why the Secretary-General fixed fifteen as the minimum age of criminal responsibility was not made explicit, but it seems that the intention was to mirror the provisions of the two Additional Protocols and the CRC, on the ground that if children under fifteen are too young to be recruited, they must be too young to be held responsible for their actions. The Secretary-General's draft also provided that:

'At all stages of the proceedings, including investigation, prosecution and adjudication, an accused below the age of 18 (hereinafter "a juvenile offender") shall be treated with dignity and a sense of worth, taking into account his or her young age and the desirability of promoting his or her rehabilitation, reintegration into and assumption of a constructive role in society.'[43]

There followed a number of guarantees for juvenile offenders. Only exceptionally should a juvenile offender be denied bail. A juvenile offender should be tried before a specially constituted 'Juvenile Chamber'. A juvenile offender's trial should be

---

[40] Ibid., paras. 34-35.

[41] 'Report of the Security Council mission to Sierra Leone', *UN Doc.* S/2000/992, 16 October 2000, para. 50.

[42] Ibid., para. 54(b).

[43] Article 7(2), draft Statute, ibid., enclosure.

separated from those of any co-accused adults. The parent or legal guardian of a juvenile offender should be permitted to participate in the proceedings. The Special Court should provide protective measures, including but not limited to the protection of his identity and *in camera* proceedings, to ensure the juvenile offender's privacy. The Court could not punish a juvenile offender by imprisonment. These provisions closely followed those concerned with juvenile justice in the International Covenant on Civil and Political Rights and the Convention on the Rights of the Child.[44]

The Secretary-General's advocacy of these provisions cannot be seen as unreserved. In his report, he simply stated that he considered 'that it would be most prudent to demonstrate to the Security Council for its consideration how provisions on prosecution of persons below the age of 18 ... before an international jurisdiction could be formulated.'[45] Indeed, he concluded by saying that: 'ultimately, it will be for the Prosecutor to decide if, all things considered, action should be taken against a juvenile offender in any individual case.'[46] However, all the Security Council did to Article 7 was to shorten it so that it read that:

> 'Should any person who was at the time of the alleged commission of the crime below 18 years of age come before the Court, he or she shall be treated with dignity and a sense of worth, taking into account his or her young age and the desirability of promoting his or her rehabilitation, reintegration into and assumption of a constructive role in society, and in accordance with human rights standards, in particular the rights of the child.'[47]

This was, it might be thought, less satisfactory than the Secretary-General's draft, as it failed to set out the human rights standards that should apply to the trial of any juvenile offenders.[48] Even more significantly, the revised Article 7 failed to include any minimum age of criminal responsibility for crimes within the Special Court's jurisdiction. However, the wording of the revised provision implied that any such prosecutions would be exceptional. Such a reading is confirmed in the Security Council's comments on the Secretary-General's draft: 'the simplified and more general formulations suggested were considered appropriate because the Council considered that the Special Court should concentrate on prosecuting persons who played a leadership role in the conflict in Sierra Leone.'[49] Instead, the Council considered that the Truth and Reconciliation Commission established under the

---

[44] See in particular ICCPR Articles 10(2b), 10(3), 14(1) and 14(4); and CRC Articles 37(b), 37(c), 37(d), 40(1), 40(2bii), 40(2bvii) and 40(4).

[45] Ibid., para. 36.

[46] Ibid., para. 38.

[47] Letter dated 22 December 2000 from the President of the Security Council addressed to the Secretary-General, *UN Doc.* S/2000/1234, Annex.

[48] Although it has been suggested that the intention was to make the prosecution of child soldiers before the Special Court less likely, on the ground that too detailed provisions for such trials would legitimise such proceedings and encourage their use.

[49] Ibid., para. 1.

Lomé Peace Agreement[50] should play the major role in dealing with juvenile offenders.

In his reply to the Security Council, the Secretary-General suggested amendments to the revised Article 7. He stated that even if jurisdiction of the Court was limited to persons bearing the greatest responsibility for crimes committed during the conflict in Sierra Leone, the determination of which individuals bore such responsibility would be made, in the first instance, by the Prosecutor, and would therefore 'have to be reconciled with an eventual prosecution of juveniles ... even if such prosecutions are unlikely.'[51] The Secretary-General expressed his understanding that the Security Council's revised draft was not intended to allow the prosecution of persons for crimes committed below fifteen years of age and that the reference to human rights standards encompassed all the guarantees of juvenile justice set out in his draft,[52] and suggested that Article 7 be amended to read that:

> '1. The Special Court shall have no jurisdiction over any person who was under the age of 15 at the time of the alleged commission of the crime. Should any person who was at the time of the alleged commission of the crime between 15 and 18 years of age come before the Court, he or she shall be treated with dignity and a sense of worth, taking into account his or her young age and the desirability of promoting his or her rehabilitation, reintegration into and assumption of a constructive role in society, and in accordance with international human rights standards, in particular the rights of the child.
> 2. In the disposition of a case against a juvenile offender, the Special Court shall order any of the following: care guidance and supervision orders, community service orders, counselling, foster care, correctional, educational and vocational training programmes, approved schools and, as appropriate, any programmes of disarmament, demobilization and reintegration or programmes of child protection agencies.'

Paragraph 2 reproduced *verbatim* the provisions of Article 7(3f) of the Secretary-General's original draft. The Secretary-General's suggested amendments were accepted by the Security Council and the Government of Sierra Leone and were incorporated into the Statute of the Special Court.

Article 1(1) of the Special Court's Statute provides that its function is 'to prosecute persons who bear the greatest responsibility' for the atrocities committed during the conflict in Sierra Leone. Security Council Resolution 1315,[53] which requested the Secretary-General to negotiate an agreement with the Government of Sierra Leone establishing the Special Court, stated that this Court:

> '[S]hould have personal jurisdiction over persons who bear the greatest responsibility for the commission of the crimes referred to in paragraph 2 [crimes against humanity,

---

[50] *UN Doc.* S/1999/777.

[51] Letter dated 12 January 2001 from the Secretary-General addressed to the President of the Security Council, *UN Doc.* S/2001/40, para. 2.

[52] Ibid., paras. 7-8.

[53] UNSC Resolution 1315 of 14 August 2000.

war crimes and other serious violations of international humanitarian law, as well as crimes under relevant Sierra Leonean law committed within the territory of Sierra Leone], including those leaders who, in committing such crimes, have threatened the establishment of and implementation of the peace process in Sierra Leone.'[54]

The Secretary-General's draft omitted the leadership criterion, arguing that the term 'persons most responsible' should be viewed as including not only the political and military leadership but also others responsible for particular grave or serious crimes.[55] On this reading, according to the Secretary-General, children could fall within the Court's personal jurisdiction.[56] However, the Security Council restored the reference to those persons who played a leadership role,[57] and the Special Court's Statute again categorises 'those leaders who, in committing such crimes, have threatened the establishment and implementation of the peace process' as amongst those persons most responsible. Given this focus, it was always unlikely that any juvenile offenders would be tried before the Special Court.[58] The general view, expressed by both the Security Council and the Secretary-General, was that juvenile offenders were best dealt with by the Truth and Reconciliation Commission.[59] It came as no surprise, therefore, that early in his tenure the Prosecutor stated that, as a matter of policy, he did not intend to indict persons for crimes committed when children.[60]

3.   CONCLUSIONS

A number of general conclusions can be drawn from this rather disparate material. States are obliged to establish a minimum age of criminal responsibility, which should be fixed and not determined on an individual basis by reference to an accused's personal characteristics. However, although international law dictates that states have a minimum age of criminal responsibility, it does not purport to tell them what that age should be. It does, however, offer a number of guidelines. Firstly, the age should not be so low as to result in the punishment of children for offences in respect of which, at the time of their commission, they were too young to under-

---

[54] Ibid., para. 3. See also chapter 9 of this book, by David Crane.

[55] 'Report of the Secretary-General on the establishment of a Special Court for Sierra Leone', *UN Doc*. S/2000/915, 4 October 2000, para. 30.

[56] Ibid., para. 32.

[57] Letter dated 12 January 2001 from the Secretary-General addressed to the President of the Security Council, *UN Doc*. S/2001/40, para. 1.

[58] See the comments of Hans Corell, UN Under-Secretary-General for Legal Affairs, in C. McGreal, 'Unique Court to Try Killers of Sierra Leone', *The Guardian*, 17 January 2002, and D. Crane, Special Court Prosecutor, in R. Dowden, 'Justice Goes on Trial in Sierra Leone', *The Guardian*, 3 October 2002.

[59] See above, text to n. 41, and Letter dated 12 January 2001 from the Secretary-General addressed to the President of the Security Council, *UN Doc*. S/2001/40, para. 9.

[60] Special Court for Sierra Leone, Public Affairs Office, press release, *Special Court Prosecutor Says He Will Not Prosecute Children*, 2 November 2002.

stand the consequences. This would seem to be a general principle of law. Secondly, there may be a trend to standardising the minimum age of criminal responsibility somewhere in the mid-teens (thirteen, fourteen, fifteen). This was the approach taken by the minority in the *T.* and *V.* Cases and by the UN Secretary-General (with whom the Security Council agreed) when drafting the Statute of the Special Court for Sierra Leone.[61] Thirdly, even children above the age of criminal responsibility should be treated differently from adults. Here the drafting history of the Statute of the Special Court is particularly relevant. The Statute closely follows Article 40 of the Convention on the Rights of the Child and emphasises that the purpose of juvenile justice is rehabilitation. The Secretary-General's draft also set out a list of guarantees of juvenile justice. Indeed, in some respects it went further than the relevant human rights instruments: providing that all trials of children be held *in camera* and prohibiting the Court from imprisoning juvenile offenders. In the final version of the Statute much of this language disappeared but a requirement that the Court adhere to international human rights standards was retained. Moreover, according to both the Security Council and the Secretary-General, prosecution before the Special Court should be a last resort. Their attitude that juvenile offenders be dealt with by the Truth and Reconciliation Commission mirrors CRC Article 40(3b), which provides that States shall seek to promote, 'whenever appropriate and desirable, measures for dealing with such children without resorting to judicial proceedings.'

However, even if the Statute and practice of the Special Court can be seen as an example of 'best practice', states are still left with a considerable amount of discretion. Indeed, the to-and-fro between the Secretary-General and the Security Council, and the variety of opinions expressed by the government of Sierra Leone, local civil society and international NGOs serve to show serious differences about and uncertainties as to how children alleged to have committed serious crimes should be dealt with.

Difficulties arising

That States retain considerable discretion as to when to fix their minimum age of criminal responsibility can be seen as giving rise to difficulties. It is generally admitted that the perpetrators of genocide, war crimes and crimes against humanity are subject to universal jurisdiction.[62] Any state into whose hands they fall may prosecute and punish them. Indeed, state parties to the 1949 Geneva Conventions and 1977 Additional Protocols are obliged to do so in the case of persons who have committed grave breaches of these Conventions and Protocols.[63] In cases involving child soldiers, at present it would appear perfectly proper for states to apply

---

[61] Which was, of course, adopted by the Security Council and the government of Sierra Leone.

[62] See I. Brownlie, *Principles of Public International Law*, 5th edn. (Oxford, Oxford University Press 2003) pp. 303-305.

[63] Articles 49, 50, 129, 146 and 1949 of the Geneva Conventions and Article 85 of Additional Protocol I.

their own domestic law as to the minimum age of criminal responsibility providing such law falls within the broad limits set out above. This might be seen as likely to lead to arbitrariness and unfairness. To a large extent, whether a child soldier can be prosecuted for international crimes would seem to depend on the minimum age of criminal responsibility of the state prosecuting him. A suspect found in a country with a low minimum age of criminal responsibility might be prosecuted, when his comrades, who had escaped to a state with a higher one, could not be. Alternatively, a child soldier might be under the age of criminal responsibility of the state in which he committed atrocities, but having fled elsewhere, to somewhere with a lower minimum age, might open himself to criminal prosecution.

States have hardly shown themselves eager to prosecute child soldiers who fall into their hands, so it might be argued that the possibility that child soldiers will face prosecution for international crimes is merely theoretical. In recent years, however, at least some states have displayed a greater willingness to prosecute international crimes, even in cases where their own nationals had not been involved either as perpetrators or victims. In addition, under Article 1F(a) of the 1951 Convention relating to the Status of Refugees, states are obliged to refuse refugee status to any persons 'with respect to whom there are serious reasons for considering that ... he has committed ... war crime or a crime against humanity.' Former child soldiers have been excluded from refugee status by the application of Article 1F.[64]

There are thus a number of good reasons – both practical and theoretical – why agreement should be sought on a minimum age of criminal responsibility for international crimes.[65] As this paper has shown, there exist at least some foundations upon which to build. However, seeing the issue of how best to deal with children who commit atrocities through the prism of criminal responsibility is often unhelpful.

One of the reasons why concern has grown about the involvement of children in armed conflict is the growing belief in children's rights: that children are rights-bearers and that their rights must be respected regardless of what their parents or other adults might think. It does not necessarily follow from this that children are always viewed as having the capacity to exercise their rights, but the two ideas have tended to go hand-in-hand. This can be seen, most prominently, in Articles 12(1) and 13-15 of the Convention on the Rights of the Child, which respectively require that: 'States Parties [to the Convention] shall assure to the child who is capable of

---

[64] See United Nations High Commissioner for Refugees, 'The Exclusion Clauses: Guidelines on Their Application' (December 1995), reproduced in P.J. van Krieken (ed.), *Refugee Law in Context: The Exclusion Clause* (The Hague, T.M.C. Asser Instituut 1999) p. 22; and S. Kaepferer, 'Exclusion Clauses in Europe – A Comparative Overview of State Practice in France, Belgium and the United Kingdom', 12 *International Journal of Refugee Law* Suppl. 1 (2000) p. 214. For discussion of child soldiers as asylum seekers and refugees, see M. Happold, *Child Soldiers in International Law* (Manchester, Manchester University Press 2005) pp. 160-169.

[65] Although even then problems could arise if the minimum age of criminal responsibility for domestic crimes is not standardised, as in many cases conduct amounting to an international crime will also be criminal under the relevant domestic law.

forming his or her own views the right to express those views freely in all matters affecting the child, the views of the child being given due weight in accordance with the age and maturity of the child', and declare that children have the right to freedom of expression; freedom of thought, conscience and religion; and freedom of association and peaceful assembly. The traditional view of a right-holder is of a rational individual capable of making decisions for his or herself and responsible for the consequences of his or her actions. Yet children's rights campaigners have often resisted the criminal prosecution of children on the grounds that it is not in children's best interests. This has led to comments that such a position is an attempt to have one's cake and eat it. On the one hand, children are said to have the capacity to do good things, such as participating meaningfully in drafting a child-friendly version of the report of the Truth and Reconciliation Commission for Sierra Leone,[66] as presented in chapter 4 of this book by Saudamini Siegrist. On the other hand, it is argued that they are too immature to be held responsible for the bad things they do, such as committing atrocities during the civil war in that country.

There are good reasons, from a children's rights perspective, for seeing children as moral actors and, hence, accountable for their actions. However, accountability does not always involve criminal responsibility, and even if held criminally responsible for their actions, children should not necessarily be dealt with in the same way as adults.

---

[66] See 'Children and the Truth and Reconciliation Commission for Sierra Leone: Recommendations for policies and procedures for addressing and involving children in the Truth and Reconciliation Commission' (2001), available at <http://www.unicef.org/emerg/SierraLeone-TRCReport.pdf>; Truth and Reconciliation Commission for Sierra Leone, *Truth and Reconciliation Commission Report for the Children of Sierra Leone: Child-Friendly Version* (Accra, Graphic Packaging September 2004) p. 8, <http://www.unicef.org/infobycountry/sierraleone_23937>.

Chapter 6
WHAT DO THEY KNOW? CHILD-DEFENDANTS AND THE AGE OF CRIMINAL RESPONSIBILITY: A NATIONAL LAW PERSPECTIVE

Claire McDiarmid*

The age of criminal responsibility is a deceptively easily expressed term which represents an important legal principle: that young children are not to be held accountable for acts which would, if carried out by adults, constitute offences. In most legal systems which make use of it, the age signifies the point at which minors may be held criminally responsible for their crimes in largely the same way as adults. These matters are often regarded as uncontroversial[1] but, if we begin to unpick the legal principle and theory underlying them, it becomes clear that, as a concept, the age of criminal responsibility is a rather more complex legal construct than this might suggest.

This chapter examines four possible models for the age of criminal responsibility in national legal systems. It will then consider, in a little more depth, what it actually means to have criminal responsibility. Finally, it will look at the link between criminal responsibility as defined and a child's chronological age. The list of the four models presented is not intended to be exhaustive. The age of criminal responsibility may well operate differently in specific legal systems. Each model, however, does reveal something of the overall purpose and effect of the age, if only by raising questions about this.

1. MODEL 1: IRREBUTTABLE PRESUMPTION OF LACK OF CRIMINAL CAPACITY

In this first model, the age of criminal responsibility acts as an absolute dividing line between childhood and adulthood as far as the criminal justice system is con-

---

* Claire McDiarmid is Lecturer in Law at The Law School, University of Strathclyde, United Kingdom.

[1] Academic commentators on the legal concept of insanity, e.g., often use children as an example of a group of people who obviously lack criminal capacity. See, e.g., V. Tadros, 'Insanity and the Capacity for Criminal Responsibility', 5 *Edinburgh Law Review* No. 3 (2001) pp. 325-354 at p. 327.

K. Arts & V. Popovski (eds.), International Criminal Accountability and the Rights of Children
© 2006, Hague Academic Coalition, The Hague, The Netherlands and the Authors

cerned. It carries with it a presumption that, below the age set, the child is incapable of committing crime. Younger children, therefore, cannot be prosecuted because they are presumed not to understand sufficiently the nature of the crime. This appears to be the model favoured by the 1989 United Nations Convention on the Rights of the Child (CRC) and the 1985 United Nations Standard Minimum Rules for the Administration of Juvenile Justice, the so-called 'Beijing Rules'. Article 40(3) of the CRC states that 'States Parties shall seek to promote … (a) The establishment of a minimum age below which children shall be presumed not to have the capacity to infringe the penal law.' Similarly, Rule 4.1 of the Beijing Rules states: 'In those legal systems recognizing the concept of the age of criminal responsibility for juveniles, the beginning of that age shall not be fixed at too low an age level, bearing in mind the facts of emotional, mental and intellectual maturity.' This model is problematic in that it tends to perpetuate an image of children, as a group, as completely lacking in basic understandings and skills. In other words, children below the age of criminal responsibility are simply presumed to have no understanding whatsoever of criminal behaviour. Clearly, this may not be true of children as a general rule and it is certainly untrue in individual cases. However, the model's advantage is to be found precisely in the fact that there *is* a theory underlying the blanket exemption from criminal liability. In claiming that all children below the age lack criminal capacity, it provides a rationale for that exemption.

Certainly in the United Kingdom, there is a discernible tendency to stigmatise children who commit serious crimes. This reached its height with the murder of James Bulger in 1993.[2] If children below a certain age are exempted from criminal liability then, from the point of view of stigma it is at least slightly better to state that this is because they are legally incapable of offending. This may seem a slight point but it assumes importance in relation to the second model proposed here.

2.   MODEL 2: AGE AS THE (BARE) GATEWAY INTO THE ADULT SYSTEM

The age of criminal responsibility can also simply mean the age at which the child ceases to be subject to any juvenile justice system or other special provision made for children who offend and is, instead, subject to the same form of criminal process as his or her adult counterpart. All legal systems with dedicated juvenile justice systems utilise this model because, obviously, once individuals age sufficiently to be no longer regarded as children by the culture to which they belong, there is no justification anymore for the application of juvenile justice. However, because this is so self-evident, many legal systems will not term this point of transition between types of procedure the 'age of criminal responsibility'. Instead, that term is reserved for a lower age which is linked, at least notionally, to the child's lack of

---

[2] See, e.g., B. Franklin and J. Petley, 'Killing the Age of Innocence: Newspaper Reporting of the Death of James Bulger', in J. Pilcher and S. Wagg (eds.), *Thatcher's Children: Politics, Childhood and Society in the 1980s and 1990s* (London, Falmer Press 1996) p. 134.

criminal capacity as described in model 1. Accordingly, in practice, many legal systems operate a model which is a hybrid of models 1 and 2.

For example, some states in the United States operate a 'waiver procedure' whereby a minor who still qualifies, by reason of age, for the juvenile system, can be processed and ultimately sentenced as an adult, usually for a serious crime, where the court considers that (s)he has an understanding of the act.[3] Similarly, other legal systems retain an option to prosecute in adult proceedings children aged above the (model 1-type) age of criminal responsibility but below the age where those proceedings are automatically applied.[4]

Ignoring these hybrid arrangements and returning to the basic mechanism represented by this model 2, the dividing line which the age draws between juvenile and adult proceedings is absolute and the only issue raised is which of these types of procedure to use. Therefore, no question is raised about capacity or capability to commit crime. It is contended, however, that this is an important omission because legal systems should provide a rationale, in terms of legal capacity, for treating children differently. It is partly because there is uncertainty over the child's understanding, by comparison with the adult's, that the issue of exemption from criminal liability, or differential treatment, arises in the first place. On the other hand, this model usually draws its dividing line at a later point in childhood than that utilised by model 1,[5] thus allowing the child to have moved closer to a mature understanding of criminal behaviour. Also, because it is concerned solely with the type of procedure to be applied, it concentrates thinking on the child's role in the criminal process, a point which is central to the third model.

3. MODEL 3: AGE AS CONFERRING AN IMMUNITY FROM PROSECUTION ONLY

Similarly to model 1, this model sets an age of criminal responsibility below which no child may be prosecuted. However, the child is only declared to be immune from prosecution during that period. As soon as (s)he attains the age, the immunity ceases and, at least in theory, it is open to the prosecuting authorities to bring a case against him or her for a crime committed earlier, during the period of immunity.[6]

---

[3] P.H. Witt, 'Transfers of Juveniles to Adult Court: The Case of HH', *Psychology, Public Policy and Law* (September/December 2003) p. 361.

[4] This is the position in Scotland and England. E.g., in New Zealand the age of criminal responsibility is ten, but the age of jurisdiction for the Youth Court is fourteen. Children charged with murder or manslaughter who are aged over ten but under fourteen are usually prosecuted using adult procedure, though the preliminary hearing may be held in a Youth Court. See Neighbourhood Support, 'New Zealand Fact Sheet: Citizen's Arrest and Self-Defence', <http://www.ns.org.nz/40.html>.

[5] E.g., in England the age of criminal responsibility *per se* (i.e., as described in model 1) is ten. See Children and Young Persons Act 1933, s 50 as amended by Children and Young Persons Act 1963, s 16. However, the jurisdiction of the Youth Court continues until the child attains the age of eighteen (and longer in certain cases). See Children and Young Persons Act 1933, s 45 (as amended by the Courts Act 2003. s 50) and R. Ward, *Young Offenders: Law, Practice and Procedure* (Bristol, Jordans 2001) pp. 2-6.

[6] This model has recently been proposed for Scotland by the Scottish Law Commission which exists, similarly to the Law Commission for England and Wales, to 'suggest reforms to improve, sim-

This model finds its theoretical justification[7] in the fact that very young children are likely to lack the ability to understand the trial process and to defend themselves against the charge. Following the case brought by Robert Thompson and Jon Venables (the killers of James Bulger) in the European Court of Human Rights,[8] it is no longer merely desirable that the trial process should be comprehensible to a child-defendant in states which are signatories to the 1950 European Convention on Human Rights (ECHR). It is now essential, under Article 6 of the European Convention, that such defendants should be able 'to participate effectively in the criminal proceedings against [them].'[9] Compliance with this principle requires more than simply ensuring that the child-defendant is legally represented.[10]

A notable advantage of this model is that it draws attention to the fact that children may not have the advocacy skills to answer the charge against them effectively. The more traditional concept of criminal capacity, in terms of understanding of the nature of the crime, with which model 1 is concerned, may sometimes overlook this point. However, this is the only issue with which model 3 engages. Once the child attains the age of criminal responsibility, and is, at least notionally, old enough to be deemed to possess these skills, (s)he becomes, at least in theory, answerable for the crime.

There are a number of legal and practical reasons why it is unlikely that such charges would be brought. For example, Article 6 of the European Convention on Human Rights states that '[i]n the determination ... of any criminal charge against him [sic], everyone is entitled to a fair and public hearing within a reasonable time ...'. Failing to prosecute for a number of years might well constitute unreasonable delay in terms of this provision. Nonetheless, the possibility of later prosecution remains. This seems unfair, in that the child concerned would have the prospect of proceedings hanging over his or her head for a number of years. Also, it may not serve the public interest particularly well in that the quality of witnesses' memories is likely to deteriorate over time.

Finally, although there is a theoretical dimension and rationale to this model in terms of the child's answerability for the crime, immunity from prosecution suggests privileging a status (similarly to the immunity from prosecution accorded to diplomats) rather than acknowledging that it is inappropriate to attach criminal responsibility because of an absence of understanding of some essential aspect of the crime, or of criminal behaviour in general, on the part of the defendant. Where the political climate is punitive towards child-offenders, it is particularly important that the criminal law should provide a robust rationale for its refusal to prosecute those

---

plify and update the law of Scotland'. See Scottish Law Commission, *Report on Age of Criminal Responsibility* (Scot Law Com No. 185, especially paras. 3.1-3.20).

[7] For a full discussion of the theory underlying this model see G. Maher, 'Age and Criminal Responsibility', 2 *Ohio State Journal of Criminal Law* No. 2 (2005) pp. 493-512.

[8] 30 *European Human Rights Reports* 121 (2000).

[9] Ibid., at p. 126.

[10] Ibid.

aged under the age of criminal responsibility. If there is no link to criminal capacity, this rationale is lacking.

4.   MODEL 4: ABSOLUTE INCAPABILITY FOLLOWED BY REBUTTABLE PRESUMPTION OF INCAPABILITY

The final model to be presented here is that represented by the *doli incapax* presumption. This echoes the first model in that it provides one age carrying an absolute presumption of incapacity to commit crime. Between this age and the age of (usually) fourteen, a further, rebuttable presumption operates that the child is *doli incapax*, that is incapable of crime. This presumption often operates on a sliding scale so that the closer the minor-defendant is to the age of fourteen, the less evidence is required to rebut the presumption.[11] The standard procedure is to require the prosecution to lead this evidence in the same way as to prove, beyond reasonable doubt, that the defendant committed the *actus reus* (the criminal act itself) of the offence with the relevant mental element or element of fault.

The *doli incapax* presumption is still applied in a number of jurisdictions including South Africa and Australia.[12] Certainly in English law, where it applied for around 800 years until its abolition in 1998,[13] the presumption was flawed. There were contradictions in the case law as to the issue which required proof. Although ultimately it appeared to be settled that the question was whether the child understood the act to be seriously wrong as opposed to merely naughty,[14] many other possibilities were canvassed along the way. For example, in 1981 one case held that the test was knowledge that the act was morally wrong.[15] This was then directly contradicted three years later.[16] More concerningly, in some cases, evidence that the child had committed the offence was enough to rebut the presumption,[17] thereby robbing it of any meaning or value. In other cases, the prosecution simply proved that the child was of normal development and the court accepted the implicit argument that a normal child of the age of the defendant ought to have the necessary understanding to be convicted.[18] All of these questions are one-dimensional and

---

[11] *R* v. *Coulbourn* (1988), 87 *Criminal Appeal Reports* 309.

[12] See respectively K. Johansson and T. Palm, 'Children in Trouble With the Law: Child Justice in Sweden and South Africa', 17 *International Journal of Law, Policy and the Family* No. 3 (2003) pp. 308-337; and Th. Crofts, 'Doli Incapax: Why Children Deserve Its Protection', 10 *E-Law* No. 3 (2003) available at <http://www.murdoch.edu.au/elaw/indices/title/crofts103_abstract.html>.

[13] See respectively A. Morris and L. Gelsthorpe, 'Much Ado About Nothing – A Critical Commentary on Key Provisions Relating to Children in the Crime and Disorder Act 1998', 11 *Child and Family Law Quarterly* No. 3 (1999) pp. 209-221; and Crime and Disorder Act 1998, s 34.

[14] *R* v. *Gorrie* (1919), 83 *Justice of the Peace* 136, affirmed by the House of Lords in *C (a minor)* v. *DPP* (1995), 2 *Weekly Law Reports* 383.

[15] *JBH and JH (minors)* v. *O'Connell* (1981), *Criminal Law Review* 632.

[16] *JM (a minor)* v. *Runeckles* (1984), 79 *Criminal Appeal Reports* 255.

[17] *F* v. *Padwick* (1959), *Criminal Law Review* 439; *T* v. *DPP* (1989), *Criminal Law Review* 498.

[18] *A* v. *DPP* (1992), *Criminal Law Review* 34.

indulge the law's liking for a yes or no answer, at the expense of a thorough investigation of the child's actual understanding of the key elements of the crime itself and of criminal liability generally.

Despite the fact that the presumption itself may not always have operated well in practice, this model for the age of criminal responsibility is attractive. It provides a complete protection against criminal prosecution for the very youngest children whilst at the same time, ensuring, at least in theory, that only those older minors who do have the appropriate understanding of the criminal act are held to account. In fact, this may well be the best model for ensuring fairness to the minor-defendant whilst at the same time balancing the public interest in justice being seen to be done, but this is only the case if the evidence led to rebut the presumption is insightful as to the child's actual understandings. This, in turn, requires that the questions which the legal system asks the presumption to answer are predicated on a proper understanding of the nature of criminal responsibility.

5.   WHAT IS CRIMINAL RESPONSIBILITY?

That being the case, it becomes necessary to examine, in more detail, the concept of criminal responsibility. For a defendant of any age to be criminally responsible, the first prerequisite is proof (to the criminal standard which, in many common law systems, is 'beyond reasonable doubt') that (s)he committed the crime with which (s)he is charged. This will, usually, require evidence that (s)he carried out the relevant criminal act (for example the killing where the offence is murder; the attack where the offence is assault), together with evidence of the requisite mental attitude or fault element – generally a form of intention or recklessness or knowledge. For example, killing someone completely by accident is unlikely to constitute a criminal offence. It only becomes murder if the killer intended to kill, or perhaps was seriously reckless as to the consequences of his or her actions.

Where the defendant is a 'sane' adult, proof of the physical act, combined with proof of the relevant mental element is often enough to render the accused criminally liable for the offence. However, there is a third dimension to criminal responsibility which underlies these first two points. The defendant must also have 'criminal capacity'. Broadly, this means that (s)he must have an understanding of the criminal act in context and of its immediate and wider consequences. The concept has been particularly well-defined in H.L.A. Hart's model, as consisting of

> 'both a cognitive and volitional element: a person must both understand the nature of her actions, knowing the relevant circumstances and being aware of possible consequences, and have a genuine opportunity to do otherwise than she does – to exercise control over her actions, by means of choice.'[19]

---

[19] N. Lacey, *State Punishment: Political Principles and Community Values* (London, Routledge 1988) p. 63.

As noted above, where the defendant is an adult, these abilities are often presumed. For minors, it is necessary to be more prescriptive about the skills and abilities required to constitute criminal capacity. Since, clearly, very young children are able to perform actions which would, in themselves constitute criminal offences (such as hitting, biting, damaging property – even killing),[20] their incapability or incapacity must relate to the mental element in crime. The blanket nature of the presumption of incapability made by the age of criminal responsibility often means, however, that there is no need to specify exactly what it is that the legal system assumes that the child cannot do. Is it that she or he cannot intend, or be reckless or have guilty knowledge, or any of the other states of mind which attach fault and which turn an otherwise innocuous action into a criminal offence? Or, is it that (s)he does not understand the relevant action, or its context, or its consequences, or the role of the criminal justice system? Or, again, is it that, due to his or her young age, (s)he did not have a fair opportunity to avoid committing the act?

In relation to defendants who are minors, some of the issues which require specific investigation are:

1) the developmental ability to conform actions to the requirements of the criminal law. In other words, has the child-defendant developed the appropriate internal, cognitive abilities to restrain and control his or her actions? The development of cognition in children is one of the key areas examined by the developmental psychologist, Jean Piaget. Effectively, it comprises the conscious mind's efforts to synthesise and apply all that the child learns so that earlier developmental acquisitions can be applied to solving problems which are encountered subsequently.[21] If cognition is insufficiently developed in the individual child, (s)he will be unable to conform his or her actions to the requirements of the criminal law.
2) understanding of the distinction between right and wrong both morally and legally, and of degrees of wrongdoing – that it is more reprehensible to kill a baby than a cat for example;
3) causation. Does the child have sufficient understanding of the physical world to know that his or her initial wrongful action may have knock-on effects and what these are likely to be?
4) understanding of criminality and criminal consequences. Does the child understand that his or her action carries with it wider consequences than simply the immediate physical effect – for example that its seriousness may involve the police and lead to prosecution?

---

[20] E.g., in May 1993 a four-week old baby was killed by a three-and-a-half year old boy by dropping the baby down a flight of stairs and then dropping him off a table. See *Sydney Morning Herald Magazine*, 8 June 1996, p. 31.
[21] For a clear summary see H.W. Maier, *Three Theories of Child Development: The Contributions of Erik Erikson, Jean Piaget and Robert R Sears and Their Applications* (London, Harper and Row 1969) chapter 3.

5) rationality or answerability – is the child able to order his or her thinking so that (s)he can explain the act? In other words, is the child able to answer for the crime in the court setting?

6) does the child-defendant have the developmental ability to formulate the relevant mental element?

Consideration of these issues – and possibly others – is a prerequisite of determining whether the minor had criminal capacity. Those who lack these abilities and understandings lack criminal capacity. The important point here is that the child's criminal capacity is a complex and multi-layered matter which ought not to be dismissed lightly within the court process, particularly in view of the fact that a finding of criminal liability carries with it consequences which may include the deprivation of liberty.

Almost by definition children are, or are very likely to be, less developed physically, mentally, emotionally, intellectually and morally than adults. It is reasonable, therefore, for a legal system to be asked to assess the criminal capacity of the child in every case. It may also be the case that the numbers of children who are prosecuted are small so that such an investigation would not overload criminal justice systems which are already stretched.[22] This is not to deny that individual adult-defendants may possess criminal capacity in varying degrees, nor is it to invest any undue value in the chronological age at which any individual legal system confers adulthood for these purposes. For adult-defendants whose lack of understanding is seriously problematic, whether in relation to the nature of the act itself, or to the trial process, provision is often made for a plea of 'insanity' whether as a defence to the crime charged or as a bar to the trial taking place. Such pleas do not always operate effectively for child-defendants.[23]

In order to be fair to children then, a finding of criminal responsibility for them should be based on a recognition of the complexity of the concept and an investigation into the extent to which they can be held to possess it.

6.   CRIMINAL RESPONSIBILITY AND AGE

If it is accepted that criminal responsibility consists in proof of commission of the act, with the relevant mental attitude and criminal capacity as just outlined, how is this to be linked up to an age of criminal responsibility? The answer is 'with some difficulty'! Looking at the age in individual legal systems only reveals the diversity

---

[22] E.g., the Scottish Law Commission estimated that only around 0.5% of Scottish children charged with criminal offences are referred to the (adult) courts. Over 99% are referred, instead, to the children's hearings system. See Scottish Law Commission, *Report on Age of Criminal Responsibility* (Scot Law Com No. 185, at para. 3.10).

[23] See C. Connelly and C. McDiarmid, 'Children, Mental Impairment and the Plea in Bar of Trial', 5 *Scottish Law and Practice Quarterly* No. 2 (2000) pp. 157-168.

of choices made. In South Africa the age is seven (with the *doli incapax* presumption then operating to the age of fourteen)[24] while in Luxembourg it is eighteen. Between these extremes we find, among many other examples, Scotland at eight, England and Wales at ten, the Netherlands at twelve, Sweden at fifteen and Portugal at sixteen.[25] Clearly then the age does not particularly represent the point at which each of these systems assumes the child's maturity – the range is too wide to be explained away by cultural differences. Rather, this breadth demonstrates that the meaning, purpose and effect of the age is only discernible within the context of a particular system. It is also worth noting that, while the age may operate as an absolute cut-off point below which prosecution is precluded, this does not mean that legal systems routinely do nothing about younger children who offend. In Sweden, for example, where the age is fifteen, there is sophisticated social welfare provision which holds that 'it is the municipality that has the main responsibility for children below the age of 15'.[26] In Scotland, they could be referred to a children's hearing, not on the ground of having committed an offence itself but possibly on another ground such as being beyond the control of their parents.[27]

Of course, the age of criminal responsibility is not the only line which the law draws to delineate childhood from adulthood. Most legal systems draw similar lines in relation to, for example, the consumption of alcohol, the age of consent in sexual matters, the ability to drive or marry, and the right to vote. Some may set an age where children are deemed able to formulate and express opinions in matters arising under the civil law.[28] What is striking about these ages in many legal systems is that they are often set (sometimes much) higher than the age of criminal responsibility, yet it assumes a much more complicated set of understandings on the part of the child. In this respect, it is interesting to note the commentary on the Beijing Rules on the setting of an age of criminal responsibility:

'The minimum age of criminal responsibility differs widely owing to history and culture. The modern approach would be to consider whether a child can live up to the moral and psychological components of criminal responsibility; that is, whether a child, by virtue of her or his individual discernment and understanding, can be held responsible for essentially antisocial behaviour. If the age of criminal responsibility is fixed too low or if there is no lower age limit at all, the notion of responsibility would become meaningless. *In general, there is a close relationship between the notion of*

---

[24] Johansson and Palm, *supra* n. 12, section 2B.

[25] United Kingdom Parliament, *Joint Committee on Human Rights, Tenth Report: The UN Convention on the Rights of the Child*, 2003, footnote 64, available at <http://www.publications.parliament.uk/pa/jtselect/jtrights/117/11706.htm>.

[26] Johansson and Palm, *supra* n. 12, section 2A. There is also a little-used process which allows a court to determine whether a younger person has committed a crime, for the sole purpose of establishing guilt.

[27] Children (Scotland) Act 1995, s 52(2)(a).

[28] In Scotland this age is twelve, though younger children can express views if they are able and wish to do so. See ibid., s 16(2)(c).

responsibility for delinquent or criminal behaviour and other social rights and respon-
sibilities (such as marital status, civil majority, etc.) '.[29]

'Efforts should therefore be made to agree on a reasonable lowest age limit that is applicable internationally.'

Overall, the age of criminal responsibility can only be arbitrary because all children
mature at different rates and using an age at all means that a minor who is a day
short of the relevant birthday will escape criminal liability altogether whilst his
one-day-older counterpart can be held accountable. This is unlikely to reflect the
reality of the maturity of individual children. But exactly the same situation arises
in any area where the law uses chronological age as a dividing line – for example,
the right to vote. It is only because juvenile offending is often highly politicised that
this is sometimes seen as a particular disadvantage of this model.

If a legal system is to use an age, then presumably it would be better if this were
to comply with the commentary on the Beijing Rules and, accordingly, be brought
into line with other key ages of legal significance. In some jurisdictions however,
the United Kingdom certainly being one, the whole arena of youth crime is politicised
so that there appears to be no political will to raise the age of criminal responsibility. Paradoxically, this politicisation renders the provision of an age which relates to
the child's age at the time of commission of the offence, all the more necessary to
protect the very young from politically motivated prosecution. In Cincinnati Ohio,
in 1994, a twelve-year old child was indicted for a homicide which she allegedly
committed when aged three.[30] No further proceedings were instituted after the charge,
but this illustrates the danger that prosecution of very young children may be attempted in order to assuage public opinion. Contrary to the justification sometimes
put forward for such intervention, the (adult) criminal justice system is not an appropriate mechanism through which to obtain 'help' for troubled children.[31]

7. CONCLUSION

The age of criminal responsibility exists to protect children from prosecution for
acts of which they are deemed to have lacked understanding. In this respect, it
promotes the child's interests but, in order to have credibility, it must at some level
have the support of the society in which it operates. It is not infrequently the case
that there is a weight of evidence establishing that a child actually carried out the
criminal act, thereby engendering a public outcry against the young perpetrators.

---

[29] Emphasis added. It should be noted that neither this Commentary, nor the Rules themselves are
binding on states which are signatories to them. The UN invites, but does not require states to adopt the
Rules.

[30] 'Can a Three-Year Old Child Commit Murder?', *Montreal Gazette*, 9 March 1994, p. A1.

[31] See United Kingdom Parliament, *supra* n. 25, paras. 35 and 36.

While legal systems, at least nominally, treat youth as mitigatory,[32] societies some-times seem to regard it, instead, as increasing the perpetrators' blameworthiness. The killing of James Bulger in Liverpool, England, in 1993 is an example of this. The setting of an age of criminal responsibility in national legal systems should not be influenced by this. Instead it should look to the understanding and development of children and to the other key chronological ages used – of majority, marriage, driving and the like – seeking to ensure minimal disparity with these. This is encouraged by the commentary on the Beijing Rules cited above. The age of criminal responsibility may ignore the individual child's actual abilities and understandings, and stifle discussion of the component elements of the child's criminal capacity but it remains a necessary safeguard for young citizens. Where it should be set is a much more difficult question.

---

[32] See, e.g., *R* v. *Storey and Others* (1984), 6 *Criminal Appeal Reports (Sentencing)* 104, which recognised, in English law, that the length of a sentence imposed on a juvenile should be adjusted to reflect his or her youth.

Chapter 7
THE CRIMINAL RESPONSIBILITY OF FORMER CHILD
SOLDIERS: CONTRIBUTIONS FROM PSYCHOLOGY

Angela Veale*

1. INTRODUCTION

As pointed out in the two previous chapters of this book, the criminal responsibility of minors is a contested subject, both internationally and nationally. In legal terms, key issues are whether children may be held accountable for criminal actions, including consideration of the capability or otherwise of forming the requisite intent and duress. As the two previous chapters have also shown, there is no international consensus with respect to the age of criminal responsibility. In Ireland, the matter is governed by common law and the presumption that a child under seven years does not have the capacity to commit an offence. Under Part 5 of the Children's Act (2001) there was a provision to raise the minimum age to twelve years.[1] However, the Irish Minister for Justice has repealed this provision and replaced it with an age of criminal responsibility of ten years to be included in a Bill before the Government in the autumn of 2005. In England and Wales the age of criminal responsibility is ten years (in Scotland it is eight), in France it is thirteen years, Norway fifteen years, Spain sixteen and in Belgium and Luxembourg eighteen years. Therefore, a child perpetrator of crime would be more fortunate to live in some countries compared to others as immunity may be available on the basis of chronological age alone.

For crimes of genocide, Article II of the 1948 Convention on the Prevention and Punishment of the Crime of Genocide defines genocide as 'acts committed with intent to destroy, in whole or in part, a national, ethnical, racial or religious group, as such.' McCarney outlines arguments that support a presumption that child soldiers are incapable of forming the requisite intent to commit genocide. His arguments include the following: that the age of many of the children sheds doubt on whether children can understand what genocide is; that they have been so traumatised

---

* Angela Veale is a Lecturer at the Department of Applied Psychology, National University of Ireland, Cork.

[1] D. Griffin, 'The Juvenile Conundrum: Ireland's Responses', *Cork Online Review* (2004) available at <http://colr.ucc.ie/2004xii.html>.

K. Arts & V. Popovski (eds.), International Criminal Accountability and the Rights of Children
© 2006, Hague Academic Coalition, The Hague, The Netherlands and the Authors

by their experiences that they can no longer distinguish between right and wrong; and that the power dynamics of social norms which demand the obedience of children to adults has to be taken into account in any consideration of 'intent'.[2]

As is also explained in chapter 5 by Matthew Happold, the 1989 Convention on the Rights of the Child (CRC) requires that States parties establish 'a minimum age below which children shall be presumed not to have the capacity to infringe the penal law' but does not give guidance as to what that age should be. With respect to child perpetrators of crime, the CRC's key principles are to promote their reintegration and their return to a constructive role in society. Furthermore, the CRC calls on state parties to seek measures for dealing with child perpetrators without resorting to formal judicial proceedings, such as through diversionary practices.

This chapter seeks to ask the following questions. What are the appropriate responses to children and young persons who have perpetrated violence and committed gross human rights violations in the context of armed conflict? What tensions or areas of complementarity exist between justice and child welfare agendas? In addressing the issue of minors who participate in the commission of gross human rights violations, is there a necessary or useful distinction to be made between legal justice and social justice, where social justice serves a broader agenda of promoting young people's reintegration in civil society? All of these questions will be explored from the angle of the contribution of psychological perspectives to the broader issue of societies' responses to children who, as members of armed groups, have participated in committing gross human rights violations. This chapter will critically examine recruitment and choice, and consider issues relating to the age of criminal responsibility and to developmental status. It will also examine the evidence for or against the need to incorporate restorative justice perspectives in addition to existing reintegration methodologies, which include quite sophisticated psychosocial community-based rehabilitation and reintegration models. Finally, in utilising concepts from cultural psychology, this chapter explores what function a cultural restorative justice perspective could contribute for those who were involved in perpetrating crimes as minors. Who should administer such a justice initiative? The argument will be that it has to be fundamentally local, situated in cultural meanings and community-led. This raises questions as to what constitutes a 'community'? What kind of justice for what goal? And finally, what is the relative contribution and role of the child welfare, psychosocial professionals, justice professionals and communities themselves?

2.   CHILD AGENCY AND RECRUITMENT

Forced abduction as a tool of war has been used in many contexts, including Cambodia, Northern Uganda, Sierra Leone and elsewhere. The Khmer Rouge rendered

---

[2] W. McCarney, *Child Soldiers: Criminals or Victims? Should Child Soldiers Be Prosecuted for Crimes Against Humanity?*, paper presented to the Child and War Conference (Sion, Switzerland, International Institute for the Rights of the Child 2001) p. 7.

children and young people the prime instruments of state violence and terror during their rule. In Sierra Leone, many children were abducted and made to terrorise the civilian population. In Uganda, the Lord's Resistance Army is believed to consist of over 90 per cent of abducted children with 200 core fighters and approximately 3,000 child combatants.[3]

Within social research and child psychology, there is a broad theoretical push against theorising 'incompetent children'. Accounts which stress children's power and agency are also having an influence within discourses on children and conflict. There are a number of research accounts which document children's voluntary participation in fighting. In Sierra Leone, Wessells[4] noted that many minors joined the Civil Defence Forces to revenge atrocities committed against family members by the Revolutionary United Front, or to defend their families and communities, using violence and the commission of atrocities as tools. In Palestine, Jason Hart documented how minors see their involvement in the political struggle as stemming from a sense of grievance and injustice and a desire to defend their community:

'Young people growing up in the Occupied Palestinian Territories are often willing participants in the national struggle. Their political consciousness is developed to an extent and from an age that commonly takes outsiders by surprise.'[5]

Boyden goes further and notes that children's active participation in political violence may in certain circumstances be an active coping strategy that serves a protective psychological function compared to an alternative of frustration, poverty hopelessness, and learnt helplessness. Commenting on her observations in Sri Lanka, she noted:

'It is also worth highlighting that assuming an active role, in itself, is known to have beneficial psychological effect when children have been exposed to conflict ... During discussions, a group of mothers revealed that 15 of their children had, as they put it, "gone over to the other side". By this they meant that the youngsters had chosen to leave the village by night and cross over into the area controlled by the LTTE [Liberation Tigers of Tamil Eelam] in order to enlist. There was no suggestion they had been forced. Rather, ... family problems and frustration at life in the community had added to the pressures of poverty in encouraging the young to take this course of action.'[6]

---

[3] See J. Boyden, 'The Moral Development of Child Soldiers: What Do Adults Have to Fear?', 9 *Peace and Conflict: Journal of Peace Psychology* No. 4 (2002) pp. 343-362; M. Wessells and J. Davidson, 'Reintegration of Former Youth Soldiers in Sierra Leone: Challenges of Reconciliation and Post-Accord Peace Building', in S. McEvoy-Levy (ed.), *Troublemakers or Peacemakers? Youth and Post-Accord Peace Building* (Notre Dame, University of Notre Dame Press 2006). Z. Lomo and L. Hovil, *Behind the Violence: The War in Northern Uganda*, Monograph Series No. 99 (Pretoria, Institute for Security Studies 2004).

[4] Wessells, ibid.

[5] J. Hart, *Children's Participation in Humanitarian Action: Learning from Zones of Conflict* (Oxford, Refugees Studies Centre, University of Oxford 2004) part 1, p. 12.

[6] J. Boyden, et al., *Children Affected by Armed Conflict in South Asia: A Review of Trends and Issues Identified Through Secondary Research*, Working Paper No. 7 (Oxford, Refugee Studies Centre, University of Oxford 2002) <http://www.rsc.ox.ac.uk/PDFs/workingpaper7.pdf>, p. 53.

In summary, what is the anthropological or psychological evidence regarding children's capacity to be rational and responsible participants in a conflict? It is clear that recruitment patterns are not homogenous. There are multiple routes to involvement in conflict that range on a continuum from forced to agentive participation. Much of the research evidence cited above, which highlights the rational and purposive quality of children's voluntary participation in a conflict, has an agenda of arguing strongly for the participation and inclusion of those who fought as minors in post-conflict peace-building initiatives. This contrasts with many psychosocial accounts that show former child soldiers as traumatised by their experiences.

The very little outcome evidence that exists on the psychosocial well-being of former child soldiers is mixed. In Northern Uganda, MacMullin and Loughrey[7] found that of the youths who had gone through rehabilitation and reintegration programmes, former abductees had higher levels of anxiety and/or depression, and were less confident than their peers who were never abducted. However, other research from Northern Uganda found that teachers reported that many formerly abducted children were stronger and more confident than those children who had never been abducted as they had demonstrated the strength to survive.[8] In another study carried out by a group of non-governmental organisations in Gulu, Uganda, formerly abducted girls said that, compared to girls who had never been abducted, they considered themselves equal to men. They could sow, harvest and construct a granary, they felt their moral values to be stronger, they were more hard-working and enduring and had no faith in witchcraft.[9] General Dallaire has strongly argued that ex-child fighters have developed important skills and leadership experience and, in his experience, are more confident, self-reliant, mature and developmentally advanced than many of those who remained with their families in communities or displacement camps and never fought. His concern is that such young people should not be marginalized in post-conflict social reconstruction.[10] Boothby noted that a group of 14-year old boys he encountered in one programme did not wish to be repositioned as 'children' post-demobilisation. They wished to refuse education as they felt they had earned the right to be in the army.[11]

This analysis of former child soldiers has many parallels with women's experiences as fighters. In research conducted in Ethiopia with female former child soldiers of the Ethiopian Peoples' Revolutionary Democratic Front (EPRDF), women

[7] C. MacMullin and M. Loughry, *The Psychosocial Adjustment of Formerly Abducted Child Soldiers in Northern Uganda*, Field Report (Kampala, International Rescue Committee 2002).

[8] A. Veale and A. Stavrou, *Violence, Reconciliation and Identity: The Reintegration of Lord's Resistance Army Child Abductees in Northern Uganda*, Monograph No. 92 (Pretoria, Institute for Security Studies 2003) <http://www.iss.za>.

[9] G. Onyango, et al., *Uganda Girl Mothers of Northern Uganda'*, paper presented at the Conference 'Girl Mothers in Fighting Forces and their Post-War Reintegration in Southern and Western Africa* (Bellagio, Italy, Rockefeller Foundation Bellagio Center 12-18 April 2005).

[10] General R. Dallaire, *Voices Out of Conflict: Young People Affected by Forced Migration and Political Crisis*, unpublished presentation (Cumberland Lodge, Windsor Great Park 26-28 March 2004).

[11] N. Boothby, *The Demobilization and Reintegration of Child Soldiers into Civilian Society*, unpublished paper, 1995.

who had volunteered to be part of fighting forces between the ages of ten to fourteen, and who had fought proudly and fiercely, then felt betrayed and marginalized at the point of peace-building as the agenda they fought for as women was discounted in peace-building.[12]

A core challenge, therefore, in any discussion of the criminal responsibility of children in contexts of political violence – if child agency is recognised as possible, and particularly in peace-building – is whether it is possible to maintain a stance on child perpetrators of gross human rights abuses as passive, lacking rational thinking skills, and demonstrating an inability to consent, on the basis of them being minors.

Whatever the form of recruitment, there is documented evidence of minors being involved in perpetrating atrocities. In some cases, minors have even directed other children to perpetrate human rights abuses that would allow the establishment of a doctrine of command responsibility. In some conflicts, such as in Liberia, children's actions as fighters have had significant political and military consequences.

Singer has noted that in many conflict contexts, there is a readily available pool of child labour:

'Warlords can transform children into soldiers and thus transform an insignificant force into an army. E.g. Charles Taylor in Liberia. In the early 1990s he turned an "army" of 150 amateur soldiers armed with small arms into a force of thousands by the recruitment and use of child soldiers, to become Liberia's president, demonstrating the potential payoff. Through child soldiers, he was able to use a small gang to gain a kingdom.'[13]

3. DEVELOPMENTAL TRANSITIONS AND THE ROLE OF ARMED GROUPS

Within this discussion, it is essential to look at the recruitment of child soldiers in a broader demographic, economic, political and cultural context. In many conflict contexts in Africa, for example, population demographics show that 50 per cent or more of the population may be eighteen years or under. Such children potentially represent a massive recruitment pool for armed groups.[14]

From a psychological perspective, this has to be understood in terms of developmental transitions. A central question in developmental psychology has been to identify the nature and timing of people's transitions from one phase of development to the next, for example from childhood to adulthood. Such transitions are cultural community events as individuals change their roles in their communities'

---

[12] A. Veale, *From Child Soldier to Ex-Fighter: Female Fighters, Demobilisation and Reintegration in Ethiopia*, Monograph, No. 85 (Pretoria, Institute for Security Studies 2002).

[13] P. Singer, 'Caution: Children at War', *Parameters* (Winter 2001-2002) pp. 40-56 at p. 48. Available at <http://carlisle-www.army.mil/usawc/Parameters/01winter/singer.htm>.

[14] A. McIntyre (ed.), *Invisible Stakeholders: The Impact of War on Children* (Pretoria: Institute for Security Studies 2004).

structure.[15] This may be marked by transition ceremonies or new levels of status and responsibility. If examined across cultures, chronological age is not a marker that systematically delineates stages of development as there is a great deal of variety in transitions in different cultural communities. Transitions are dependent on the values and expectations of a cultural group. Transitions in development can be identified by the changing relations of children with others in their community.

Conflict impacts massively on developmental transition opportunities from childhood to adulthood. Normative means of achieving adult responsibility may not be open to many young people in conflict afflicted regions, displaced persons or refugee camps. Education, a chance to be economically independent and to gain status may not be easily accessible. Participation in an armed group might provide many more possibilities. The question of most relevance here is the following: should local and international communities allow impunity for anything that happens as part of this developmental transition, if it happens below a certain age?

4.   ASSUMPTIONS INHERENT IN INTERNATIONAL LEGAL AND PSYCHOSOCIAL RESPONSES REGARDING THE CRIMINAL RESPONSIBILITY OF CHILDREN

In a comprehensive review of international legal instruments, McCarney argues that international instruments tend to support a view of the child soldier as a victim.[16] International legislation criminalizes those that recruit children under fifteen years into armed forces, while the optional protocol to the CRC prohibits any forced recruitment of children under eighteen years into armed forces. The doctrine of command responsibility holds that adult commanders are criminally responsible for the actions of child soldiers.

Within the child welfare and child rights discourse, concepts relating to incapacity and 'victimhood' are also dominant. A UNICEF report notes:

'When it comes to children – especially children under 15 – so-called 'voluntary recruitment' is always a misnomer. Child rights advocates maintain that children's participation in armed forces will always involve some form of pressure, be it cultural, political, or simply the need to ensure their safety or daily subsistence.'[17]

And also:

'Children, mostly from poor families, may be coerced into participating in crimes, either threatened, indoctrinated, manipulated or drugged ... The recognition of child perpetrators as victims can establish that they are not rational actors in a particular

---

[15] B. Rogoff, *The Cultural Nature of Human Development* (Oxford, Oxford University Press 2003) p. 150.

[16] W. McCarney, *supra* n. 2.

[17] *International Criminal Justice and Children* (Rome, No Peace Without Justice and UNICEF Innocenti Research Centre, 2002) p. 73.

case and can thus mitigate their legal responsibility for the crimes they have allegedly committed'.[18]

Psychosocial programming is also characterised by a strong assumption of 'victimhood' and of societies' responsibility to rehabilitate and reintegrate former child soldiers.

According to Jarge and McCallin, emphasis must be placed on understanding the situation of children, and the effects of their participation in armed conflict within the context of their ongoing developmental processes: 'The events that children experience as soldiers are horrific ... child soldiers have suffered extreme trauma.'[19] Broader social discourses also support this view. Archbishop Desmond Tutu has noted:

'We must not close our eyes to the fact that child soldiers are both victims and perpetrators. They sometimes carry out the most barbaric acts of violence. But no matter what the child is guilty of, the main responsibility lies with us, the adults. There is simply no excuse, no acceptable argument for arming children.'[20]

However, is it in *all* former child soldiers' best interests to be treated within international legislation and psychosocial programming as victims, as lacking the capacity to understand their actions, as incapable of forming intent and therefore as not culpable for their actions?

5. Impunity?

There are significant concerns about granting impunity. Clark notes that impunity permits and even encourages the continued recruitment of child soldiers.[21] Mawson argues that if child or adult perpetrators believe that they can get away with atrocities, there is little incentive not to commit further violence, particularly if there are gains to be made, thus leading to a spiral of violence.[22] Furthermore, ignoring atrocities committed by minors could undermine the wider administration of justice, and the scope for justice systems to maintain credibility.[23] Brett has concerns that, in the absence of considering their cases in the civilian justice system, child soldiers

---

[18] Ibid., p. 30.

[19] E. Jareg and M. McCallin, *The Rehabilitation of Former Child Soldiers. Report of a Training Workshop for Caregivers of Demobilised Child Soldiers, Freetown, Sierra Leone* (Geneva, International Catholic Child Bureau 1993).

[20] Archbishop D. Tutu, *No Peace Without Forgiveness* (New York, Random House 1999).

[21] C. Clark, *Discussion Paper: Juvenile Justice and Child Soldiering* (London, Coalition to Stop the Use of Child Soldiers – no date).

[22] A. Mawson, Children, *Impunity and Justice: Some Dilemmas from Northern Uganda*, presentation to the Conference on 'Children in Extreme Circumstances' (London, London School of Economics 27 November 1998).

[23] Ibid.

may be subjected to a military legal system in which there may be little or no compatibility with international human rights norms and standards of juvenile justice.[24] There are also concerns that impunity for minors, but not for others, could set up categories of 'the misled' and categories of adult 'guilty' parties that ignores local social perceptions that individuals have engaged in similar acts of violence and are similarly accountable.[25] Finally, McCarney asks, what happens to the doctrine of command responsibility when the person who controls the child soldiers is a child him or herself?[26]

With respect to sexual violence, which is widespread and systematic in many conflicts, the issue of impunity regarding rape and sexual violence has hardly been raised. Yet addressing this at a national, regional or community level must be key to building restorative relations if young men and women are to have any possibility of being able to work together in peace-building.

There is a broader empirical question on the issue of impunity, and that is to what extent reintegrated former child soldiers who have gone through rehabilitative psychosocial programmes, have been accepted back within their communities of origin in the absence of any justice discourse?

6.   SOCIO-ECONOMIC AND PSYCHOLOGICAL REINTEGRATION OF FORMER CHILD SOLDIERS: THE EMPIRICAL EVIDENCE?

In many contexts, such as Rwanda and Sierra Leone, communities have been reluctant to receive all the youths involved in atrocities with impunity. After the Rwandan genocide, a community survey concluded that communities believed that children are culpable and must be punished to ensure accountability and 'adherence to the established social order'. They also believed that children had voluntarily committed acts of violence, and that anyone with enough strength to commit the crimes should be treated as an adult.[27]

In Northern Uganda, a general amnesty has been applied and there is a broad peace discourse of forgiveness. The majority, but not all, of returned children have gone through reintegration programmes. In an in-depth survey of 183 formerly abducted children in Northern Uganda, Rodriguez and others found that longer periods spent in the bush were associated with former abductees experiencing more problems on reintegration.[28] Exactly half of those who had reported feeling wel-

---

[24] R. Brett, 'Causes, Consequences and International Responses', in E. Bennett, et al. (eds.), *ACT Against Child Soldiers in Africa: A Reader* (Pretoria, Institute for Security Studies 2000).

[25] Mawson, *supra* n. 22.

[26] W. McCarney, *supra* n. 2.

[27] Save the Children Fund, *Children, Genocide and Justice* (Kigali, Save the Children USA 1995) p. 3.

[28] C. Rodriquez, et al., *Seventy Times Seven: The Impact of the Amnesty Law in Acholi* (Uganda, The Acholi Leaders Peace Initiative, Yje Women's Desk of Caritas Gulu and the Justice and Peace Commission of Gulu Archdiocese 2002).

comed had been inducted for four months or less, and only 5 per cent were inducted for four or more years. Only 8 per cent of those inducted for less than five months reported bad experiences, whereas induction of six years or more represented 63 per cent of bad experiences, such as abusive language, being avoided or isolated, or feeling intimidated or threatened. Males were less welcomed than females, with 70 per cent of females who claimed that they felt welcomed on their return, compared to 57 per cent of the males. The authors noted:

'The final negative experience that returnees reported from the community is jealousy from those who are still missing family members and struggle openly with accepting those that have returned ... There is clearly a difference between how the community perceived they are welcoming returnees and how returnees feel they are being welcomed ... It is also hard to find examples of forgiveness.'[29]

A core task that must be negotiated upon reintegration is that of acknowledging the identity transformations that have occurred between the child and community as a result of their participation in an armed group.[30]

Furthermore, one should realise that, if some individuals are marginalized, not forgiven, and these are individuals who have been inducted for longer periods, for whom a significant part of their development through adolescence occurred within armed forces, these individuals are arguably at a higher risk of re-recruitment by civil defence forces, government forces and other armed groups.

More empirical evidence needs to be gathered to examine the effectiveness of psychosocial programmes for community acceptance and reintegration. However, it seems that a 'restorative justice' orientation could potentially serve a role in acknowledging and addressing identity transformations as a result of children's involvement in conflict, for former child soldiers who have been with armed groups for a long period, who have been involved in perpetrating gross human rights violations in the absence of ongoing coercion, and where community reintegration is unlikely to be achievable without acknowledgement and possibly some form of reparation.

7. CRIMINAL RESPONSIBILITY, AGE AND DEVELOPMENTAL STATUS

What can psychological research contribute to the question of the age of criminal responsibility and a consideration of developmental status in holding individuals accountable for acts committed as minors? The simple equation of age with a particular developmental level, a level of knowledge, competencies, cognitive understanding or emotional maturity is not supported in developmental research.[31] Rogoff

---

[29] Ibid., p. 17.

[30] A. Veale and A. Stavrou, *supra* n. 8.

[31] S. Greene and M. Hill, 'Researching Children's Experiences: Methods and Methodological Issues', in S. Greene and D. Hogan (eds.), *Researching Children's Experiences* (London, Sage 2005).

has comprehensively demonstrated that different cultures have very different values and expectations of the skills, behaviour, and emotional maturity expected of children of different ages.[32] Within that, there are differences in terms of the competencies and maturity demanded of boys versus girls. Further, there are different competencies and maturity demands of children within different socio-economic groupings and societally-provided opportunities to develop such skills. Normatively, therefore, there is a wide range of abilities and developmental competency and maturity amongst children of the same chronological age.

As mentioned earlier, cultural expectations of child competency, maturity and understanding vary widely. These are linked to expectations of role transitions and observations of readiness or ableness to take on adult roles and responsibilities. In Rwanda, focus group discussions were carried out to explore cultural constructions of 'childhood' and local understandings of whether child perpetrators of genocide were viewed as responsible for their actions. There was consensus that a child was 'one who has not reached social maturity'. All agreed that it was a person aged less than six years, and 'a child is one who does not have the capacity to distinguish between good and bad'. One group maintained that between eight and ten years a person can retain ideas and imitate them, and between eight and fourteen years can remember messages given to him or her by one person and repeat them correctly to another. A child becomes an adult between fifteen and eighteen years. However, if an individual has committed rape, no matter at what age, then this person can no longer be a child as the physical act of rape is inconsistent with the power dynamics and behavioural norms defining a 'child'.[33] In many African countries, an individual may continue to be regarded as a 'child' up to the age of thirty-five years, for example if he or she is economically dependent on his/her parents, is in full time education, or has not taken on the roles and responsibilities associated with adulthood. A 15-year old who is living independently and is shouldering adult responsibilities may be viewed as an adult.

Any age-based approach is problematic for other reasons also. There is the issue of 'ageing out'. As is likely, how should justice orientation deal with individuals who, as former child soldiers, were involved in the perpetration of gross human rights abuses, and who, while within the armed group or subsequently, have reached eighteen years or over. Do they remain within a framework established for dealing with offences by juveniles? Challenges related to age at the commission of crime would come up in societies where it is difficult to determine age and where official documents such as birth certificates are difficult to trace or have never existed. There is also a broad question about the capacity to participate in and understand judicial proceedings. Again, such a question is not likely to be answered by direct reference to age. Trauma, for example, can impact significantly on developmental maturity and memory, resulting in developmental regression, memory distortion,

---

[32] B. Rogoff, *supra* n. 15.
[33] Save the Children Fund, *supra* n. 27, p. 7.

difficulty in forming a coherent narrative, as well as the possibility of retraumatisation through remembering.

In summary, there are so many influential variables that a judgment on the developmental and psychological capability to participate in a restorative justice initiative would probably need to be considered on a case-by-case basis, and in a manner grounded culturally in local understandings of childhood and youth. An arbitrary cut-off age of eighteen years does not make cultural sense and a broader culturally-based definition of 'youth' would have more applicability.

8. CONCLUSION

Can minors be held criminally responsible? In some cases it may be in the long-term best interests of former child soldiers and their communities of origin that minors be held accountable: where former child soldiers spent a number of years as an active participant within an armed group, where he or she was responsible for the commission of gross human rights violations, held a position of responsibility or authority, where the individual is deemed to be psychologically capable of participating.

Fundamentally, any restorative justice initiative has to be situated in local cultural meanings and understandings of children, of recruitment dynamics, of developmental transitions, of what is developmentally expected, and of cultural mechanisms for acknowledging wrongdoing and means of reparation. Age as a distinctive criterion for the form of restorative justice is problematic. As we have seen above, cultural constructions of what constitutes a 'child' are extremely contested. A justice orientation may need to be flexible enough to go beyond legalistic boundaries of child/adult to incorporate a locally defined category of 'youth'.

Cultural-psychological dynamics of justice, healing and forgiveness are central. For example, shaming is a central dynamic of many restorative healing approaches. In Nigeria, according to a key informant, shaming as a juvenile justice mechanism could lead to further social-relational difficulties in communities as it is not the individual who is shamed, but the extended family and clan. However, in Nigeria also, community solutions may mean some form of Sharia law in which juvenile rights under international conventions may not be respected. At all times there is a strong argument to be made for the integration of local and international practices. International juvenile justice has made significant progress in establishing procedures which protect children's rights in justice processes. Any local or national restorative procedures should be developed in accordance with international juvenile justice legal standards.

Almost without exception, psychosocial intervention and child welfare literature have been lacking discussion of justice issues. Yet, psychosocial programming might be the place to position such initiatives. Many such programmes are culturally and community-based and therefore may have the expertise to front restorative justice initiatives at a local or national level.

At a political level, international bodies and state parties cannot ignore the massive recruitment pool that is created as a result of armed conflict, political instability, and a lack of economic opportunities within civilian society for children's developmental transition to adulthood status, economic responsibility and respect.

Part III
Practice Unfolding
in International Courts

Chapter 8
THE RIGHTS OF CHILDREN AND THE INTERNATIONAL CRIMINAL COURT

Luis Moreno-Ocampo*

1. INTRODUCTION: THE INTERNATIONAL CRIMINAL COURT'S MISSION REQUIRES COOPERATION

The only way for the International Criminal Court (ICC) to succeed in its mission is by being part of a network of people working together. In relation to this network, this chapter presents the policies of the Court, and particularly the policies of the Office of the Prosecutor, to the extent relevant to the rights of children. What is the ICC, and especially the Office of the Prosecutor, doing in relation to the rights of children in international criminal procedures, and how do they work together with other relevant actors in this field?

The mission of the Office of the Prosecutor is twofold. Firstly, there is the classic mission of investigation and prosecution of crimes. Secondly, and by far the most complicated task, is to have a broader impact, by helping to put an end to impunity and thereby contributing to the prevention of crimes. A key element of the latter task is, through our investigation and prosecution work, to promote national efforts and international cooperation to prevent, investigate and punish crimes.

Although we are a global institution, we have to remain small in size. Our small size will help us to stay nimble and responsive, and to avoid becoming a local bureaucracy. The need to be global and small forces both the Court and the Prosecutor to rely on global networks and on the networks of states. Diplomats are a key constituency in such networks; so, too, are national police forces, national forensic institutions, national prosecutors and national judges. Many institutions within states have to be part of our networks. A range of different non-governmental organisations play various roles relevant to our networks. The academic world is important as we need an epistemic network to transform knowledge into policy, to make it operational and to disseminate it. The media help with dissemination. The private sector is a key partner too, because actors in the private sector can also be global citizens.

---

* The first Chief Prosecutor of the International Criminal Court. Previously, as a prosecutor in Argentina (1984-1992), Mr. Moreno-Ocampo was among others involved in precedent-setting prosecutions of top military commanders for mass killings and other large-scale human rights abuses.

K. Arts & V. Popovski (eds.), International Criminal Accountability and the Rights of Children
© *2006, Hague Academic Coalition, The Hague, The Netherlands and the Authors*

Big companies have interests around the world, and they have to learn how to support human rights and the protection of life. One example is that of Unilever, a Dutch company that lost its branch in the Democratic Republic of Congo. For many years it produced $10 million annually in the Congo. However, it was forced to close its branch because of the war. This example demonstrates that there is a connection between values, interests and money, and that the ICC and the Office of the Prosecutor have to include diverse groups in their networks.

The Rome Statute creates more than a Court; it creates a global justice system based on states. What happens in The Hague – the legal capital of the world – is very important, but at the same time, this is only a small part of what is happening in the world. Thus, we have to create a global network, working in The Hague, but also in each state where there are problems. The ICC needs cooperation from each state. We need cooperation with our investigations, and we also need cooperation to increase our impact. For example, because this Court will only hear a few cases each year, we have to learn how to maximize the impact of each case. We are likely to have cases in the near future which will expose the problem of child soldiers. The first such case concerns enlisting, conscripting and using children under fifteen to participate actively in hostilities in the Democratic Republic of Congo.[1] We must learn how to maximize the possibilities for one, two or three cases a year, to have a global impact. We can do this through, for example, communication, research and training, and cooperation with states and global institutions.

2.   THE ROME STATUTE AND CHILDREN

The Rome Statute is a miraculous achievement. It reflects agreement among a growing number of states to cooperate in order to ensure accountability for genocide, crimes against humanity and war crimes. Bringing criminal enforcement from a national level to a global level was a quantum leap. For students today, for whom the ICC was already in place before they started their studies, this may seem an obvious development. For older generations, it is a breakthrough. For future generations, it will be a self-evident and normal feature of the international system.

The Rome Statute creates a global justice system based partly on states and partly on an international court with international judges. For the first time in human history, we have a permanent court, with eighteen judges from all continents deciding cases based on international law. This is a very important step. The Statute reflects a development of common standards and a commitment to the enforcement of these standards. There is agreement on the basic standards of the Statute, even among some non-state parties. In Iraq, for example, Rome Statute standards were used in the drafting of arrangements for the Iraq High Tribunal.

---

[1] The accused was first brought before the ICC on 20 March 2006. For more details on this case, see, e.g., Pre-Trial Chamber I, 'Situation in the Democratic Republic of the Congo', *The Prosecutor* v. *Thomas Lubanga Dyilo*, ICC-01/04-01/06, 10 February 2006.

With regard to crimes specifically related to children, Article 6(e) of the Rome Statute states that genocide includes the forcible transfer of children of one group to another group. Article 8(2)(b)(xxvi) of the Rome Statute states that conscripting or enlisting children under the age of fifteen years into the national armed forces, or using them to participate actively in hostilities, is a war crime. The importance of this provision cannot be overestimated: there are many countries in which this crime is taking place and something must be done in order to address this practice. It is not just the decisions of the judges that are very important: it is also very important for national armies around the world to comply with this norm.

There are some indications that the Court is having an impact. Recently, during a meeting with generals in charge of legal matters, one of the generals highlighted the impact of the Court. He informed me that his chief commander called him after the establishment of the Court and instructed that the general must be present each time operations were planned, in order to ensure respect for international treaties. NGOs also contribute to ensuring compliance with international treaties by monitoring and exposing country situations in which children under the age of fifteen are being enlisted. These examples relate closely to one of the ideas that the Office of the Prosecutor wishes to promote: that it is not just about the Court rendering judgments, but also about what we can do to deter crimes even before a case arrives at the Court.

Another important provision regarding children under the Rome Statute is Article 26, which excludes jurisdiction over any persons who were below the age of eighteen at the time of the alleged commission of the crime. Article 68 provides for the protection of victims and witnesses and their participation in proceedings. One of the innovative features of the Court is that victims can participate in proceedings. Although victim participation in proceedings is common in civil law countries, it is unusual in common law countries, and it is altogether new in the international criminal law arena. Judges will decide the extent and terms of victim participation in trials before the ICC. It is very important to listen to the victims, as the trial is not just for the prosecutor or for lawyers – it is also for victims.

In addition to the Rome Statute, there are several other treaties that contain provisions which are relevant to the protection of children. For example, Article 3(1) of the 1989 United Nations Convention on the Rights of the Child stipulates that:

'In all actions concerning children, whether undertaken by public or private welfare institutions, courts of law, administrative authorities or legislative bodies, the best interests of the child shall be a primary consideration.'

And, according to CRC Article 3(2):

'State Parties undertake to ensure to the child such protection and care as is necessary for his or her well-being, taking into account the rights and duties of his or her parents, legal guardians, or other individuals legally responsible for him or her, and, to this end, shall take all appropriate legislative and administrative measures.'

Article 1 of the CRC Optional Protocol on the Involvement of Children in Armed Conflict (2000) requires states parties to 'take all feasible measures to ensure that members of their armed forces who have not attained the age of 18 years do not take a direct part in hostilities.' Article 2 prohibits compulsory recruitment into the armed forces.

3. THE EXERCISE OF JURISDICTION BY THE INTERNATIONAL CRIMINAL COURT: PROSECUTION VERSUS PEACE?

By way of a preliminary remark on this matter, the current state of the international system should be noted. As part of the debates on 'peace' and 'justice', people state with regard to our cases:

> 'Please justice, but just not now. We have to negotiate to make peace in this conflict. During the negotiations, I do not want your prosecutor to try and arrest the person with whom I am dealing, so please wait.'

In current international relations, it is normal in peace negotiations to offer positions to the leaders of the different rival groups although they may have been involved in the commission of crimes. Imagine that in the Netherlands the Minister of Justice identifies a group of people who are serial killers. The minister negotiates with them, and offers them a position in the cabinet if they stop committing the crimes. A failure to do so, however, will result in the minister sending the case to the prosecutor. It is impossible to consider this type of negotiation in national systems, and yet this is normal practice in the international arena. This example illustrates the position and shortcomings of the current international system. We must also realise that it will not always be easy for people living elsewhere to understand what is happening in, for example, Uganda, where children walk kilometres every night to sleep in Gulu in order to avoid being killed during the night. We work in a world with enormously different problems in different parts of the globe, complex realities and complications, and a rudimentary system of international organisation. In the field of peace and security, we do have the Security Council with fifteen member states – five of whom have a veto – which is in charge of matters within the realm of peace and security.

The Security Council brings me to the topic of initiating proceedings. The Security Council created the *ad hoc* Tribunals for the former Yugoslavia and Rwanda. Because of this background, some states thought that the Court should also work only by the referral of a case by the Security Council. This model, however, was not accepted in the Rome Conference that established the ICC. In addition to the Security Council, states parties to the Rome Statute can also bring a case to the Court. These two ways in which a case can be brought before the Court reflect the reality that states remain the main actors in, and the subjects of, international law.

The new idea in Rome was that of allowing the Prosecutor to commence a case, *proprio motu*, when a crime was committed by a national or on the territory of one of the states parties. However, before the Prosecutor may decide to initiate a case, he has to analyse the crimes committed, as well as their admissibility. He has to determine explicitly that the state involved is unable and unwilling to prosecute, and the gravity threshold of the crime. Authorisation by the Pre-Trial Chamber is required in order for the Prosecutor to initiate a case. The system is thus one of checks and balances between the Prosecutor and the Pre-Trial Chamber. This third way in which the Court may exercise jurisdiction is controversial, primarily because it makes the Court relatively independent from states and from the Security Council.

4.   A GLOBAL JUSTICE SYSTEM: INTERVENTION, NON-STATE ACTORS AND GENDER DIMENSIONS

It is useful to return to the idea of networks and to the idea of a global justice system based in national systems set out at the beginning of this chapter. In March 2005, Kenya was the 98th state to ratify the Statute. It is important to focus not only on what is happening at the Court, but also on what is happening at the national level.

The ICC is a court of last resort. It will intervene very selectively, when the state does not (genuinely) act. Once the Court intervenes, the positive impact of its intervention should be maximized in other states. The Prosecutor has the role of the investigator, and the judges decide the cases, but civil society and other national actors have a very critical role as well. This role extends to monitoring what happens, or to reporting to the Prosecutor when crimes have occurred that may call for intervention by the Court. The Prosecutor can receive communications from any person in the world. After the judges render a decision, concerted efforts are required to expand the impact of the decision throughout the world.

It is very important to note that the international criminal justice system is not just about genocide, war crimes and crimes against humanity. The gender dimension is extremely important. There have been significant developments in the jurisprudence regarding rape and other gender crimes because of the great work of Navanethem Pillai, Elizabeth Odio Benito and other judges at the International Criminal Tribunal for the Former Yugoslavia (ICTY) and at the International Criminal Tribunal for Rwanda (ICTR). At Nuremberg, the Prosecutor was reluctant to present rape cases before the judges, because he feared they would feel embarrassed. Although rape has for centuries been used as a weapon of war, rape and gender-based violence had for a long time not been litigated before the courts. The practice of the ICTY and the ICTR has drastically changed this. Interestingly, this may have occurred in part because women judges were leaders in these matters, and they directed some of the necessary changes, including definitions of what constitutes rape. In Chile, a group connected with gender initiatives at the international criminal tribunals are not just working on such initiatives at the Court. They are also trying to transfer the contemporary definition of rape to the domestic legislation. The idea of transposing the standards developed by the international community into the national system is extremely important. This is where the Court could have a broader impact.

5. THE OPERATION OF THE INTERNATIONAL CRIMINAL COURT WITH REGARD TO CHILDREN

Within the ICC, the different organs have different missions and responsibilities and thus different ways and means for taking up children's issues and rights. The Registry has two main sections that are involved in children's issues. The Victims and Witnesses Unit of the Division of Court Services evaluates the security situation, and is in charge of the relocation of witnesses. The Special Gender and Children's Unit – which will be referred to in greater detail below – is also responsible for putting in motion an emergency response system, if required. The other section at the Registry involved in children's issues is the Division of Victims and Counsel, which, through its Victims Participation and Reparations Section, deals with the participation of victims in proceedings and with compensation. The compensation aspect will be another interesting and innovative feature of the practice of the Court, because the Court deals not only with those responsible for committing crimes, but also has the possibility to compensate individuals or communities. The judges still have to decide the modalities of how to award compensation, but the Court may in this way help to rebuild communities after trials.

Chambers have critical roles in relation to the participation of victims and other specific issues. When necessary, according to Article 57(3c) of the Rome Statute, the Pre-Trial Chamber provides for the protection and privacy of victims and witnesses. This means that the Pre-Trial Chamber controls the protection of victims and witnesses, especially children.

Within the Office of the Prosecutor, a Special Gender and Children's Unit was created. It forms part of the investigation division, and is very operative. It comprises a group of persons specialized in dealing with those who have suffered trauma, especially victims of gender-based violence and children. They support those involved before the meetings with ICC officials, during these meetings and thereafter. In collaboration with different NGOs, UNICEF and other experts, the Special Unit is currently developing guidelines on how to treat children. Each investigator at the Office of the Prosecutor will receive training concerning these guidelines, as each investigator will have to learn how to deal with children. The Special Unit will also be in charge of cases where there are child witnesses. We are attempting to avoid children having to testify, but where this cannot be avoided the Special Unit will be involved. Guidelines are also being prepared for people working in the field to provide us with feedback on these matters. We are learning from other courts as well, including the Special Court for Sierra Leone.

We have prepared basic guidelines, the basis of which is that the protection of victims is one of the main duties of the Court. This means that victims cannot be exposed, that the number of victim witnesses has to be minimized and that each witness, especially child witnesses, has to be provided with maximum protection. The ICC does not have a police force or an army, so it cannot physically protect victims and witnesses. Therefore it works with partners. To reduce risks, a thorough evaluation of the situation is conducted before any contact is made with a potential witness. Parental consent is a condition for the pre-assessment of or for interviewing children, after which the situation is assessed. This means that before investigators conduct interviews, the Special Unit goes into the field to assess the viability of interviewing any child witnesses.

All witnesses under the age of eighteen years are assessed with regard to their physical, mental and psychological condition. These assessments are conducted by associate victims experts and professional psychologists. The same procedure is followed with people who have been raped and with other traumatized witnesses. A few examples of situations with which we are dealing and in which we protect the persons involved can clarify this. In one case, a girl was in a rehabilitation centre for a few months and planned to return home. Our advisor considered that it was not a good idea to interview her then, so the interview was postponed. In some cases girls have refused to be interviewed and we have respected their wishes. In other cases, victims have taken the initiative of approaching our investigators asking to be interviewed.

6. CONCLUDING REMARKS

This chapter has presented the workings of the International Criminal Court, with special emphasis on its operational activities that involve children. We must work together in order to be successful. The ICC needs non-state actors to help states to develop their own systems, which is something the Court cannot do. While you can always help us to improve the system and organisation within the Court, you are also key to maximizing the global impact of the relatively few cases that we will be able to deal with.

Chapter 9
STRIKE TERROR NO MORE: PROSECUTING THE USE OF CHILDREN IN TIMES OF CONFLICT – THE WEST AFRICAN EXTREME

David Crane*

1. INTRODUCTION

It was a clear hot day. The meeting hall in the school for the deaf located up country near Makeni rippled with the heat of over five hundred persons. I had been speaking to the students, faculty, and others in one of the many town hall meetings that I conducted throughout Sierra Leone. The purpose of these meetings was to provide a vehicle for the people of this small and fragile nation to talk to their Prosecutor about the war, the crimes, their pain and other issues related to our work. As I finished answering a question from a student near the front, a shy and small arm was raised in the middle of the hall. I walked back to the student. He meekly stood up, head bowed and he mumbled, loud enough for those around him to hear: 'I killed people, I am sorry, I did not mean it'. I went over to him, tears in my eyes, and hugged him and said: 'Of course you didn't mean it. I forgive you'.[1]

Only in the past ten years has the international community begun to grapple with the scourge of the use of children in armed conflict,[2] after the 1996 Graça Machel report to the Secretary-General of the United Nations first laid out a comprehensive program for immediate action to protect children during times of armed conflict.[3]

---

* David M. Crane was the founding Chief Prosecutor of the Special Court for Sierra Leone between April 2002 and July 2005. He lived and worked in Freetown, Sierra Leone for 36 months. Currently he is Distinguished Visiting Professor of Law at Syracuse University College of Law.

[1] The event took place in March of 2004 in Makeni, Sierra Leone. The child was twelve years old and was deaf. The catholic sister who was headmistress told me that this young man had never spoken of his involvement in the civil war, but he had been having a behavioural problem, running away, sometimes for weeks. This is just one story from the lost generation that many of the children of Sierra Leone in the 1990s belong to.

[2] See also chapter 3 by Vesselin Popovski. Conscripting or enlisting children under the age of fifteen, or using them to participate actively in hostilities, is a war crime now and is within the jurisdiction of the International Criminal Court (ICC). Rome Statute, Article 8(2)(b)(xxvi) and (e)(vii). For further details, see the previous chapter by Luis Moreno-Ocampo.

[3] G. Machel, 'The Impact of War on Children', *UN Doc.* A/51/306 of 26 August 1996, available through <www.unicef.org/graca>.

K. Arts & V. Popovski (eds.), International Criminal Accountability and the Rights of Children
© 2006, Hague Academic Coalition, The Hague, The Netherlands and the Authors

The report in its introduction dramatically declared:

> 'These statistics are shocking enough, but more chilling is the conclusion to be drawn
> from them: more and more of the world is being sucked into a desolate moral vacuum.
> This is a space devoid of the most basic human values; a space in which children are
> slaughtered, raped, and maimed; a space in which children are exploited as soldiers; a
> space in which children are starved and exposed to extreme brutality. Such unregu-
> lated terror and violence speak of deliberate victimization. There are few further
> depths to which humanity can sink.'[4]

For the first time in history those who bear the greatest responsibility for war crimes,
crimes against humanity, and other serious violations of international humanitarian
law that took place during the horror that was the conflict in Sierra Leone, have
been charged with the use of child soldiers.[5] The use of children in armed conflict
is an age old issue.[6] Modern international norms, however, have identified and
outlawed their use. The Special Court for Sierra Leone is on the cutting edge of
international criminal law in holding accountable those warlords, commanders, and
politicians who turned to children, some as young as six years old, to carry out
orders that in some cases resulted in war crimes and crimes against humanity. This
paper will highlight the ground-breaking efforts by the Special Court for Sierra
Leone (SCSL), to bring to justice those who destroyed a generation of children in
that struggling and hapless backwater of a country during the 1990s.[7]

However, it will first be important to step back and discuss the conflict in general. This puts the use of children in context and helps to understand the role children played in the tragedy that was the civil war in Sierra Leone. We will then

---

[4] Ibid. at 5.

[5] Article 4(c) Statute of the Special Court for Sierra Leone, on conscripting or enlisting children
under fifteen into armed forces or groups or using them to participate actively in hostilities.

[6] According to Article 1 of the 1989 UN Convention on the Rights of the Child 'a child is every
human being below the age of eighteen years unless under the law applicable to the child, majority is
attained earlier.' As to child soldiering, see, generally, G. Machel, *The Impact of War on Children: A
Review of Progress* (London, Hurst 2001) e.g., at p. 7: 'A child soldier is any child – boy or girl – under
the age of 18, who is compulsorily, forcibly or voluntarily recruited or used in hostilities by armed
forces, paramilitaries, civil defence units or other armed groups. Child soldiers are used for forced
sexual services, as combatants, messengers, porters and cooks.' As per the Cape Town Principles,
adopted 30 April 1997: 'Child soldier … means any person under 18 years of age who is part of any
kind of regular or irregular armed force or armed group in any capacity, including, but not limited to
cooks, porters, messengers and those accompanying such groups, other than purely as family members. It includes girls recruited for sexual purposes and forced marriage. It does not, therefore, only
refer to a child who is carrying or has carried arms. "Recruitment" encompasses compulsory, forced
and voluntary recruitment into any kind of regular or irregular armed force or armed group.'

[7] In the 2005 version of the United Nations Development Programme's 'Human Development
Index' (HDI), Sierra Leone ranks 176th, followed by Niger as the last on the list. The HDI is a compos-
ite index that measures a country's average achievements in three aspects of human development: life
expectancy, illiteracy and school enrolment, and standard of living (per capita GDP). In the 2004
version of the HDI, Sierra Leone ranked 177th and last. In terms of quality of life it is essentially one of
the worst places in the world to live with an average life expectancy of approximately 40. For more
details see <http://hdr.undp.org>.

discuss various relevant indictments and charges. All of the indictees were charged with the unlawful recruitment of children into an armed force. Several of the indictees challenged this charge on jurisdictional grounds during the pre-trial phase, but were rebuffed by the Special Court for Sierra Leone's Appellate's Chamber. From there we will review the current state of the law regarding the use of child soldiers, in order to finish with a look into the haze of an uncertain future.

The world is only beginning to understand this scourge that is such a black mark on mankind. We cannot let the world's children strike terror. The rights of children and accounting for crimes against them and humanity are linked to all of our attempts to ensure that children grow up healthily and secure from impunity. It is my belief that children under fifteen *per se* are legally not capable of committing a crime against humanity and are not indictable for their acts at the international level. The atrocity is not what the child has done, but the opportunity, conditions, and circumstances that allow them to commit these horrors.

2. THE CONFLICT

Sierra Leone sits along the West African coast that stretches from Senegal to Nigeria before turning gently south into Central Africa.[8] It is a small nugget in a corroded string of nations along this coast linked together by a colonial past, with a history of bad governance, conflict, and disease. The common thread that holds this odd geographic necklace together is varying degrees of corruption.[9] West Africa, generally, and Sierra Leone in particular, possesses vast natural resources.[10] Rich in diamonds, rutile and bauxite, among other minerals, these important commodities are Sierra Leone's curse. Corruption and diamonds were the catalysts that ignited a conflict that resulted in the murder, maiming, mutilation, and rape of over half a million human beings in Sierra Leone.[11]

Living in a failed state, Sierra Leoneans have no faith in their governmental institutions or in the rule of law. Since independence, the leprosy of corruption has eaten the country alive for over forty years, the last decade in the convulsive throes of an internal armed conflict. Sierra Leoneans struggle daily just to survive to the end of the week. For many of these citizens there is no hope. It was this very loss of hope that warlords, criminal organisations, and cynical politicians took advantage of as part of their plan to execute the civil war in the 1990s.

Fresh from the terror training facilities and camps in Libya, young ruthless leaders were sent south to begin a decade long campaign to take over politically, by force if necessary, the entire region of West Africa. Lying prostrate before Moammar

---

[8] J.L. Hirsch, *Sierra Leone: Diamonds and the Struggle for Democracy* (Boulder, Lynne Riener, 2001) pp. 22-24. See generally, T. Lucan, *A Visual History of West Africa* (London, Evans, 1981).

[9] Hirsch, ibid., at pp. 25-28.

[10] *Sierra Leone Country Handbook*, United States Marine Corps, pp. 52-55.

[11] Ibid.

Gadhaffi, the struggling former colonies of France and Great Britain were vulnerable to unrest, conflict, and overthrow. This decade long plan of unrest started in 1990 and 1991. Charles Taylor, an escaped detainee from the United States, slipped quietly into Liberia and began years of civil war there. Along with another graduate of the Libyan terror camps, a former wedding photographer and corporal in the Sierra Leonean Army, Foday Sankoh, Taylor looked west over the border of Sierra Leone to the alluvial diamond fields in the Kono and Koinadugu districts. Diamonds would help keep both his revolution and his bank account well financed.[12]

With backing and planning assistance from Ghadaffi and Blaise Campore, President of Burkino Faso, Taylor assisted Sankoh in launching two strikes into the eastern portion of Sierra Leone in March 1991. He was admonished by Taylor to vigorously recruit the civilian population to the cause, by terror and force, if necessary. What followed after that day was a back and forth death struggle that lasted over ten years between various warring factions, each brutalizing civilians, particularly women and children. Never really having a political purpose or goal, this internal armed conflict, started by Charles Taylor and the Revolutionary United Front (RUF), evolved into a terror campaign in the hope of gaining and maintaining control of not only the diamond fields, but the entire nation for this joint criminal enterprise.

During this bizarre spectacle pain, suffering, and agony reached new dimensions. The atrocities committed almost defied description in any language. 'Believe the unbelievable' is what I told the chamber responsible for the trial of the leadership of the Civil Defense Forces (CDF) in the opening statement that began their prosecution. No more horrific a tale is the one just told in the introduction to this chapter, however this is only illustrative of years worth of using boys and girls as soldiers and support personnel who raped, maimed, mutilated, and murdered their way across Sierra Leone in such military operations as 'Pay yourself' and 'No living thing'.

A favourite tactic to induce children to join their force was for the rebels to move in and surround a village. The children were made to kill their parents and then were driven into the bush and forced to serve as soldiers, in many instances for years. The numbers are not fully known, but it was in the thousands. These children, ranging from six to eighteen years of age, roamed the battlefields hopped up on cocaine or marijuana destroying their own country. Over time the various warring factions became their home and their families. All sides to the conflict in Sierra Leone used children.

When the conflict staggered to its bloody conclusion in 2002, an entire nation lay in ruins. These child fighters found themselves with no families, little to no education, and a society unable to assist them in starting to rebuild their lives. Many

---

[12] For an excellent general overview of the conflict within Sierra Leone, see L.A. Smith, et al., *Conflict Mapping in Sierra Leone, Violations of International Humanitarian Law from 1991 to 2002* (No Peace Without Justice, Sierra Leone Conflict Mapping Programme, Freetown 2004) available through <www.specialcourt.org/SLMission/CMFullReport.html>.

were physically and psychologically damaged. The lost generation of Sierra Leone now sits by pocked-marked roads with no hope, waiting for the next 'Pa' to lead them back into the only life they know: fighting, raping, pillaging, and murdering their fellow citizens.[13]

A forty-two year old secretary, in an interview on 20 May 1999, told a Human Rights Watch researcher about child soldiers used in the invasion and destruction of Freetown in January of that same year: 'We feared them. They were cruel and hard hearted; even more than the adults. They don't know what is sympathy; what is good and bad. If you beg an older one you may convince him to spare you, but the younger ones, they don't know what is sympathy, what is mercy. Those who have been rebels for so long have never learned it.'[14]

3. THE SPECIAL COURT FOR SIERRA LEONE

The Special Court is an innovative step in the evolution of international war crimes tribunals designed to prevent future atrocities. Even with the establishment of the International Criminal Court, the SCSL is a model that can work in the future to combat impunity in troubled areas of the world.

The Court is a new kind of 'hybrid' tribunal that is independent of the United Nations and any state.[15] It is considered the next generation of war crimes tribunal. Established through an Agreement between the United Nations and the Government of Sierra Leone in January 2002, the Court is both international and national.[16] The signing of the Agreement was the culmination of a year and a half of discussions since August 2000, following a United Nations Security Council resolution

---

[13] See *Youth, Poverty and Blood. The Lethal Legacy of West Africa's Regional Warriors*, Human Rights Watch, Vol. 1, No. 5(A), March 2005. The report in its opening paragraph at p. 1 sums up the problem: 'Since the late 1980's, the armed conflicts in Liberia, Sierra Leone, Guinea and Cote d'Ivoire have reverberated across each country's porous borders. Gliding back and forth across these borders is a migrant population of young fighters – regional warriors – who view war as mainly an economic opportunity. Their military "careers" most often began when they were abducted and forcibly recruited by rebels in Liberia or Sierra Leone, usually as children.'

[14] *Getting Away with Murder, Mutilation, and Rape: New Testimony from Sierra Leone*, Human Rights Watch Report, Vol. 11, No. 3(A), June 1999, at p. 54. The interviewee goes on declaring: 'Once a rebel, a small boy in full combats, couldn't have been more than twelve, called everyone out of the house across the street. The papa of the family, Pa Kamara, said, "please my son, leave my family", but the boy said, "listen, we can do anything we want in Freetown. We don't have mothers, we don't have fathers. We can do anything we wanna do". And that is how Pa Kamara died; the rebel boy shot him, in front of his wife, his children, his grandchildren. They are wicked, those boy soldiers. They spare no human life.'

[15] UNSC Resolution 1315 (2000), 14 August 2000. See also, 'Report of the Secretary-General on the establishment of a Special Court for Sierra Leone', *UN Doc*. S/2000/915, 4 October 2000.

[16] Agreement between the United Nations and the Government of Sierra Leone on the Establishment of a Special Court for Sierra Leone, 16 January 2002. See also, The Special Court Agreement, 2002, Ratification Act, 2002.

directing the Secretary-General to enter negotiations to create the Court. The national parliament passed a law to implement the treaty in March 2002.[17]

The Court's Registrar, Robin Vincent from the United Kingdom, and the Prosecutor were appointed by the United Nations Secretary-General in April 2002. The Deputy Prosecutor, Desmond DeSilva was appointed by the Government of Sierra Leone in the fall of 2002.[18] The Court's Chambers are a combination of five international and national justices in the Appellate Chamber and three international and national justices each in the two Trial Chambers. The first eight justices (five in the Appeals Chamber and three for trial chamber one) were sworn into office in early December 2002. The second Trial Chamber was sworn in January 2005.[19]

The Court's mandate is to try those who 'bear the greatest responsibility' for serious violations of international humanitarian law, including the laws of war; crimes against humanity, including widespread or systematic murder, enslavement, rape, sexual slavery and other forms of sexual violence, torture, and other inhumane acts; and certain crimes under Sierra Leone law.[20] Cases can be brought against anyone who committed crimes or was responsible for crimes committed in the territory of Sierra Leone since 30 November 1996.[21] The mandate is very specific and there are a few short years to finish it. With the current plan and strategy, this will be accomplished in an effective and efficient manner, hopefully within a politically acceptable timeframe.

Unlike the two existing *ad hoc* international criminal tribunals, the Special Court's budget is drawn mainly from voluntary contributions rather than assessments from UN member states. The entire four year budget for the Court, including the construction of a permanent court site, will be approximately $100 million. Thus far, over 30 countries have generously provided financial or in-kind contributions. With an annual budget of around $25 million, a tenth of what the other tribunals spend each year, the Court must be more efficient and operate with a leaner staff and less resources.

Most importantly, the Special Court sits in the country where the violations occurred. This is exactly the right place for the Court to be – in the heart of Sierra Leone, delivering justice directly for the people who suffered during the civil war. The courtroom is open to the public and an ambitious outreach and public informa-

---

[17] Ibid.

[18] In May 2005, Mr. DeSilva was appointed by the UN Secretary-General to succeed David M. Crane as Prosecutor for the Special Court for Sierra Leone. He will serve until the Court completes its' work on or around the winter of 2007.

[19] Statute of the Special Court for Sierra Leone, Article 11, 'Organization of the Special Court'.

[20] Ibid., Article 1 para. 1: 'The Special Court shall, except as provided in subparagraph (2), have the power to prosecute persons who bear the greatest responsibility for serious violations of international humanitarian law and Sierra Leonean law committed in the territory of Sierra Leone since 30 November 1996, including those leaders who, in committing such crimes, have threatened the establishment of and implementation of the peace process in Sierra Leone.' For a discussion of the minimum age of criminal responsibility and the SCSL Statute, see chapter 5 by Matthew Happold.

[21] Ibid.

tion program is already in place to keep Sierra Leoneans informed and engaged in the work of the Court. This is, first and foremost, their Court.

The Court hopes to make a lasting contribution to promoting accountability and the rule of law long after its work has finished. Thus, capacity-building and legacy activities constitute an important part of our work. Courtroom facilities are completed and will be turned over to the people of Sierra Leone at the conclusion of the trials. In addition, the Court hired a high percentage of Sierra Leonean professionals (the Office of the Prosecutor employs more Sierra Leoneans than any other nationality) and we have reached out to the local legal community to design initiatives to bolster legal reform in the country. These include facilitating scholarship opportunities and training programs in international humanitarian law, as well as a fruitful partnership with the local law school.[22] Trials may end, but the Special Court will never truly leave Sierra Leone.

4. THE INDICTMENTS AND THE CHARGES

As the Prosecutor I arrived in Sierra Leone in early August 2002. Criminal investigations began two weeks later, according to plan.[23] On 3 March 2003, eight indictments were signed.[24] These indictments were confirmed by a trial chamber judge in London on 7 March. At noon on Monday, 10 March – just seven months after the Prosecutor's arrival – members of the investigations team, along with the Sierra Leone Police launched 'Operation Justice' and took down simultaneously all the indictees who were in Sierra Leone at the time, including the Minister of Interior, Samuel Hinga Norman. A total of 13 indictments have been issued. Two indictees are currently outside of Sierra Leone with outstanding international warrants for

---

[22] The Legacy Program for the Office of the Prosecutor (OTP) for 2005/2006 consists of: putting various Sierra Leonean Legal texts on DVD and distributing them to the law school and the bar association; a monthly lecture series for the local bar given by members of the OTP; a street law program teaching high school students key aspects of Sierra Leonean criminal law; and a codification project of customary law. The major legacy initiative that started back in 2004 and continues to this day is the innovative witness management program. This program trains Sierra Leonean Police (SLP) the nuances of caring for, protecting, and monitoring witnesses' pre-trial, trial, and post-trial. The unit formed in the OTP will be transferred in total to the SLP and become a first-ever organisation caring for witnesses within the jurisdiction of the SLP.

[23] In May 2002 the Prosecutor developed a general prosecutorial strategy which he presented for the first time at a roundtable sponsored by the United States Institute of Peace that same month. While doing this he also developed a ten-phase plan that detailed the milestones and sequence of critical events that would take place in the set-up, investigation, indictment, pre-trial, and trial stages of the Court's mandate. Currently they are in phase ten and have started executing a 'phase 11' called the exit strategy.

[24] In a moving ceremony in the office of the Chief Prosecutor, eight indictments were signed in front of all of the investigators and trial counsel. I recall saying to them in a short opening before I signed the indictments that 'the ghosts of a 100,000 people stand with us in this room today'. Some of my staff were weeping openly. Beethoven's 'Ode to Joy' was being played on my stereo as we signed the indictments one at a time.

their arrest. The six indictees arrested in March 2003, plus three more over a period of several months, are in a detention facility at the Court compound in Freetown facing three joint criminal trials. Investigations are ongoing and further indictments may follow.

We have been encouraged by the response to the indictments by the people of Sierra Leone. The peace has held and many have spoken out in support of our work. According to polls, over two-thirds of the population believe the Special Court is necessary, with another two-thirds believing it will deter future conflict.[25]

Each of the indictees have been jointly and severally charged with the use of child soldiers among other international crimes. The extent of that involvement was widespread and systematic. Each of the indictees had command responsibility of the combatants that they led, to include child soldiers. The various combatants over the period of the conflict had Small Boy Units (SBUs). Some of these SBUs had specific duties to perform. In the burning of Freetown, January 1999, children were part of squads specifically ordered to mutilate, to burn, and to pillage. Child soldiers were seen throughout the three weeks of occupation carrying burlap bags full of body parts, trailing blood along the way. They were required to bring the bags to their commanders.

The leadership of the Revolutionary United Front are charged, in Count 12 of their amended indictment, for the recruitment and use of child soldiers, specifically conscripting or enlisting children under the age of fifteen years into armed forces or groups, or using them to participate actively in hostilities. Similarly, the leadership of the Armed Forces Revolutionary Council (AFRC) are charged in their further amended indictment in Count 12, as well. The dreaded leadership of the Civil Defense Force is charged in Count 8 of their indictment.[26] The former President of Liberia, Charles Taylor is charged with the recruitment and use of child soldiers and so is the fugitive indictee, Johnny Paul Koroma. The deceased indictees Foday Sankoh and Samuel Bockerie were likewise charged.

All of the indictees, allegedly, are individually criminally liable for the use of children in times of armed conflict both under either of two theories: aiding and abetting, as articulated in Article 6(1) of the Statute of the Special Court for Sierra Leone or, in the alternative, command responsibility under Article 6(3) of the Statute. Each of the indictees is charged with the recruitment and use of children during all times relevant to the indictment. As Charles Taylor had directed Foday Sankoh in Liberia in February 1991, children were rounded up early to bulk up the forces in Sierra Leone. Later in the conflict the Civil Defense Force, particularly the Kamajors, initiated children into their ranks. Children served on all sides throughout the conflict that lasted 10 long years.

---

[25] According to an informal poll taken by an NGO in June 2003.

[26] *The Prosecutor* v. *Samuel Hinga Norman, Moinina Fofana, Allieu Kondewa*, Case No. SCSL-03-14-I (Indictment); *The Prosecutor* v. *Issa Hassan Sesay, Morris Kallon, and Augustine Gbao*, Case No. SCSL-2004-15-PT (Amended Consolidated Indictment); *The Prosecutor* v. *Alex Tamba Brima, Brima Bazzy Kamara, and Santigie Barbor Kanu*, Case No. SCSL-2004-16-PT (Further Amended Consolidated Indictment).

The various charges in the indictments stem from the enumerated crimes within the SCSL Statute. The specific crime of using child soldiers can be found in Article 4 of the Statute, 'other serious violations of international humanitarian law'. This provision allows the Prosecutor to indict a person for three international crimes, ranging from intentionally attacking civilians; various crimes against peacekeepers or humanitarian assistance workers; and the recruitment and use of child soldiers. The Prosecutor has used all three in the various joint criminal indictments.

5. THE CHALLENGES

During the pre-trial phase, in the summer of 2003, several of the indictees made various jurisdictional challenges to the charges in the indictments and to the Court itself. On 26 June 2003, one of the indictees, Hinga Norman, specifically challenged the charge against him relating to the use of child soldiers as not being a crime at the time of its alleged commission. Another indictee intervened as well. This preliminary motion was referred to the Appeals Chamber pursuant to Rule 72(E) of the Rules of Procedure and Evidence of the Special Court, after the response by the Prosecutor which was filed on 7 July 2003. Amicus curiae briefs were filed by both the International Human Rights Clinic of the University of Toronto and by UNICEF.[27] An oral hearing was held on 6 November 2003, with a follow on post-hearing submission by the Prosecutor on 24 November 2003.[28]

On 31 May 2004, the Appeals Chamber of the Court dismissed Norman's motion. The Appeals Chamber held that child recruitment had been criminalized under customary international law by the time frames relevant to the indictment, thus protecting the legality and specificity principles questioned by Norman. For the first time in legal history a high court had ruled that the recruitment of child soldiers was a crime under international law.[29]

---

[27] Amicus Curiae Brief of University of Toronto International Human Rights Clinic and interested International Human Rights Organizations, 3 November 2003. Also, Amicus Curiae Brief of the United Nations Children's Fund (UNICEF), 21 January 2003.

[28] 'State practice demonstrates full awareness and abhorrence to the practice of recruiting children, and a firm commitment to ensuring that those responsible for such recruitment are held liable under criminal law. The prohibition on recruitment and use of child soldiers below 15 has been universally recognized. Most States have enacted legislation for the implementation of their minimum age for recruitment and use of children in hostilities. Some States have explicitly criminalized child recruitment. The prohibition was therefore well established and its violation considered a criminal act. [...] and demonstrates opinio juris in the acceptance by States that this norm is legally binding.'

[29] *Prosecutor* v. *Sam Hinga Norman*, Case No. SCSL-2004-14-AR72(E), Decision on Preliminary Motion Based on Lack of Jurisdiction (Child Recruitment), 31 May 2004: 'Therefore, child recruitment was criminalized before it was explicitly set out in treaty law and certainly by the time frame relevant to the indictments.' The principle of legality and the principle of specificity are both upheld. Justice Gelaga King wrote a separate concurring opinion and Justice Geoffrey Robertson dissented stating that the crime of child recruitment did not enter into international criminal law until the Rome Treaty [for the International Criminal Court] in July 1998, thus declaring that the applicant should not be prosecuted for any offense of enlistment before that date. For an interesting point of view related to

6. THE STATE OF THE LAW

The decision by the Appeals Chamber correctly reflects the state of the law.[30] The case of children in warfare is not a new phenomenon. Children have followed armies for centuries as support personnel – pages, water carriers, and as musicians, particularly as drummers. In navies throughout Europe children were seconded to warships by nobility to learn a trade and careers as officers, and others were pressed into seamanship.

With the advent of the various Hague rules governing weapons in war in the late 19th and early 20th centuries, the rules of warfare began to take on a universal status, and coupled with the Red Cross movement the role of the combatant became a legal term of art. The status of the non-combatant also began to take shape.[31] Yet the specifics as to the age of combatants were not well defined early in the regulation process. The focus of the international community was more on the regulation of weapons that would cause unnecessary suffering and the types of targets combatants could engage.[32]

After World War I and into World War II, the shift away from universal rules relating to weapons and targets began, and by the end of the horrors of these two world wars the focus was now rightfully on non-combatants. With the founding of the United Nations in 1945, there was now a permanent body that could be a voice for non-combatants, particularly for children.

Shortly after the founding of the United Nations, with its broad mission to assist mankind in peace and security, the universal rules began to narrow and define in more specific terms the special status of non-combatants. The cornerstone to these rules became the Geneva Conventions of 1949, which by their nature, were devoted to persons who are 'out of the combat' – prisoners of war, the shipwrecked,

---

the *Norman* decision, see A. Smith, 'Child Recruitment and the Special Court for Sierra Leone', 2 *Journal of International Criminal Justice* (2004) pp. 1141-1153.

[30] See generally, Smith, ibid. See also, the 1977 Additional Protocols to the Geneva Conventions of 1949, the 1989 Convention on the Rights of the Child and its Second Optional Protocol of 2000, the 1998 Rome Statute for the International Criminal Court and the 1999 ILO Convention No. 192 Concerning the Prohibition and Immediate Action for the Elimination of the Worst Forms of Child Labour.

[31] Hague Convention No. III Relative to the Opening of Hostilities, 18 October 1907; Hague Rules No. IV Respecting the Law and Customs of War on Land, 18 October 1907; Annex to Hague Convention No. IV embodying the Regulations Respecting the Laws and Customs of War on Land, 18 October 1907; Hague Convention No. V Respecting the Rights and Duties of Neutral Powers and Persons in Case of War on Land, 18 October 1907.

[32] For a general review of the history of the development of the laws of armed conflict, see L. Friedman, *The Law of War: A Documentary History*, Vol. II (New York, Random House 1972); L. Kotzsch, *The Concept of War in Contemporary History and International Law* (Geneva, Droz 1956); J. Stone, *Legal Controls of International Conflict* (London, Stevens and Sons 1954); J. Norton Moore, et al., *National Security Law* (Durham, Carolina Academic Press 1990); L. Oppenheim, *International Law Vol. II Disputes, War and Neutrality* 7th edn. (London, Longmans, Green and Co. 1952); G. von Glahn, *Law Among Nations* (New York, Macmillan 1992); M. Walzer, *Just and Unjust Wars* (New York, Basic Books 1977); Dept. of Army, *Field Manual 27-10*, 'The Law of Land Warfare' (18 July 1956).

and civilians.[33] It is here that we begin to see that children become protected under international law. Also, by this time the international commitment to the principles of human rights were laid out in the Universal Declaration of Human Rights, which echoed the fundamental principles of the dignity of human beings found in the Geneva Conventions as well.[34] The world then plunged into the Cold War with a new standard of protection of the rights and status of non-combatants in times of war.

However, the tragedy of the Cold War was the third world 'flashpoints' that resulted in various conflicts. Children were once again the victims. In the middle of the Cold War many colonies became independent and the long process of having these new emerging nations, struggling just to feed their populations, review, debate, and adapt the universal principles related to the governing of armed conflict began in third world capitals.

In the 1970s the world paused long enough to reconsider the 1949 Geneva Conventions, and to shape them to reflect the realities of modern armed conflict. The debate was significant and the results important, as it brought into the fold much of the third world by their agreeing to the two new Protocols.[35] Once again the bar had been identified and, indeed, it had been raised. Most of the nations of the world agreed to the new standards.[36] In the Protocols we see the specific prohibition of the use of children in armed conflict. The criminality of the act of using children in conflict, however, is not specifically laid out. Yet the implication is that the violation of the Geneva Conventions related to civilians as non-combatants, coupled with the Additional Protocols, implies a grave breach when using children in combat. Such breaches impose a duty to investigate and prosecute upon all the signatories to the Conventions and the Protocols.[37]

---

[33] Geneva Convention for the Amelioration of the Condition of the Wounded and Sick in Armed Forces in the Field, 12 August 1949; Geneva Convention for the Amelioration of the Condition of the Wounded, Sick and Shipwrecked Members of Armed Forces at Sea, 12 August 1949; Geneva Convention Relative to the Treatment of Prisoners of War, 12 August 1949; Geneva Conventions Relative to the Protection of Civilian Persons in Time of War, 12 August 1949.

[34] Adopted and proclaimed by UNGA Resolution 217 A (III) of 10 December 1948. The first clause of the Preamble to this important document declares: 'Whereas the recognition of the inherent dignity and of the equal and inalienable rights of all members of the human family is the foundation of freedom, justice, and peace in the world ...'.

[35] Protocol Additional to the Geneva Conventions of 12 August 1949, and Relating to the Protection of Victims of International Armed Conflicts, 10 June 1977; Protocol Additional to the Geneva Conventions of 12 August 1949, and Relating to the Protection of Victims of Non-international Armed Conflicts, 19 June 1977.

[36] However, e.g., the United States has not ratified either of the protocols.

[37] The obligation to prosecute grave breeches of the laws of armed conflict or extradite can be found in the Geneva Conventions of 1949: Wounded and Sick (GWS), Art. 49(2); GWS Sea, Art. 50(2); Prisoners of War (GPW), Art. 129(2); Civilians, Art. 146(2). Universality of jurisdiction over those who commit grave breaches of the customary principles of the laws of armed conflict has been around even prior to 1949. See Israel District Court of Jerusalem, *Israel* v. *Eichman*, 12 December 1961, reprinted in L. Friedman, *supra* n. 32, pp. 1627, 1631-1635; see also W.B. Cowles, 'Universality of Jurisdiction over War Crimes', 33 *California Law Review* (1945) pp. 177-218.

The subsequent Convention on the Rights of the Child (CRC) and its Second Optional Protocol began to highlight the prohibition against the use of children in armed conflict. The CRC appears to criminalize the concept of child recruitment. By this time one certainly can argue that the act of child recruitment as a crime had crystallized into customary international law.

Despite this political and legal recognition by states that child recruitment was a universal crime, in practice child recruitment went on unabated. Millions of children died in the 1980s and 1990s, mostly in Africa where children played a significant role in various armed conflicts. In 1996, the already cited Graça Machel Report stunned the United Nations, highlighting the full extent of the problem throughout the world in the way it did. There were calls for action and a plan began to evolve to monitor the recruitment of child soldiers.

In the late 1990s the world once again sat down together and began to develop a mechanism to prosecute war crimes and crimes against humanity. The Rome Statute created the International Criminal Court which is now mankind's attempt to stamp out impunity wherever it rears its ugly head. The Rome Statute specifically states that the recruitment of children under the age of fifteen is another serious violation of international humanitarian law.[38]

At the same time the Rome Statute was being drafted, the President of Sierra Leone reached out to the United Nations for help in punishing those who committed atrocities in the conflict that had ravaged his country in the 1990s. As explained above, children had played a special and tragic role in the conflict. They were for example recruited or conscripted under great duress to fight as soldiers or act as support personnel. Many committed war crimes, some of them unimaginable for a child. As stated earlier, in response the SCSL Statute came to list, in Article 4, the now universally recognised crime of child recruitment. It mirrors the Rome Statute in that regard. All of the indictees that were undergoing trials in 2005 were charged with this crime. This is an historic first, indeed.

7.   CONCLUSION: THE FUTURE

Despite the assertion that the recruitment of child soldiers is an international crime, even today the tragedy continues worldwide, particularly in Africa. Between 1986 and 1996 over two million children were killed in armed conflict.[39] Countless more have been killed since then, many of them in places such as Sierra Leone. Only when the rule of law is enforced will abusers of children be held accountable at the international level and this crime begin to diminish. Forty-two armed groups in eleven countries were specifically singled out in a February 2005 report by the UN Secretary-General's special envoy for children in armed conflict, Olara Otunnu. He

---

[38] International Criminal Court, *UN Doc.* ICC-ASP/1/3, Article 8(2)(e)(vii).
[39] See the Graça Machel Report, *supra* n. 3, at p. 5.

stated that these groups should be punished for war crimes or crimes against humanity for what they have done to children.[40]

The Norman decision will certainly assist in the advancement of jurisprudence in the area of child recruitment. The International Criminal Court, which has a provision on child recruitment in its Statute that is identical to that found in the SCSL's Statute, will look upon the groundbreaking work of the Special Court for Sierra Leone as a cornerstone in their charging of cynical warlords, politicians, and governments who continue to ignore the clear prohibition of this criminal conduct.[41]

The 2005 report by the United Nations called for monitoring and reporting of children in armed conflict to ensure that the law is complied with worldwide, as was spelled out in the action plan of the report.[42] It highlights six 'grave violations' that should be monitored in particular.[43] The report also laid down standards that constitute a basis for monitoring, the types of parties whose activities should be monitored, and the responsibilities of who is to gather, vet, and compile information at the country level.[44] The latter will mainly be done by the field teams in the various countries where the United Nations is located.[45]

Certainly there is an increasing awareness of the scourge of child soldiers and a shift internationally towards action. The United Nations must be in the forefront of this effort backed by a unified Security Council that takes swift and decisive action when confronted with the issue. International courts will have to aggressively charge this crime in future indictments or the practice of using child soldiers will not stop. For, children need to play and grow in a nurturing environment so that they will 'strike terror no more'.[46]

I will close with another tragedy in this 10-year long tale of horror. It involves a child. He lived in a village in the Kono district. They were told that the rebels were going to attack. The witness testified that he fled into the bush with his parents and brother, but they were caught by the RUF. The rebels took his younger brother and himself to Kaiama along with thirteen other boys. The rebels lined the fifteen chil-

---

[40] For more information about the work of the special envoy and the involvement of the UN Security Council, see chapter 3 by Vesselin Popovski.

[41] See 'Amicus Curiae Brief of the United Nations Children's Fund' related to the Fourth Defense Preliminary Motion on Lack of Jurisdiction (Child Recruitment), *The Prosecutor* v. *Sam Hinga Norman*, SCSL-2003-08, 21 January 2004 at 8.

[42] 'Children and Armed Conflict: Report of the Secretary-General', *UN* Doc. A/59/695-S/2005/72, 9 February 2005 at p. 14.

[43] Ibid., at p. 16. The grave violations are: killing and maiming of children; recruiting or using child soldiers; attacks against schools or hospitals; rape or other grave sexual violence against children; abduction of children; and, denial of humanitarian access to children.

[44] Ibid., at pp. 16-17.

[45] Ibid., at p. 18.

[46] For further reading on children and armed conflict, see, generally: *In the Firing Line: War and Children's Rights* (London, Amnesty International 1997); P.J. Braken and C. Petty, *Rethinking the Trauma of War* (London, Save the Children UK 1998); R. Brett and M. McCallin, *Children, the Invisible Soldier* (Stockholm, Radda Barnen 1996), G. Machel, *supra* n. 6; *International Criminal Justice and Children* (Rome, No Peace Without Justice and UNICEF 2002).

dren up and offered them a choice: join one line if they wanted to be a rebel, another line if they wanted to be freed and allowed to go home. All fifteen of these boys, and they were just boys, joined the line for freedom. It was the wrong choice. They were accused of sabotage to the revolution. To keep them from escaping each was held down, screaming, and one-by-one had AFRC and/or RUF carved into their chests with the blade of a sword. The witness was now just marked property and treated as such. What took place marks the limits of our language to communicate and falls outside the realm of expression. However, the Special Court for Sierra Leone attempts to do so, by hearing one witness at a time, by the dozens, to show how the beast of impunity fed the conflict in Sierra Leone.[47]

---

[47] David M. Crane, 'The Opening Statement against the Leadership of the Revolutionary United Front in an Amended Joint Indictment', Case No. SCSL-2004-15-PT, *Prosecutor* v. *Sesay, Kallon, Gbao*, delivered 5 July 2004 at 15.

Chapter 10
'AS IF IT WAS HAPPENING AGAIN': SUPPORTING ESPECIALLY VULNERABLE WITNESSES, IN PARTICULAR WOMEN AND CHILDREN, AT THE SPECIAL COURT FOR SIERRA LEONE

An Michels*

1. INTRODUCTION

'I did not want to come to the Special Court because when something happens to you and you start explaining, you feel the pain as though it was happening anew. I am feeling the pain as I did before. If you don't say anything to anybody, you don't have to feel it again.'[1]

'I'm happy that I had the courage to testify; now they will all know, there will be justice and the dead can finally rest.'[2]

The Special Court for Sierra Leone (SCSL) is a so-called hybrid tribunal, established by an agreement between the government of Sierra Leone and the United Nations. Its mandate is to bring to justice those who bear the greatest responsibility for crimes committed since the end of November 1996. How do victims of gross human rights violations, in particular women and children, perceive their participation in a war crimes tribunal? How do they need to be protected and supported? Is there not a paradox between the importance of these 'especially vulnerable witnesses' – mainly victims – as providers of evidence, the burden which the judicial process places on their shoulders and the limited mandate and resources which a tribunal like the Special Court for Sierra Leone has to address the needs of victims in general?

---

* An Michels is the former Head of the Psychosocial Support Team of the Witnesses and Victims Unit of the Special Court for Sierra Leone (2003-2005). She currently works as a consultant for UNICEF and other organisations on issues related to victim support in transitional justice mechanisms.

[1] Special Court for Sierra Leone, Testimony of Protected Witness TF1- 256, April 2005.

[2] Quote from post-trial interviews with a protected witness, Special Court for Sierra Leone, October 2004. All examples mentioned in this chapter are drawn from the author's experience as the head of the psychosocial team of the Witnesses and Victims Section. The views expressed in this article are the personal views of the author and do not represent the views of the Special Court for Sierra Leone.

K. Arts & V. Popovski (eds.), International Criminal Accountability and the Rights of Children
© 2006, Hague Academic Coalition, The Hague, The Netherlands and the Authors

This chapter seeks to contribute to this debate by describing the challenges that women and children face as witnesses before the Special Court for Sierra Leone, by presenting the measures put in place to protect and support them, and by analyzing some of their experiences.

2. WHO ARE THE 'ESPECIALLY VULNERABLE WITNESSES'?

The character of the conflict in Sierra Leone, the context in which the Court is operating and its set-up create many challenges, especially for the involvement of witnesses (and victims in particular) in the process. After a conflict that left behind very little documentary evidence, both the Prosecution and the Defence have to rely almost exclusively on witness statements for establishing their case. The burden on witnesses during the proceedings is therefore significant. Unlike other international tribunals, the Special Court for Sierra Leone sits in the country where the atrocities took place, a situation that creates additional difficulties for the protection of witnesses and victims. Perpetrators and victims are often still living together in small communities and the capacity of the local police is very limited. It is also clear that, generally, the witnesses are physically and mentally vulnerable. There is a high prevalence of trauma among the general population as a consequence of the horrendous atrocities committed during the ten-year civil war.[3] The majority of Sierra Leoneans still have very limited access to health care and education and suffer from widespread poverty. These aspects directly impact on their physical and mental health.[4]

Both of these factors – the functioning of the Court and the general vulnerability of witnesses – create a heavy burden for all witnesses testifying before the Special Court. From a psychological point of view, every witness who might face the risk of being retraumatised by the judicial process, because of his or her history and/or mental state, can be considered a vulnerable witness. However, some categories of witnesses are 'especially vulnerable'. During the stage of the proceedings when the Prosecutor is presenting the case, victims form the majority of the witnesses. However, the definition of who exactly is a victim is not always clear after a conflict where, for example, children and adults were abducted and/or forced to join the fighting forces on a large scale. Especially child ex-combatants can often be considered as both victims and (alleged) perpetrators. Although it is psychologically and morally important to respect this ambiguity, in the context of international judicial mechanisms there is a common understanding among child rights advocates that child ex-combatants are to be treated as victims of conflict, and definitely not

---

[3] Médecins Sans Frontières International, 'Mental Trauma in Sierra Leone', 2000, article available at <http://217.194.25/msfinternational>.

[4] See, e.g., the United Nations Development Programme's Human Development Index (HDI), available at <http://hdr.undp.org>, for concrete indicators. Sierra Leone was ranked last but one and last, respectively, in the 2005 and 2004 HDIs.

as those who bear the greatest responsibility. Many share the view that international judicial mechanisms are not well suited for prosecuting children who have allegedly committed crimes under international law.[5]

The position of children as victims and witnesses is even more important because, for the first time ever before the Special Court, the crime of child recruitment is being prosecuted by an international tribunal, as was analyzed in the previous chapter by David Crane.[6] Children, and more specifically child ex-combatants, therefore form a very important but also particularly vulnerable group of witnesses. Not only can they provide crucial evidence about the alleged recruitment of child soldiers, but they may also be able to provide important elements to prove the command responsibility of indicted persons. Child soldiers frequently fulfilled roles close to their commanders, for example as bodyguards.

Women and girls who have been victims of the crimes of sexual assault, sexual slavery or forced marriage – the last-mentioned being a crime that has also never been previously addressed by an international tribunal – form another group of important but vulnerable witnesses. The ambiguous status of some of the victims of forced marriage as so-called 'bush wives' increases their vulnerability and complicates their reality. Many of them are being perceived by their community as collaborators or even perpetrators because of the protection and status from which they benefited during the conflict. These 'forced' relationships often entailed attachment and loyalty to their husband/the perpetrator as well, and the presence of 'rebel children'. For these reasons some of the women never separated.

It is striking that the choice of witnesses generally reflects a typical gender division: boys are called to testify about being a child ex-combatant, women and girls testify about sexual violence. This division obviously also reflects the fact that girls were by and large overlooked in the Disarmament, Demobilisation and Reintegration process in Sierra Leone, at least during the first phase thereof.[7] On the other hand, although sexual crimes are also committed against men and boys,[8] during the war in Sierra Leone women and girls were the primary targets of sexual crimes. This added to their pre-existing social vulnerability, which was among other things due to the high prevalence of sexual and domestic violence before the war and structural discrimination in Sierra Leonean society.[9]

---

[5] *International Criminal Justice and Children* (Rome, No Peace Without Justice and UNICEF Innocenti Research Centre, 2002) p. 54.

[6] In March 2006 the International Criminal Court followed suit with the case *The Prosecutor* v. *Thomas Lubanga Dyilo*, concerning child recruitment in the Democratic Republic of Congo.

[7] D. Mazurana and C. Kristopher, *From Combat to Community: Women and Girls of Sierra Leone* (Cambridge, M.A., Hunt Alternatives Fund 2004).

[8] G. Machel, *The Impact of War on Children* (London, Hurst 2001) p. 55.

[9] Physicians for Human Rights, 'War-Related Sexual Violence in Sierra Leone: PHR/UNAMSIL's Population Based Study', 2001, available at <http://www.phrusa.org/research/sierra_leone/report.html>, pp. 24 and 45.

3. WHICH POTENTIAL RISKS AND PROBLEMS DO ESPECIALLY VULNERABLE
    WITNESSES FACE?

Many of the victims of the war in Sierra Leone suffer mentally.[10] They show symptoms of Post-Traumatic Stress as a consequence of exposure to the recurrent and long-lasting traumatic events during the war. Many of them suffer from feelings of anxiety, anger, hopelessness or a lack of control; nightmares and intrusive thoughts; sleeping problems, increased irritability or a lack of emotional responsiveness. They often isolate themselves and tend to avoid places, people or activities that are associated with the events in question. The trauma has an important impact on their daily occupation and their ability to cope with situations of poverty, relations with their families and communities and their vision of the future.[11]

It is well known that, while testifying in court, victims and vulnerable witnesses face the risk of being 'retraumatised'. Recalling traumatic events in a stressful environment can cause an exacerbation of symptoms during and after testimony. It could also lead to more severe mental problems like depression in the months after giving evidence. Increased stress or the resurfacing of traumatic stress can also impact on the testimony itself, by affecting the ability to communicate, bringing about nervousness, stuttering, confusion, intense emotions, black-outs and difficulties in instantly recalling information, which can influence the capacity to speak.

Child witnesses

Child witnesses, mostly child ex-combatants, are particularly vulnerable and demand special attention and care. Their traumatic experiences have a deep mental impact that can affect them until and throughout adulthood. Most of the child witnesses who were assessed by the psychologist and the psychosocial counsellors of the Witnesses and Victims Section during the pre-trial stage showed symptoms of behavioural disorders and affect-deregulation. They also suffered from intrusive thoughts and nightmares, and, in a few cases, they reported suicidal thoughts.

Most child ex-combatants have to bear a double burden: they were both victims and perpetrators and have to deal with the complex mental and moral consequences of that fact. The process of emotional attachment to parents and other relatives – crucial in the psychological development of a child – was often severely disturbed. During the war, rebel leaders regularly became attachment figures for these children. In spite of the suffering and abuse, the children involved developed an ambiguous loyalty to the rebel leaders as 'insiders'. Under these circumstances, child witnesses can experience their testifying in Court against these leaders as a form of disloyalty towards primary attachment figures, even at an unconscious level.[12] Es-

---

[10] Ibid.

[11] 'Diagnostic Criteria of the DSM IV-TR' (Lisse, the Netherlands, Swets and Zeitlinger 2001) – in Dutch.

[12] R.E. Fioravanzo, 'TRC and Children, a Psychosocial Approach', in UNICEF, *Children and the TRC for Sierra Leone* (Freetown, UNICEF 2001) pp. 77-83.

pecially a public and direct confrontation can be very disruptive to children and might resurface attachment problems towards their parents, other relatives and carers. Accordingly, while giving evidence stress levels might increase significantly.

Child ex-combatants themselves reported that stigmatisation as a 'rebel' by the community is often an obstacle to developing normal social contacts and to reintegrating into society. Some of them fear rejection and a threat from the community if it were to become public that they are testifying before the Special Court and/or if the content of their testimony became known. They are often worried that their newly re-established relationships with family and the community and their education could be disrupted by this knowledge or as a result of being forced to leave for security reasons.

Women and girls

Women and girl victims of sexual assault have to live with the physical and psychological consequences of extremely brutal and humiliating acts, often carried out in public. Almost all these witnesses show symptoms of post-traumatic stress and report strong feelings of shame and/or guilt. Some of these women can be described as being severely traumatised. Talking about these experiences, even in a safe counselling environment, in many cases provokes intense emotions. For many of these women the idea of publicly testifying in Court is something which is very difficult and frightening. This feeling is made worse by the fact that in Sierra Leone the victims of sexual violence are often stigmatised by the communities or even rejected by their families. In many cases the sexual violence was never reported to the family. Some victims reported that even their partner did not know what happened to them.

For some witnesses, testifying directly against the perpetrator can be extremely stressful. This direct confrontation can be very emotional and even psychologically disturbing for the women. Seeing and being in the presence of the perpetrator can trigger traumatic memories and feelings of fear. So, for the women involved stress can increase significantly during evidence.

As was pointed out earlier in this chapter, girls who were abducted by fighting forces were often forced to 'marry' one of their abductors. They reported instances of repeated and long-lasting sexual abuse. They suffer not only from the consequences of the sexual violence as such, but also from the psychological impact of the relationship with commanders and the power they had over the girls, including over their fate and life. The internal conflict from which these girls often suffer is just as important as the social stigma and the lack of recognition as a victim. There is the resulting shame and the guilt, but also the emotional attachment to the 'husband', often reinforced by the presence of 'rebel children'. The women and girls find themselves in a position of having an ambiguous loyalty towards their husband/the perpetrator, a relationship frequently marked by abuse, but also by protection and status. For, being a rebel's wife often saved their lives and granted them special benefits like access to food. Testifying about these facts can be emotionally demanding but sometimes also liberating.

4. WHAT TYPE OF SUPPORT AND PROTECTION IS PROVIDED FOR ESPECIALLY
   VULNERABLE WITNESSES AT THE SPECIAL COURT FOR SIERRA LEONE?

The role of the witnesses and victims section

Before a witness takes the stand he or she has gone through a long process of
providing statements, identification and confirmation as a witness, preparation for
trial, and, in some cases, pre-trial protection. The last-mentioned might occur if
there is a suspicion of a threat against the witness. The mandate of the Witnesses
and Victims Section is 'to produce witnesses for the Court in the best physical and
mental state possible and to ensure that they suffer no harm, loss or threat as a result
of their testimony.' It is the main Section of the Court that deals with witnesses and
potential witnesses before, during and after trial. As stated in the Special Court's
Rules of Procedure and Evidence, the Witnesses and Victims Section has to provide
witnesses and potential witnesses with adequate protective measures and security
arrangements and to develop short and long-term plans for their protection and
support. Apart from providing physical protection to witnesses, the Witnesses and
Victims Section also has an obligation to take care of the Court's witnesses in a
broader sense as '[i]t ensures that witnesses receive relevant support, counseling
and other appropriate assistance, including medical assistance, physical and psychological rehabilitation, especially in cases of rape, sexual assault and crimes against
children.'[13] To accomplish this task, the Rules of Procedure and Evidence provide
that 'the Section shall include experts in trauma, including trauma related to crimes
of sexual violence and violence against children.' The psychologist who fulfils this
role works together with a team of Sierra Leonean counsellors, paramedical and
support staff. The Witnesses and Victims Section cooperates with both non-governmental and intergovernmental organisations. In addition to the direct protection and
support provided to witnesses and victims, another important role of the Section is
that it can 'also recommend to the Court the adoption of protection and security
measures for them.' Given the importance of victims as a major group of witnesses,
the Section in general, and the psychologist in particular, can advise the Court and
the Parties on victim-friendly and child-friendly procedures, especially on protective measures designed to prevent the retraumatisation of vulnerable witnesses as a
result of testifying in Court.

Support strategies

In order to minimise the risk of retraumatisation for vulnerable witnesses it is crucial that witnesses have a feeling of safety and control over the situation throughout
the process. It is therefore of great importance that a safe and protective environment is created in the period before, during and after giving evidence. Protection of

---

[13] See Rules 34(A) and (B), Rules of Procedure and Evidence, Special Court for Sierra Leone,
available at <http://www.sc-sl.org>.

privacy and anonymity can ensure safety and the perception of safety by the witness. It also avoids a potential disturbance of family relationships or even rejection by the community. Building up a relationship of trust with support staff is crucial in helping vulnerable witnesses to go through the process.

In order to implement these principles from the very first contact which a witness has with the Court, and thereafter, guidelines have been designed by the Witnesses and Victims Section for the support and protection of vulnerable witnesses. Through a system of vulnerability checklists, filled in by investigators and lawyers, it became possible to detect vulnerable potential witnesses early on in the pre-trial stage. Psychosocial assessments of these witnesses were carried out and in many cases they formed the starting point for establishing a supportive relationship between the psychologist and counsellors and the vulnerable witness. Intensive support during the trial-phase, for example by the presence of a member of the psychosocial team in the waiting room and/or the courtroom, is crucial. In the case of child witnesses, collaboration was set up between the Office of the Prosecutor, the Witnesses and Victims Section and different child protection agencies and organisations in order to ensure the effective protection of potential child witnesses in the investigative stage. The Witnesses and Victims Section followed up the support and protection of children, in close collaboration with the Office of the Prosecutor.

Protective measures

In view of the particular context in which the Special Court for Sierra Leone operates, witnesses in general need a high level of protection. In the three ongoing cases against the Civil Defense Forces (CDF), the Revolutionary United Front (RUF) and the Armed Forces Revolutionary Council (AFRC), the Court therefore decided on a series of protective measures for witnesses. Based upon the conviction that anonymity and confidentiality are the most effective protection mechanisms, it was decided not to disclose the identity of the witnesses to the public. Therefore witnesses testify by using a pseudonym and they are shielded from the public by a screen. Secondly, the full identity of the witnesses is only disclosed to the Defence 42 or 21 days – depending on the features of the case involved – before giving evidence.

Apart from these general protective measures, different levels of protection are provided before and after testifying, ranging from surveillance to the relocation of witnesses, depending on the outcome of the risk assessment of individual witnesses. In addition to measures to protect witnesses from a threat or physical harm, the Court has recognised that certain groups of witnesses, such as women, victims of gender-based violence and children, need extra protective measures to prevent their testimony from resulting in further psychological harm or suffering.

Closed circuit television for child witnesses

All possible means are used to protect child witnesses during their testimony, in order to ensure privacy and anonymity, to minimise direct confrontation with the accused and to prevent disruptions in their social environment. In particular younger children, whose mental development is more immature and whose understanding of the process is limited, need maximum protection.

To ensure this protection the Special Court decided that all children, defined as all persons under the age of eighteen, would testify through the use of closed circuit television.[14] The child sits in a separate room in front of a camera and on a split screen sees himself and the person in the Courtroom who is asking questions to the child. Those in the Courtroom see the child on their monitor while the public can only hear the child's voice. Although the Court procedures with a closed circuit television are identical to a hearing in open Court, it reduces the stress which the child experiences and increases her/his comfort level. By only showing the person who is talking to the child the information input is filtered, the Courtroom environment is less overwhelming and the child can concentrate more easily on the questions asked. A direct and open confrontation with the accused is avoided. It is as if there is a mental protective screen between the child witness and the persons present in the Courtroom.

One of the problems with limiting the use of closed circuit television to child witnesses under eighteen is that it is often difficult to establish the exact age of a child in a country like Sierra Leone. Child ex-combatants, who often spent several years with the fighting forces during a crucial time in their development, might show a significant difference between their mental age and their biological age. Often there will have been a gap in their mental and physical development, due to the particularly harsh life in the bush and traumatic experiences. On the other hand, these children or adolescents can easily give the false impression of 'being an adult' on a behavioural level, while, for instance, their emotional development is sometimes seriously disturbed. By linking the use of closed circuit television solely to the biological age of the child, it is difficult to take these other developmental aspects (which are important indicators for the risk of retraumatisation) into account and to ensure maximum protection. However, in at least one case so far the use of closed circuit television has been granted to a witness who was slightly older than eighteen.

Specific measures for victims of sexual assault and gender crimes

Women, victims of sexual assault or gender crimes, need privacy and anonymity to testify, in order to prevent retraumatisation and social rejection. Direct confrontation with the accused should therefore be avoided as much as possible. This is true

---

[14] *Prosecutor* v. *Sam Hinga Norman, Moinana Fofana, Allieu Kondewa*, Decision on Prosecution Motion for Modification of Protective Measures for Witnesses, 8 June 2004.

in particular for some women who are directly testifying against their perpetrators. In particular, women and girls who have suffered from long-lasting sexual abuse should have as much choice as possible concerning the way in which they should testify. This can help them to regain some feeling of power.

A Special Court decision can allow these women to testify with the use of a voice distortion system.[15] The use of voice distortion in combination with the use of a screen ensures that the identity of the women is not disclosed to the public and, equally important, gives the women the feeling of being protected from the public and of having a sense of privacy. In a few cases the Court has allowed a support person – a counsellor from the Witnesses and Victims Section with whom a relationship of trust has been built up – to sit next to the witness in the witness box during testimony. Although verbal exchange is kept to a strict minimum, the physical presence of a support person is very helpful for creating a feeling of safety and for calming the witness during difficult phases of the examination or cross-examination. Additionally, the Office of the Prosecutor, the Witnesses and Victims Section and the Translation Unit try to ensure that, as far as possible, female lawyers, support officers and interpreters deal with the victims of gender-based violence. In a culture where talking about female sexuality in mixed company is very much a taboo subject, such measures help to a certain extent to reduce feelings of shame during preparation and during the testimony. In one case, a victim of sexual violence also reported after giving evidence that the fact that she could testify in her own local language was very helpful in creating a feeling of safety. The idea that almost no one could understand her words and that the persons present in Court as well as the public could not therefore hear her story 'directly from her own mouth' was instrumental in this.

5. How Do 'Especially Vulnerable Witnesses' Perceive their Participation in the Special Court?

Although it is too early to make a final assessment of the impact of testifying before the Special Court for Sierra Leone on witnesses and victims, it is possible to give a first but prudent indication of how victims perceive their participation as witnesses. The post-trial debriefings and a first limited number of follow-up interviews show different tendencies. The question whether especially vulnerable witnesses experience their testimony as an empowering or as a retraumatising experience, should therefore be approached thoughtfully.

Many vulnerable witnesses experience difficulties during and/or after giving evidence. They become very emotional or feel inhibited when they have to talk about the traumatic events that happened to them. In the majority of cases a short

---

[15] *Prosecutor* v. *Issa Hassan Sesay, Augustine Gbao and Morris Kallon*, SCSL-2004-15-T, Decision on Prosecution Motion for Modification of Protective Measures for Witnesses, 5 July 2004, disposition paras. 3 to 6.

break is sufficient to overcome these difficulties and to continue with the evidence. So far, only one witness has had difficulties in starting to give evidence because of fear and overwhelming emotions. However, a day later she could begin to give evidence normally. Some of the witnesses report that they have experienced flashbacks and that they were clearly reliving the traumatic events while testifying. For example, one victim had to explain to the Court how he had witnessed his wife being raped several times before she was killed and he had a limb amputated. During a break and after giving evidence he reported that at one point in his testimony 'it was as if it was all happening again when I was sitting in that Courtroom, the images and the noises came back when I was talking.' He had clear symptoms of dissociation, provoked by the testimony. Some victims showed increased symptoms of traumatic stress during the days after giving evidence. They experienced sleeping difficulties, nightmares, increased agitation or feelings of depression. One witness developed psychotic reactions in the weeks after his testimony, preceded by intense feelings of anxiety as a consequence of giving evidence. Most likely, he had a history of psychotic episodes.

The adversarial system has a special impact on vulnerable witnesses. Many witnesses, especially victims, experience being cross-examined as painful and humiliating. Although they generally understand the purpose of cross-examination and accept that it is inherent in the process of being a witness, they sometimes feel that it minimizes their suffering. Especially repeated questions about the traumatic events themselves often trigger serious emotional reactions. A few victims felt frustrated at the end of the testimony. They were wrongly under the impression that they would be given an opportunity to address the Court and to talk about how they felt about the process of justice and being a witness. After being told by the judges that it was not allowed for them to go beyond answering questions concerning the content of their testimony, they felt disappointed. The often rather lengthy process from being present in Freetown in a safe location to waiting as a standby-witness in the Court's waiting-room is generally a burden for witnesses too.

So far, children and adolescents have done relatively well as witnesses. Thanks to intensive support and the availability of appropriate protective measures, they have managed to cope well with the stress of testifying. It is not surprising that the level of understanding of the judicial process is an important factor in this. Children or adolescents who had a more limited understanding of the procedures and consequences of their testimony seemed to suffer more from stress. Understanding the need for cross-examination as part of a fair trial, for instance, is crucial in this respect. The more children felt that cross-examination was a personal attack and that they could be 'punished' because of their testimony, the more the feelings of shame and guilt affected them after giving evidence.

On the other hand most victims report a sense of relief immediately at the end of giving evidence, because 'it is over' and because they managed to tell their story. This feeling is in most cases still present a few days after giving evidence. Some victims grew in confidence during their testimony: once through the difficult or painful part of their statement, they felt more empowered and relaxed. This is definitely often the case for women and girls who testify about sexual assault or gender-based violence. Once they feel during their testimony that they are in control of the events, in contrast to the time of the sexual abuse, they often show tremendous emotional strength. Also, some women experienced their exposure to the accused, in some cases also the alleged perpetrator, as a moment of catharsis. This feeling was reinforced by the special environment of a courtroom. In post-trial debriefings some women and girls referred to this shifting of roles, the sense of power they experienced and the exposure as important factors in their recovery.

6. INVOLVEMENT OF VICTIMS IN THE SPECIAL COURT: A PARADOX?

As a retributive justice mechanism, the primary role of the Special Court is to punish perpetrators. In its focus on putting on trial those who bear the greatest responsibility, victims play an important role as the providers of evidence. However, the judicial process is not victim-centred. This situation creates various paradoxes. There is the burden created by the tension between the importance of the witness statements as evidence and the general vulnerability of victims and witnesses. But there is also the paradox that witnesses and victims play a crucial and often difficult role in the proceedings through the process of examination and cross-examination, while on the other side the Special Court for Sierra Leone has important limitations in its mandate that prevent it from addressing some of the real needs and problems of victims. Although the Court has important provisions on support to victim-witnesses and compensates witnesses for their involvement, unlike the International Criminal Court[16] the Court has neither the mandate nor the funds to provide victims in general with any form of reparation or compensation. The victim's role is therefore confined solely to being a witness in the proceedings.

However, in spite of the significant limitations in its mandate, it is clear that the Court has an important role towards victims because its success will not only be judged by its decisions but also by the perception of its work by the victims of the conflict. Firstly, by prosecuting those who bear the greatest responsibility for the crimes committed, the work of the Court intends to bring an end to impunity and wants to send this message to all layers of the population. Placing a special focus on crimes against women and children can contribute not only to the development of case law in this domain, but can in particular give the necessary recognition to women and children, two of the most vulnerable groups of victims. Secondly, like other restorative justice mechanisms, the Special Court can facilitate healing and reconciliation. The judicial process pursues the establishment of the truth and the recognition of suffering. Through hearing vulnerable witnesses, in particular women and children, the Court can give a voice to the victims and help to deal with the past. Its very seat in the country where the atrocities took place should give the Court more visibility and be closer to the Sierra Leonean population, which makes it more

---

[16] Article 75 of the Statute of the International Criminal Court, available at <http://www.cpi-icc.int>.

imperative to pursue these aims. Finally, the Special Court can play a role as a catalyst for efforts to reshape society, by inviting and bringing together civil society in general, and victims organisations in particular, to actively follow the process and to debate its legacy.

7. CONCLUSION

In spite of the limitations in its mandate, the Special Court for Sierra Leone can give a voice to victims, mainly by calling them as witnesses. The Prosecutor has placed strong emphasis on crimes against women and children. This is extremely important and innovative as never before have the crimes of recruiting child soldiers and forced marriages been part of indictments before an international tribunal. This focus makes women and children important providers of evidence, but also 'especially vulnerable witnesses'. They are especially vulnerable because of the particular problems that they have to deal with and the risk of being retraumatised by the judicial process. In an attempt to learn from other international tribunals, important efforts have been made by the Special Court to ensure maximum support and protection for this category of witnesses. Specific protective measures have been ordered by the Court and structures have been created to provide the necessary intensive support at the pre-trial, trial and post-trial stages.

Whether these especially vulnerable witnesses perceive their collaboration with the Court as an empowering or as a retraumatising experience is a question to which only preliminary answers can be given at this stage. Many factors play a role. Among them are the expectations of the witness, his or her personal history, as well as the quality of the support provided. The initial feedback is generally positive, but the question should be analysed further. It is a fact that testifying demands tremendous courage on the part of victims. Therefore they should be able to testify in the best conditions possible. It is clear that, also internationally, there is an increased recognition of the importance of support for especially vulnerable witnesses. Progress has been made in this regard at the Special Court for Sierra Leone. However, it is also clear that, in order to fully meet the expectations and needs of vulnerable witnesses and victims, additional efforts should be made to make international justice mechanisms truly victim-centred and more woman and child-friendly.

Rethinking procedures before international tribunals, including the methods by which evidence can be presented and the examination in chief and cross-examination of victims can be conducted, might help to make international justice mechanisms more women and child-friendly. The involvement of victims would be facilitated by the inclusion of considerations such as the psychological well-being of the witness and the risk of retraumatisation among the selection criteria for witnesses, and by ensuring psycho-social support from the investigative phase onwards and a further adaptation of the courtroom procedures to the needs of vulnerable witnesses.

In addition, the inclusion of provisions for reparation to or in respect of victims in the Rome Statute,[17] including restitution, compensation and rehabilitation, can be seen as a crucial step towards making international justice more victim-centred. Although judicial proceedings as such can be perceived by victims as a form of moral reparation,[18] explicit compensation can have a much stronger restorative influence, subject to the condition that the expectations of victims concerning the scale of reparation are well managed and a 'fair' system for preferably the allocation of community-oriented compensation is developed.

Finally, ensuring independent victim participation and legal assistance could be other key issues in changing this direction. Considering victims as a 'party' in the trial might bring them closer to being 'equal partners' in the judicial process. The Rome Statute foresees the possibility for victims to participate in the proceedings and to present observations, views or concerns to the Court.[19] These ground-breaking provisions and the presence of a comprehensive witness support programme can form important elements for the International Criminal Court to become the first truly victim-centred international justice mechanism.

---

[17] L. Walleyn, 'Victimes et Témoins de Crimes Internationaux : Du Droit à une Protection au Droit à la Parole', 845 *Revue Internationale de la Croix-Rouge* (2002), pp. 51-78.

[18] See Articles 15(3), 19(3) 68(3) and 75 of the Statute of the International Criminal Court.

[19] See also chapter 8 by Louis Moreno-Ocampo, and N. Roht-Arriaza, 'Reparations in the Aftermath of Repression and Mass Violence', in E. Stover and H. Weinstein (eds.), *My Neighbor, My Enemy: Justice and Community in the Aftermath of Mass Atrocity* (Cambridge, Cambridge University Press 2004) p. 123.

Chapter 11
CHILDREN AND INTERNATIONAL CRIMINAL LAW: THE PRACTICE OF THE INTERNATIONAL TRIBUNAL FOR THE FORMER YUGOSLAVIA (ICTY)

David Tolbert*

1. INTRODUCTION: THE ICTY AND CHILDREN

The experience of the International Tribunal for the former Yugoslavia (ICTY) with regard to children as either victims or perpetrators of serious violations of international humanitarian law is rather limited, particularly when compared to the Special Court for Sierra Leone where recently jurisprudence and practices have been much more developed – as was presented in the previous two chapters. Nonetheless, there have been a number of developments regarding children at the ICTY which merit discussion and review, especially because they established important precedents for other international courts and tribunals.

Before reviewing the ICTY's record regarding children, it is worth recalling the historical and legal context within which the ICTY was established, as this context bears a significant relevance to the Tribunal's approach to issues concerning children. The ICTY was established in 1993 by United Nations Security Council Resolution 808, adopted under Chapter VII of the United Nations Charter.[1] The Tribunal's jurisdiction extends over the laws and customs of war, including grave breaches of the 1949 Geneva Conventions, crimes against humanity and genocide committed from 1 January 1991 onwards in the territory of the former Yugoslavia.[2] Although this jurisdiction is open-ended from 1991, and while the ICTY is prosecuting cer-

---

* Deputy Prosecutor, International Criminal Tribunal for the former Yugoslavia. Formerly, David Tolbert was Deputy Registrar, Chef de Cabinet to the President and Senior Legal Adviser at the ICTY. The views expressed in this chapter are those of the author alone and not those of the United Nations or the ICTY. The author thanks Frederick Swinnen for his assistance in preparing for the remarks given at the Hague Academic Coalition Conference 'International Criminal Accountability and the Rights of Children' in The Hague in March 2005. He also expresses his appreciation to Susan Mossing for her help in the preparation of this chapter.

[1] *UN Doc.* S/RES/827, 25 May 1993.

[2] ICTY Statute, Annex to the 'Report of the Secretary-General Pursuant to Paragraph 2 of Security Council Resolution 808', *UN Doc.* S/25704, 3 May 1993, Articles 2-5. Amended version available at <http://www.un.org/icty/legaldoc/index.htm>.

K. Arts & V. Popovski (eds.), International Criminal Accountability and the Rights of Children
© 2006, Hague Academic Coalition, The Hague, The Netherlands and the Authors

tain events that occurred in the late 1990s in relation to Kosovo, the crime bases on which the Tribunal has primarily focused occurred during the years prior to the Dayton Accords,[3] that is the period from 1992 to 1995. Moreover, the Tribunal is now in its Completion Strategy[4] and the Prosecutor has issued her final indictments and completed the investigative phase of her work.[5]

The Convention on the Rights of the Child (CRC) came into force only in 1990, not very long before the Tribunal's jurisdiction commenced.[6] It obviously took some time for international lawyers and political decision-makers to take into account, in a systematic way, the rights and special circumstances of children profiled in this Convention. Thus, it was only when later courts and tribunals were established, including the Special Court for Sierra Leone (SCSL) and the International Criminal Court (ICC), that children's rights had become a central focus of international law. In the meantime, domestic policies and non-governmental organisations (NGOs) committed to children's issues also actively advanced children's causes much more than was the case before.

Even more important differences between the ICTY and certain other international courts and tribunals (particularly the Special Court for Sierra Leone), are found in the nature of the conflicts being investigated and the crimes being adjudicated. In Sierra Leone, Colombia, the Democratic Republic of Congo and other conflicts, children play(ed) a substantial role as perpetrators and pawns that simply does not parallel the conflicts in the former Yugoslavia. While in the former Yugoslavia children were frequently victims of crimes,[7] they have not been charged as perpetrators at the ICTY. In accordance with its mandate, the Prosecution at the ICTY has primarily focused, particularly in recent years, on the senior military and political leadership.[8] The ICTY is now in the process of transferring its lower level cases to courts in the region, primarily to the newly established State Court in Bosnia.[9] In the case of individuals indicted at the ICTY these transfers occur only

---

[3] The Dayton Accords were initialled at Dayton, Ohio, USA on 21 November 1995 and signed in Paris, France on 14 December 1995. They ended the armed conflict in the former Yugoslavia and are available at <http://www1.umn.edu/humanrts/icty/dayton/daytonaccord.html>.

[4] UNSC Resolution 1534, *UN Doc*. S/RES/1534, 26 March 2004.

[5] Assessment of Carla Del Ponte, Prosecutor of the ICTY, provided to the UN Security Council pursuant to para. 6 of Security Council Resolution 1534, ibid.

[6] Convention on the Rights of the Child, 20 November 1989. See UNGA Resolution 44/25, Annex, 44 *UN GAOR* Supp. (No. 49) at 167, and *UN Doc*. A/44/49 (1989). The CRC entered into force on 2 September 1990.

[7] *Prosecutor* v. *Blaskic*, Case No. IT-95-14-T, Trial Judgement, 20 April 2000. See also *Prosecutor* v. *Blagojevic et al.*, Case No. IT-02-60-T, Trial Judgement, 17 January 2005, para. 844; *Prosecutor* v. *Momir Nikolic*, Case No. IT-02-60/1-S, Sentencing Judgement, 2 December 2003, para. 137; *Prosecutor* v. *Obrenovic*, Case No. IT-02-06/2-S, Sentencing Judgement, 10 December 2003, para. 178; *Prosecutor* v. *Stakic*, Case No. IT-97-24-T, Trial Judgement, 31 July 2003, para 589; *Prosecutor* v. *Lukic et al.*, Case No.: IT-98-32-1, Trial Judgement, 26 October 1998, para. 25.

[8] *Supra*, n. 5.

[9] 'Report on the Judicial Status of the International Criminal Tribunal for the former Yugoslavia and the Prospects for Referring Certain Cases to National Courts', *ICTY Document* S/2002/PRST/21, June 2002.

when ordered by the Tribunal's Chambers pursuant to ICTY Rule 11 bis, which establishes criteria for such determinations as well as conditions of such transfers. In case of investigations that have not actually led to an indictment at the ICTY – usually lower level cases – the Prosecutor transfers dossiers and other investigative materials to prosecutors in the region for further investigation and possible prosecution.[10] Even in these lower level investigations, as a matter of principle, the ICTY does not investigate children as perpetrators. Accordingly, no significant evidence regarding children as perpetrators was obtained in the Tribunal's jurisprudence nor in its investigations generally. Consequently, there is little ICTY practice on issues relating to holding children accountable for gross violations of international humanitarian law. However, the Tribunal has addressed certain other issues relating to children as victims of crimes in the former Yugoslavia and also their roles as witnesses, which are worthy of discussion.

2. CHILD WITNESSES AT THE ICTY

At the outset, it is worth noting that the terms 'victims' and 'witnesses' are often conflated. For instance, while the Yugoslavia Tribunal, the International Criminal Tribunal for Rwanda and the International Criminal Court all have a Victims and Witnesses Unit or Section, it is important to bear in mind that these are two separate, if overlapping categories. Not all witnesses are victims. In fact many witnesses are not victims at all and some are 'insiders' or perpetrators themselves.[11]

In relation to children as witnesses at the ICTY, the Tribunal's Rules of Procedure and Evidence provide procedural and substantive approaches to a child's testimony that differ from the rules on the testimony of adults. Rule 90 of the ICTY Rules of Procedure and Evidence states that each witness must first solemnly declare that he or she will tell the truth. It further provides, in Rule 90(B), that if the witness is a child, and he or she does not understand the 'nature of the solemn declaration', then the Chamber may permit the child to testify 'without' the declaration, provided that the court is of the view 'that the child is sufficiently mature to be able to report the facts of which the child had knowledge and understands the duty to tell the truth.' However, the Rule further provides that a judgment cannot be based on such testimony alone. In other words, a conviction could not be based solely on the unsworn testimony of a child, unless there is corroboration of that testimony by an adult. At the end of the day, the Rule has yet to be applied, as so far no child witnesses have testified at the Tribunal.

Still, the Rule does raise certain issues. Rule 90(B) does not define the term 'child'. In making this determination the Chamber presumably would look to the

---

[10] See UN Press Release, GA/10297, 15 November 2004.

[11] See D. Tolbert and F. Swinnen, 'The Protection of, and Assistance to, Witnesses at the International Criminal Tribunal for the former Yugoslavia', in G. Boas and H. Abtahi (eds.), *The Dynamics of International Criminal Justice: Essays in Honour of Judge Richard May* (Leiden, Brill Academic Publishers 2005).

UN Convention on the Rights of the Child and to the local law in the former Yugo-slavia. The CRC defines a 'child' as a 'human being below the age of eighteen years unless under the law applicable to the child, majority is attained earlier.'[12] This, however, would appear to simply establish a threshold issue under Rule 90(B), as the Rule does not give different weight to a child's testimony, except in those cases where the child 'does not understand the nature of a solemn declaration'. Thus, it is quite possible under the Rule for a person under eighteen years of age to testify under oath and for his or her testimony to be given full credibility, provided that he or she understands the declaration given.

This leads to other questions: why should children who testify be considered different from other witnesses? Is this safeguard unnecessary in light of the fact that judges will ascertain the reliability of that testimony for themselves, determining whether it is credible or not, and how much weight to give it? The Rule seems to imply that children – at least those who do not fully understand the declaration, yet understand the duty to tell the truth – lack sufficient credibility. That seems to be an arguable assumption.

It is also worth noting that Rule 96 of the ICTY Rules of Procedure and Evidence specifically provides that there is no corroboration required for the testimony of a victim of sexual assault.[13] While Rule 96 clearly has a sound policy basis and reflects current trends in the law, there is a potential clash between Rule 90(B) regarding the testimony of a child and Rule 96, as there could well be cases in which the victim of the sexual assault is a child who does not fully comprehend the solemn declaration. The court would then have to determine whether the require-ments of Rule 90(B) or Rule 96 would prevail.

The ICC Rules of Procedure and Evidence have taken a somewhat different approach from those of the ICTY to the issue of children as witnesses. Similar to the ICTY, the ICC allows for the testimony of a 'person under the age of 18' with-out the solemn undertaking if he or she does not understand the nature of the decla-ration.[14] However, unlike at the ICTY, there is no restriction on the use or weight of

---

[12] Article 1 CRC, *supra* n. 6.

[13] Rule 96 of the ICTY Rules of Procedure and Evidence states that, in cases of sexual assault: no corroboration of the victim's testimony shall be required; consent shall not be allowed as a defence if the victim has been subjected to or threatened with or has had reason to fear violence, duress, detention or psychological oppression, or reasonably believed that if the victim did not submit, another might be so subjected, threatened or put in fear; before evidence of the victim's consent is admitted, the accused shall satisfy the Trial Chamber in camera that the evidence is relevant and credible; prior sexual con-duct of the victim shall not be admitted in evidence.

[14] Rule 66 of the ICC Rules of Procedure and Evidence, states:
'1. Except as described in sub-rule 2, every witness shall, in accordance with article 69, paragraph 1, make the following solemn undertaking before testifying:
"I solemnly declare that I will speak the truth, the whole truth and nothing but the truth."
2. A person under the age of 18 or a person whose judgement has been impaired and who, in the opinion of the Chamber, does not understand the nature of a solemn undertaking may be allowed to testify without this solemn undertaking if the Chamber considers that the person is able to describe matters of which he or she has knowledge and that the person understands the meaning of the duty to speak the truth.'

that testimony, provided that the 'Chamber considers that the person is able to describe matters of which he or she has knowledge and that the person understands the meaning of the duty to speak the truth.'[15] Thus, the ICC approach avoids the possibility of a child's testimony being excluded solely because he or she does not fully understand the solemn undertaking or declaration and leaves it up to the judges to accord the appropriate weight to the testimony in accordance with their usual duties.

As the above discussion shows, even in those instances where there is little or no jurisprudence on a specific point, the approach taken by the ICTY may be adopted and/or modified by other international tribunals and courts.

While the ICTY has not had experience with witnesses under eighteen years of age, there have been a significant number of witnesses who, while now over eighteen, were much younger than eighteen when the events they were testifying to actually occurred. Approximately four per cent of all witnesses that testify in proceedings at the ICTY are in the age range of eighteen-thirty.[16] Given that often a decade or more has passed between the time of the events about which they are testifying and the actual testimony, many in this group were under eighteen and some quite young at the time of the relevant events.

The ICTY's Victims and Witnesses Section recognises that these younger witnesses form a vulnerable group and has taken a number of steps to provide them with additional protection and support.[17] Young persons are frequently even more likely than others to have no experience with court proceedings, and they often bring what one Victims and Witnesses Section Support Officer described as 'heightened emotions and enormous expectations directly in relation to testifying.'[18] Given these factors, which combine with others that many witnesses suffer from such as the trauma of seeing and being confronted by the perpetrator(s) in the courtroom, the need to travel to a foreign country (younger people are often less likely to have travelled before) and the stress that comes from testifying, the ICTY's Victims and Witnesses Section (VWS) has adopted special steps for working with younger witnesses, including those who were children at the time. The most noteworthy of these policies is to allow, at the Tribunal's expense, the younger person to be accompanied to the ICTY by a significant adult figure, such as a parent, another close relative or a friend, for the whole duration of their stay in The Hague. This allows the witness to have the support of someone she or he knows and trusts, who also speaks the same language, both before and after the sometimes traumatic and life-changing event of testifying in front of the court.

In addition, the Victims and Witnesses Section (VWS) provides special counselling to younger witnesses, regarding the courtroom procedures and the terminology

---

[15] Ibid.

[16] M. Naslund, 'ICTY Developing Practice in Young Adult Witnesses', internal memorandum, on file with the author.

[17] Author's conversation with Monika Naslund, Support Officer, ICTY Victims and Witnesses Section, 15 March 2005.

[18] Ibid.

used by the judges, the defence lawyers and the prosecutors, as well as explaining the inevitable delays and procedures that occur in the proceedings, with an emphasis on the fact that these delays and complications have nothing to do with the person's testimony.[19] Finally, when necessary the VWS can always advocate with the Court on behalf of persons younger than eighteen years.

As noted above, although the ICTY does not have experience with actual testimony of children, there are a number of considerations that have been examined, and there are obviously developments in domestic jurisdictions that would be adopted should a child actually be called to testify. One step that has been taken in some domestic jurisdictions is the use of videotaped testimony as close to the time of the events as possible.[20] This would certainly be possible under the ICTY Rules of Procedure and Evidence relating to video deposition. The ICTY Rules also provide a number of other protection measures that could be used to provide extra protection in the case of a child witness, most notably the use of a video link or testimony from a remote location.[21] These as well as other measures that are at the ICTY's disposal for the protection of witnesses generally could be particularly useful with child witnesses.[22]

3. CHILD AND YOUTH VICTIMS AT THE ICTY

Another important aspect of the child related work at the ICTY is when the children are not, or not only, witnesses, but victims *per se*. There were many victims of atrocious crimes in the former Yugoslavia – more than 250,000 dead and many hundreds of thousands more persecuted and expelled from their homes, raped, tortured and otherwise mistreated[23] – and many of these were children. One need only watch Ratko Mladic rubbing the heads of young boys shortly before the massacre of Srebrenica to realise that there were many such victims of a very young age.[24]

There are a number of instances in ICTY jurisprudence where the age of the victims has been a factor in the court's consideration. The age of the victim does not generally come into play when the court is examining and determining whether a crime occurred, unless committing an act on a child is an element of the offence,

---

[19] Ibid.

[20] D. Heraghty, 'Gearing Up for Greater Use of Video Evidence', 153 *New Law Journal* (2003) p. 460.

[21] Rule 71 bis of the ICTY Rules of Procedure and Evidence, states: 'At the request of either party, a Trial Chamber may, in the interests of justice, order that testimony be received via video-conference link.'

[22] For various witness protection measures, see ICTY Rules of Procedure and Evidence: Rule 69 (Protection of Victims and Witnesses – Production of Evidence); Rule 75 (Measures for the Protection of Victims and Witnesses); and Rule 79 (Closed Sessions).

[23] See the 1996 US State Department Report, 'Bosnia and Herzegovina Country Report on Human Rights Practices for 1996', available from <http://www.state.gov/www/global/human_rights/1996_hrp_report/bosniahe.html>.

[24] 'Srebrenica Trial Video', author M. Fracassetti, V000-4458, position 02:02'02.63-02:02'00.19.

such as statutory rape or conscription of children under a certain age.[25] A murder is a murder regardless of whether the victim is old or young. There are, however, many references in ICTY jurisprudence to the age and sex of victims, and the court has specifically taken into taken account of the age and the sex of the victim as an aggravating factor in the process of sentencing. The most notable example is the *Kunarac* case, which relates to crimes committed in Foca.[26] In *Kunarac*, the Trial Chamber specifically took into account the victims' age when considering the sentence to be imposed. This case involved a gender-divided concentration camp where a number of women and girls were repeatedly raped, in some cases for long periods of time. The younger victims of rape and sexual assault ranged from what the court describes as 'very young' – aged twelve – to 'relatively youthful' – age twenty. The other victims were fifteen-and-a half, sixteen, sixteen-and-a-half and nineteen. The Trial Chamber found that, in addition to other factors, the age of these victims was an aggravating factor to be taken into account in sentencing. It also considered as aggravating factors the length of time that the rapes were repeated, the fact that there were multiple perpetrators, and, related to the age of the victims, that the crimes were 'committed against particularly vulnerable and defenceless girls'.[27]

On appeal, the accused argued that the Trial Chamber erred by considering the age of certain of the victims, relying on the law in the former Yugoslavia which allowed for marriage at sixteen years old. He also argued that there was no provision in the law that would allow for the aggravation of the sentence for a crime committed against a person over fourteen years of age and that the law only allowed for a heavier sentence in the case of victims below fourteen. The Appeals Chamber rejected these arguments. It found that the practice in the former Yugoslavia was for convictions for rape of persons under eighteen to result in longer sentences. Perhaps more importantly, the Trial Chamber has 'an inherent discretion to consider the victim's age as an aggravating factor'.[28] Moreover, even though some of the victim's ages were over eighteen, this discretion extended 'to considering' those victims at nineteen and twenty 'by reason of the closeness of that age to the protected age of special vulnerability'.[29] The Trial Chamber also observed that young women in wartime 'need special protection in order to prevent them from becoming easy targets'.[30] Thus, it is clear that according to ICTY jurisprudence, the youthful age of a victim can be a significant aggravating factor in determining the appropriate sentence for the accused. This is a significant step in the direction of further protecting children, and provides a strong precedent on which the ICC and other courts and tribunals can build.

---

[25] Articles 8(2)(b)(xxvi) and 8(2)(e)(vii), Rome Statute of the International Criminal Court, *UN Doc.* A/CONF.183/9, 17 July 1998.

[26] *Prosecutor* v. *Kunarac et al.*, Case No. IT-96-23-T and IT-96-23/1-T, Trial Judgement, 22 February 2001. See, e.g., also the *Blaskic* case, *supra* n. 7, para. 786.

[27] Ibid., para. 874.

[28] *Prosecutor* v. *Kunarac et al.*, Case No. IT-96-23 and IT-96-23/1-A, Appeal Judgement, 12 June 2002, para. 355.

[29] Ibid.

[30] Ibid.

4. CONCLUDING OBSERVATIONS

In closing this chapter, it is worth underlining the special responsibility that international courts and tribunals have *vis-à-vis* victims in pursuing international criminal justice. Victims and their families – many of whom have lost their loved ones and their children – frequently do not understand processes at the ICTY or other international courts, in The Hague or elsewhere. We have a duty to make sure that they see and understand what is being done and how it is done. In many ways, the most important task is to ensure that victims feel that justice has been done, no matter how imperfectly or belatedly. Without this, there is no chance for reconciliation or hope for the future, and we will be doomed to watching more children becoming victims and villains.

Chapter 12
BRIDGING THE GAP: MILITARY TRAINING AND INTERNATIONAL ACCOUNTABILITY REGARDING CHILDREN

Jenny Kuper*

1. INTRODUCTION

'All is fair in love and war' is not quite as true today as it once was, at least as regards 'war' or, to use the preferred term, situations of armed conflict. There is increasing, if uneven, international acceptance of the notion that there are limits to what is and what is not legal and acceptable in the conduct of such conflicts, even if this awareness is frequently not reflected in what happens on the ground. It is, however, reflected in the practice of international war crimes tribunals. For example, the International Criminal Tribunal for the former Yugoslavia (ICTY), the International Criminal Tribunal for Rwanda (ICTR), and the Special Court for Sierra Leone (SCSL), and initiatives such as the establishment of the International Criminal Court (ICC), all seek to enforce concepts of justice even in the most extreme and brutal of human undertakings. Military personnel (including soldiers and their commanders) and government officials (including heads of state) can find themselves facing trial before these tribunals, and the category of victims, witnesses, and survivors possibly involved is equally wide. As regards the latter category, one characteristic of recent war crimes trials is that greater account is being taken of children.[1] This is, to a large extent, one of the outcomes of the adoption of the 1989 Convention on the Rights of the Child (CRC), which has fostered a greater awareness of child rights and marked a change in the landscape of relevant international and national law and policy.[2]

This chapter explores the link between military training regarding children, and international criminal accountability of military personnel for violations committed

---

* Research Fellow, London School of Economics.

[1] In accordance with current standards in international law, a child is defined here as those generally under eighteen. Cases against child soldiers are not tried in these international fora.

[2] The 1999 African Charter on the Rights and Welfare of the Child (currently the only other wide-ranging international child rights treaty) is also likely to become increasingly relevant, but at present it is still in the early stage of implementation.

K. Arts & V. Popovski (eds.), International Criminal Accountability and the Rights of Children
© *2006, Hague Academic Coalition, The Hague, The Netherlands and the Authors*

against children. It argues that international tribunals can punish violations committed against children and others in situations of armed conflict, and that such tribunals can possibly deter the commission of such violations if their existence and practice is explained in the course of military training. After a few further general remarks about international criminal tribunals and their attention for children, this chapter outlines a few of the early cases heard by the ICTY and the ICTR that illustrate the approach taken towards violations of children's rights in armed conflict. Thereafter the connection between military training and the practice of international tribunals is explored, as well as the role, limits, methodology and (potential) impact of such training.

2. PRACTICE UNFOLDING IN INTERNATIONAL CRIMINAL COURTS: ACCOUNTABILITY FOR CONDUCT TOWARDS CHILDREN

Although violations against children were to some extent taken into account in international and national war crimes tribunals of many decades ago,[3] this chapter explores the practice of certain current international tribunals regarding this issue. A small sample of early cases of the ICTY and the ICTR are selected for discussion here.[4] These cases are instructive in giving an indication of the approach initially taken by international war crimes tribunals in the post-CRC era. Since these cases were heard, practice in war crimes tribunals has generally progressed towards even greater recognition and action concerning violations committed against children – as evidenced, for example, in the emerging case law of the Special Court for Sierra Leone and early initiatives of the International Criminal Court. Indeed, the former was established to address a conflict characterised by violations against children on a massive scale. Similarly, the first investigation of the ICC has been undertaken to examine a situation – in Northern Uganda – that is also characterised by numerous extreme violations against children. Moreover, the first person ever to appear before the ICC, in March 2006, was Thomas Lubanga from the Democratic Republic of Congo facing three charges relating to the enlisting and conscription of children under the age of fifteen into armed groups, and the use of children under fifteen to participate actively in hostilities.[5]

---

[3] See, e.g., regarding the Nuremberg Tribunal, J. Kuper, *International Law Concerning Child Civilians in Armed Conflict* (Oxford, Clarendon Press 1997) p. 155. Regarding Vietnam, see, e.g. the court-martial of William J Calley, Jr. Among other things, Calley was charged with killing 'one oriental human being, approximately two years of age' (*United States* v. *Calley*, US Court of Military Appeals (1973) 22 USCMA 534, 48 CMR 19).

[4] For further information on these and other relevant cases, see J. Kuper, *Military Training and Children in Armed Conflict: Law Policy and Practice* (Leiden, Martinus Nijhoff 2005).

[5] For more details on this case, see, e.g. Pre-Trial Chamber I, 'Situation in the Democratic Republic of the Congo', *The Prosecutor* v. *Thomas Lubanga Dyilo*, ICC-01/04-01/06, 10 February 2006. The ICC and the SCSL will not be further discussed here, since these were already covered in chapters 8, 9 and 10 of this book.

Further, as explained in chapters 8 to 11 of this book, the Rules of Procedure and Evidence of the various tribunals make special provision for child witnesses. Thereby they clearly anticipate, and even encourage, evidence from and about children. These rules aim to achieve a delicate balance between shielding children from the possible trauma – and perhaps even danger – of giving evidence, while still permitting their voices to be heard.

3. SELECTED CASES OF THE YUGOSLAVIA AND RWANDA TRIBUNALS

The *Blaskic*[6] and the *Kunarac* cases[7] are two especially relevant ICTY cases to consider. The *Blaskic* case concerned attacks by mainly Croatian forces against the Muslim population in the Lasva Valley in Bosnia between May 1992 and January 1994. In its judgment the Trial Chamber made no direct reference to child soldiers, but it did refer to the perception of young males as potential soldiers. For example, there were references to 'men of fighting age' who were separated from women and children. However, no definition of this term was provided, and it seems likely that this description was used on the basis of appearance only. On that basis, many so-called 'men of fighting age' could have been under eighteen, or even under fifteen.[8] On the other hand, in the trial proceedings there were many references to child civilians being killed, often with extreme brutality, for example by being burned alive. There were also references to them being harmed in other ways: being injured, arrested and detained, having their homes destroyed, and being used as human shields. Reference was made to the fact that 'men, women and children were attacked without distinction' and civilians killed 'regardless of age or gender'.[9] Interestingly, the legal element of the judgment stated, among other things, that 'in this case many crimes targeted the general civilian population and within that population the women and children. These acts constitute an aggravating circumstance.'[10] The Trial Chamber therefore regarded attacks on civilian women and children as particularly serious. It also emphasized the command responsibility of General Blaskic specifically in relation to women and children by pointing out that he knew civilians were being detained, including women and children, and that he did not make 'any effort to investigate the circumstances in which people were detained'.[11] He was sentenced to 45 years, on appeal reduced to nine years.[12]

---

[6] *The Prosecutor* v. *Tihomir Blaskic* , Case No. IT-95-14-T, Trial Chamber, 3 March 2000. For more detailed references to the information cited in the text here, see Kuper, *supra* n. 4, pp. 66-68.

[7] *The Prosecutor* v. *Dragoljub Kunarac, Radomir Kovac and Zoran Vukovic*, Case No. IT-96-23-T and IT-96-23/1-T, Trial Chamber, 22 February 2001. Again, for more detailed references see Kuper, ibid., pp. 69-71.

[8] The age of fifteen is the minimum age below which the use of child soldiers is illegal.

[9] *The Prosecutor* v. *Tihomir Blaskic*, *supra* n. 6, paras. 507 and 750 respectively.

[10] Ibid., para. 786. See also para. 783.

[11] Ibid., para 732.

[12] *The Prosecutor* v. *Tihomir Blaskic,* Case No IT-95-14-A, Appeals Chamber, 29 July 2004. Blaskic's sentence was reduced largely due to the fact that the Appeals Chamber disagreed with the Trial Chamber's

Another relevant early ICTY case was the *Kunarac* or 'rape camp' case. It concerned the Serbian occupation of the city and municipality of Foca, during the Bosnian conflict between Serbs and Muslims, between early 1992 and mid-1993. The accused were all Serbs. The case contained no explicit reference to child soldiers, but there were many references to child civilians, since many of those raped and abused were under eighteen. The witnesses in this case included rape victims aged between thirteen and seventeen at the time of the offences – most of whom were raped by numerous soldiers and others, over a period of months. One girl, subsequently sold to Montenegrin soldiers and still missing at the time of the trial, was only twelve at the time of these events. Throughout the Trial Chamber proceedings, reference was made to the rape victims as 'girls' or 'women and girls' – so repeatedly emphasizing their youth.[13]

As regards the legal aspects of the *Kunarac* case, the ICTY made history by handing down the first convictions of rape and enslavement as crimes against humanity. The Kunarac judgment also referred directly to children and to the relevant law. It cited, for example, child-specific provisions in the 1949 Geneva Conventions and the 1977 Geneva Protocols, and the Convention on the Rights of the Child in relation to 'trafficking in children'.[14] Further, the Tribunal stated it would take account of the evidence of minors even if they had trouble recalling events in detail.[15] In addition, it considered the youth of some of the victims to be 'aggravating circumstances', and expressed strong views, for example regarding abuse of the 12-year old as 'particularly appalling and deplorable.'

This case also emphasized that although Kunarac was not a 'political or military mastermind', he had 'natural authority' over his men, and therefore his 'active participation' was 'even more repugnant.'[16] Kunarac was sentenced to 28 years imprisonment. He appealed against this sentence, but his appeal was unsuccessful. It is of interest here that, in its judgment, the Appeals Chamber confirmed that the youth of rape victims constituted an aggravating factor.[17]

The third and last case to be outlined here is the *Akyesu* case that was heard by the International Criminal Tribunal for Rwanda.[18] This case differs from the ICTY cases in that Akayesu was not a military commander but the mayor of a particular

findings concerning his degree of responsibility. This sentencing decision does not therefore reflect on the ICTY's attitude towards violations committed against children.

[13] *The Prosecutor* v. *Dragoljub Kunarac, Radomir Kovac and Zoran Vukovic, supra* n. 7, paras. 28, 35-37, 40-41, 56, 63, 81, 83, 174, 178, among others.

[14] Ibid., paras. 528, 529, 531 and 536.

[15] Ibid., para. 565.

[16] This statement and the preceding one were cited in the official summary of the Judgment – see <http://www.un.org/icty/pressreal/p566-e.htm>.

[17] See *The Prosecutor* v. *Dragoljub Kunarac, Radomir Kovac and Zoran Vukovic*, Case No IT-96-23 and IT-96-23/1-A, Appeals Chamber, 12 June 2002, e.g., para. 355. The Appeals Chamber made a number of other interesting statements concerning children, but it is beyond the scope of this chapter to further consider these.

[18] *The Prosecutor* v. *Jean-Paul Akayesu*, Case No ICTR-96-4-T, Trial Chamber, 2 September 1998. For detailed references see Kuper, *supra* n. 4, pp. 71-73.

area in Rwanda. However, the Tribunal made clear that his position in the community meant the Tribunal was able to treat him as if he had been a military commander, and that civilians and military commanders can be held equally accountable in circumstances where they have authority.

The case concerns Akayesu's responsibility for the killing of, and other acts of violence towards, members of the Tutsi community by Hutu militia in 1994. Again it hardly addressed the issue of children as members of the Hutu militia, although many children did participate as combatants. However, there were many references to child civilians as victims of the violence. Numerous witnesses gave evidence regarding the massive scale of death and injury of children, among others. The judgment emphasized that 'even newborn babies were not spared. Even pregnant women, including those of Hutu origin, were killed on the grounds that the foetuses in their wombs were fathered by Tutsi men.'[19] Further, 'the Tutsi were killed solely on account of having been born Tutsi', and 'Tutsi girls and women were subjected to sexual violence, beaten and killed'.[20] In its findings, the Tribunal repeatedly referred to 'the rape of girls and women', as the ICTY did in the *Kunarac* case, using the term 'girl' to emphasize the youth of the victims.[21] Regarding the law in this case, the ICTR concluded, among other things, that genocide had been 'committed in Rwanda in 1994 against the Tutsi as a group'.[22] Akayesu was sentenced to life imprisonment.

These early cases of the ICTY and the ICTR show that the Tribunals did pay particular attention to violations committed against children, and that they considered these to be aggravating circumstances that contributed to severe sentences imposed on the accused. Nevertheless, these judgments could certainly have had a stronger child rights focus still, since the scale of the violations committed against children and young people was so enormous. In aiming to deter such violations, military training regarding children therefore should highlight the fact that international criminal tribunals clearly pay particular attention to crimes committed against children.

4. INTERNATIONAL CRIMINAL TRIBUNALS AND MILITARY TRAINING

Before further considering the link between military training and the practice of international criminal tribunals regarding children, it is worth mentioning that the training referred to here is primarily training of national armed forces, not non-governmental forces However, certain of the latter may receive pertinent training as well.

---

[19] *The Prosecutor* v. *Jean-Paul Akayesu*, ibid., para. 121.

[20] Ibid., paras. 124 and 449 respectively.

[21] Ibid., e.g., paras. 391, 403, 416, 421-422, 429-430, 433, 444-445, 452, 692, 694, 696-697 and 731.

[22] Ibid., para. 126.

It is also worth recalling the multiple roles played by international criminal tribunals. They provide a forum in which victims and survivors of violations can seek redress and some form of justice, and in which those accused as perpetrators can argue their case and, if found guilty, face punishment. This process can also enable countries to both chronicle and come to terms with their history to some extent. Further, as already indicated, international criminal tribunals may have an impact on military conduct itself. The impact can be positive, in possibly restraining combatants from committing violations for fear of punishment. It can, unfortunately, on occasion also be negative in leading combatants to commit greater crimes or take greater pains to conceal evidence of these (for example by trying to ensure that no witnesses survive), again for fear of punishment. International tribunals can only fulfil their possible preventive role if military personnel know of their existence and remit, if they know the basic rules regarding the conduct of armed conflict, and if they know they can be punished for violations.

5. ROLE AND LIMITS OF MILITARY INTERNATIONAL HUMANITARIAN LAW TRAINING

Certainly, as regards violations of International Humanitarian Law (IHL)[23] prevention is infinitely better than the 'cure' of punishment, for obvious reasons. It is in this context that military training has a crucial role to play. It is the arena in which soldiers and officers can and should learn and teach the very rules and principles that may prevent or limit violations, and hence trial and punishment for these.[24] In this way, military training can form a bridge between conduct in situations of armed conflict, and its legal and political aftermath.

Military training on international law in general rests partly on the assumption that, without such training, military personnel may remain ignorant of their legal obligations, which is clearly one factor that can lead to violation of these obligations. The International Committee of the Red Cross (ICRC) argues that '[w]hat is needed therefore is a situation in which no one – neither those who give the orders,

---

[23] There is some controversy as to the most appropriate term for describing the body of international law that regulates the actual conduct of hostilities once the use of force has started (i.e., the '*jus in bello*' as opposed to the '*jus ad bellum*': rules governing the process by which states decide whether or not to resort to the use of force). Some writers prefer the term 'law of armed conflict', but in this chapter the term 'international humanitarian law' is generally used as it is particularly apt for discussing the law regarding children in armed conflict, which has a largely humanitarian emphasis.

[24] According to M. Osiel, in 'Obeying Orders: Atrocity, Military Discipline, and the Law of War', 86 *California Law Review* (1998) p. 1022: 'legalists are right to insist that law can and does influence battlefield behaviour in important ways', including through 'threats of punishment *ex post*' (i.e., after the event). However, he sees such threats as having less impact in encouraging ethical behaviour than 'legal norms structuring day-to-day operation of combat forces' that 'achieve their effect *ex ante*' (i.e., before violations can be committed).

nor those who carry them out, nor those who let the violence happen – can say: "I didn't know".'[25]

Some of the fundamental rules of international humanitarian law may seem so obvious that one could think they need not be taught. For example, how can anyone not know that it is both morally and legally reprehensible to directly target non-combatants or to torture or gratuitously kill or injure children? Of course many soldiers and officers do know and adhere to these principles. Yet, for others, there are factors inherent in situations of armed conflict which mean that fundamental rules are not obvious. These include the simple fact that armed conflict is by its very nature a situation in which many of the usual norms of conduct do not apply, and it may be difficult to ascertain which norms do apply. Armed conflict is, to quote McCoubrey, 'in essence a descent into extra-legal violence'.[26] Or, as former officer and ICRC military trainer Roberts has written:

> '... there are not too many professions that require you as a matter of duty to be pre-pared to lay down your life .... There may be fear, fatigue, frustration, anger, hunger and stress, which in turn may prompt a desire for revenge or retribution. We must ac-cept these as part and parcel of the military life, but we can certainly try to control them as best we can.'[27]

Another obstacle to ethical conduct in armed conflict is the fact that sometimes combatants (in national armed forces as well as in other armed groups) include 'people who are virtually excluded from society – often young people without jobs, education or future prospects – and who are caught up in a spiral of violence', and who then 'find it difficult to respect a degree of dignity in others which they do not accord themselves.'[28] For combatants such as these, it may be almost impossible to ascertain the line between acceptable and unacceptable conduct in armed conflict. Then, too, some armed forces (and especially non-governmental forces) may not even aspire to conduct themselves in accordance with any international or domestic norms. They may, for example, have as their sole aim the genocidal annihilation of another ethnic group. In that context the niceties of law clearly do not feature. None-theless, most armed forces, and certainly most national armed forces, do aim to conduct themselves within some legal limits, even if this may in certain circum-stances be more evident in the words of their officers or political leaders than in their actions. International criminal tribunals have a role to play in policing those limits.

---

[25] ICRC Special Report: Stemming the Tide of Violence – ICRC Activities in Relation to the Inter-national Community's Prevention Strategies (Geneva, ICRC 1998) p. 5.

[26] H. McCoubrey, 'Jurisprudential Aspects of the Modern Law of Armed Conflict', in M. Meyer (ed.), Armed Conflict and the New Law (London, British Institute of International and Comparative Law 1989) p. 2.

[27] D.L. Roberts, 'Training the Armed Forces to Respect International Humanitarian Law: The Perspective of the ICRC Delegate to the Armed and Security Forces of South Asia', International Review of the Red Cross No. 319 (1997), pp. 433-446.

[28] ICRC, supra n. 25, p. 4.

6. BASIC RULES

The question then arises, what are the rules on which soldiers and officers should receive training, and breach of which can lead to criminal prosecution? These rules can only be briefly outlined here.[29] Fundamental rules include the notion that it is not permitted to inflict 'superfluous injury or unnecessary suffering' on either combatants or civilians.[30] Further, combatants should use only the minimum degree of force that is both necessary and lawful in order to achieve their mission, in accordance with the principles of military necessity and humanity.[31] Thus, combatants must balance military necessity against humanitarian considerations, in accordance with the principle of proportionality. Further, even in armed conflict there is a right to life. Or, to be more precise, there is the concept that no-one can be arbitrarily or unlawfully deprived of their life. This is a basic human rights principle, but it is incorporated – with different language and emphasis – into the law of armed conflict. In this context 'the right to life' means, for example, that it is unlawful to directly target civilians, and other persons (including former combatants) who are 'hors de combat', whether adult or child. Moreover, there are particular rules that emphasize that children in armed conflict are entitled to additional care and protection. Of course, and like adults, they must not be tortured, ill-treated or sexually abused.[32] According to international law, unlike adults, children generally should not be directly involved in armed conflict as combatants. Indeed, the 1998 Statute of the International Criminal Court specifically makes it a war crime to use child soldiers below the age of fifteen.[33] Other recent international law is increasingly raising the age limit to eighteen.[34] However if, despite these prohibitions, children are actively involved in armed conflict, they are entitled to special treatment when captured and imprisoned. There are specific protection measures for orphans and babies, among others.

These, then, are some of the basic rules that military personnel should learn in their training, with the message that breach of these rules can result in prosecution. For many military training purposes it is not, in fact, necessary to provide much training specifically regarding children. Depending on the circumstances, it can suffice to teach the basic IHL rules, and to emphasize that these must be applied

---

[29] For more detailed information, see, e.g., Kuper, *supra* n. 3 and Kuper, *supra* n. 4. See also D. Fleck (ed.), *The Handbook of Humanitarian Law in Armed Conflicts* (Oxford, Oxford University Press 2000); L.C. Green, *The Contemporary Law of Armed Conflict* (Manchester, Manchester University Press 2000), and F. De Mulinen, *Handbook on the Law of War for Armed Forces* (Geneva, ICRC 1989).

[30] See, e.g., Article 35(2) of Geneva Protocol I, 1977.

[31] See, e.g., A. Roberts and R. Guelff, *Documents on the Laws of War* (Oxford, Oxford University Press 2000) p. 10.

[32] Indeed, the vulnerability of children entitles them, under international law, to a particularly high standard of care in this context.

[33] See ICC Statute Articles 8(2)(b)(xxvi) and 8(2)(e)(vii).

[34] See particularly the 1999 Convention Concerning the Prohibition and Immediate Action for the Elimination of the Worst Forms of Child Labour and the 2000 Optional Protocol to the CRC on the Involvement of Children in Armed Conflict.

with particular care as regards certain vulnerable categories of people, including children. More senior personnel, such as officers, should be trained to a higher standard, and may bear a correspondingly greater burden of responsibility in any prosecutions for violations. Military lawyers, of course, should be able to ascertain the relevant law in some detail. The reality is that many such personnel do not learn these rules, either because they are fighting in non-governmental forces that consider themselves beyond the law, or because their country does not provide adequate training for its armed forces.

7.   PRACTICE ON THE GROUND: TRAINING OF NATIONAL ARMED FORCES

The next question then is whether soldiers and officers of national armed forces are actually trained in the relevant rules, either in general or specifically as regards children? Research on this question conducted by the author largely between 2001 and 2002 indicated a patchwork of varied approaches by different national armed forces to military training on children, as regards: whether any such training was provided at all; who provided the training (for example, NGOs or governments); what the training covered (for example, brief information on the 1949 Geneva Conventions, or a week-long IHL or even child rights course); and how it was provided (for example, in specific lectures or integrated into general IHL training).[35] The research looked at a representative sample of 11 different countries: Australia, Bosnia and Herzegovina, Colombia, Israel, Uganda, Sierra Leone, South Africa, Sri Lanka, Sweden, the United Kingdom, and the United States. At the time of writing, all 11 selected countries provided some IHL training for their armed forces. For the most part, this seemed to be general training with little specific focus on children. There were, however, exceptions to this. For example, Sweden provided a short lecture specifically on children to all its officers as part of their general IHL training. Uganda and Sierra Leone, both of which had undergone lengthy armed conflicts affecting large numbers of children as combatants and as civilians, were providing training concerning children to at least some sectors of their armed forces. The United Kingdom apparently provided child-specific training if the particular mission required this. The United States was the only country in the sample where, according to a senior United States army lawyer, 'no military training materials or courses discuss children as such', although he added that children would be covered under general IHL rules and training concerning civilians and combatants.[36]

The problem remains: would such training adequately equip soldiers and officers with the information they need to conduct themselves in accordance with child-related international law?

---

[35] Kuper, *supra* n. 4, chapters 8 and 9.
[36] Ibid., at p. 159.

8.   METHODOLOGY AND IMPACT OF TRAINING

Another significant point about military training is that the provision of this training does not necessarily mean that it will be effective in actually shaping military
conduct in situations of armed conflict. Training methodology is crucial, and training should be regular, varied, relevant to the specific context, and of an appropriate
length, level, structure and style to be both comprehensible and effective for the
necessary range of personnel and situations. Training that aims to change attitudes,
and develop values and instincts broadly in accordance with pertinent legal principles, is likely to be more effective than legalistic training.

Military personnel may need incentives to comply with the relevant rules. Ide-
ally they would have an innate sense of ethical conduct, but as already indicated,
this is not always the case. Sometimes they may comply with IHL rules for reasons
of reciprocity. For example, if they treat prisoners of war (POWs) in accordance
with international humanitarian law, they are more likely to be well-treated if they
themselves become POWs. In any event, Françoise Hampson argues that a soldier
should be motivated to comply with IHL in three ways:

> 'He must know that the same standards are shared by his commanding officers and
> those responsible for the conduct of the conflict. He must be used to confronting moral
> dilemmas in practice … [through] training exercises …. Finally, the soldier must know
> that a breach of the rules will entail punishment.'[37]

This statement returns, then, to the theme of the link between military training and
international criminal tribunals – in that such tribunals form part of a punitive mechanism, and can also be invoked preventively in training as a deterrent to the commission of violations.

A few further points need to be made here. One is that the effectiveness of military training is ultimately extremely hard to measure. As Roberts, former officer
and ICRC military trainer, stated:

> 'Results are very difficult to quantify. One can boast of the number of students who
> have passed through our hands or enumerate the courses held. … The true results will
> be seen only on the ground, in some far-flung corner of the region. If only 10% of
> what we teach is remembered, if a soldier as a reflex action or a senior officer as a
> function of his rank and command thinks, no matter how briefly, of the law and ap-
> plies it, then our work will have been worthwhile.'[38]

In any event, despite the difficulties and limitations of military training regarding
international humanitarian law, according to key international treaties such as the

---

[37] F. Hampson, 'Fighting by the Rules', *International Review of the Red Cross* No. 269 (1989)
pp. 115-116.

[38] Roberts, *supra* n. 27, at p. 8.

1949 Geneva Conventions and the 1977 Geneva Protocols governments are under a legal duty to provide such training for their troops.[39]

9. CONCLUSION

Military training on international humanitarian law is of course only one factor in the conduct of armed conflict, and one factor in the extent to which violations are or are not committed by military personnel. Law and related policy thus form a small part of a complex jigsaw puzzle composed of additional key elements such as international politics and finance, media pressure, cultural norms, and others. It is the sum total of these many factors that makes it more or less likely that the law will be adhered to in any given situation. That said, this chapter has outlined a way in which military training can help to bridge the gap between, on the one hand, the conduct of military personnel, and, on the other hand, proceedings before international tribunals regarding crimes committed against children. It has argued that international criminal tribunals increasingly take account of violations against children, and that such tribunals play many roles, including both punishing and arguably preventing violations. However, the latter role depends on military training that is able to make military personnel aware of the existence of these tribunals and the rules that they aim to enforce, including those for the protection of children.

---

[39] See further Kuper, *supra* n. 4, chapter 6.

Chapter 13
LITIGATING CHILDREN'S RIGHTS AFFECTED BY ARMED CONFLICT BEFORE THE EUROPEAN COURT OF HUMAN RIGHTS

Nuala Mole*

1. INTRODUCTION

All member states of the Council of Europe are parties to the European Convention on Human Rights (ECHR). The European Court of Human Rights (ECtHR) adjudicates complaints brought by individuals, or more rarely by other member states, against member states of the Council of Europe, where it is alleged that violations of their obligations under that Convention have occurred. Complaints can only be brought in relation to events that occurred after the impugned state ratified the Convention. Accordingly, many of the human rights violations that have occurred in conflicts in Europe – such as those that took place in the former Yugoslavia – are not justiciable as far as the Court is concerned. Only three ECHR provisions expressly refer to war or conflict: Article 2 (the right to life), Article 15 (allowing for a derogation from the Convention in times of emergency, including in times of war), and Protocol 13 (concerning the abolition of the death penalty in all circumstances).

The Court's case law is nonetheless of worldwide significance in considering the human rights issues which affect children in conflict and post-conflict situations. The Court is frequently acknowledged as a pre-eminent source of authoritative jurisprudence on international human rights protection. Even outside Europe, other international and national tribunals often 'borrow' from the ECtHR's case law. Other international bodies, for example, frequently develop their own case law by drawing on the principles already developed by the European Court. The terms of the ECHR itself refer back to other international human rights standards as informing the Court's approach to interpretation. ECHR Article 53 states that nothing in the Convention 'shall be construed as limiting or derogating from any of the human rights and fundamental freedoms which may be ensured under the laws of any High Contracting Party *or under any other agreement to which it is a Party*'.[1]

---

* Director, Advice on Individual Rights in Europe (The Aire Centre), London.
[1] ECHR Article 53, emphasis added.

K. Arts & V. Popovski (eds.), International Criminal Accountability and the Rights of Children
© 2006, Hague Academic Coalition, The Hague, The Netherlands and the Authors

This article thus provides that if a more comprehensive protection of human rights exists either in the national law of a party to the Convention, or in any international treaty to which the state is a party, then the relevant ECHR provision must not be interpreted in a way that would limit those rights. The European Court consequently regularly draws on the standards of other international instruments such as the United Nations Convention Against Torture or the United Nations Convention on the Rights of the Child.

Many other international human rights treaties contain provisions similar to Article 53 or provisions stating that the treaty must be interpreted consistently with other international documents.[2] Such common intentions reinforce the concept of international comity. States and international institutions strive where possible to maintain consistency in their interpretations of universally recognised human rights standards. This tendency can be seen when international institutions refer to each other's texts and case law. This cross-reference to the case law of other courts is not confined to international tribunals but occurs also in national jurisprudence, including the national jurisprudence of non–European states.[3] This chapter describes the principles found in the case law of the European Court of Human Rights which are applicable in the judicial decision making of other national and international bodies in cases involving children in conflict and post-conflict situations.

2.   EUROPEAN COURT OF HUMAN RIGHTS CASES ON CHILDREN IN CONFLICT AND POST-CONFLICT SITUATIONS

The ECtHR has developed detailed jurisprudence on the application of the European Convention on Human Rights to children.[4] However, only a few of the cases involved concern children in conflict and post-conflict situations. Although the spe-

---

[2] African Charter on Human and Peoples' Rights, Articles 60 and 61; African Charter on the Rights and Welfare of the Child, Article 46; American Convention on Human Rights, Article 29; Convention on the Rights of the Child, Article 41; Optional Protocol to the Convention on the Rights of the Child on the Involvement of Children in Armed Conflict, Article 5; Declaration on the Protection of all Persons from Enforced Disappearance, Article 21; International Convention on Civil and Political Rights, Article 5.

[3] See, e.g., *Laurence* v. *Texas*, 539 US 573 - 4&6 (2003).

[4] See, e.g., for rights of unborn children, *Poku* v. *United Kingdom*, admissibility decision 15 May 1996; *Vo* v. *France*, No. 53924/00, 8 July 2004; for neo-natal rights, *Calvelli and Ciglio* v. *Italy*, No. 32967/96, 17 January 2002; for removal at birth and other severe methods for separating children from parents, *K and T* v. *Finland*, No. 25702/94, 12 July 2001, 36 *EHRR* 18 (2003), *P, C and S* v. *United Kingdom*, No. 56547/00, 35 *EHRR* 31 (2002), *Haase* v. *Germany*, No. 11057/02, 8 April 2004; for older children and medical negligence or improper treatment, *Powell* v. *United Kingdom*, No. 45305/99, 4 May 2000, *Glass* v. *United Kingdom*, No. 61827/00, 9 March 2004; for neglect and ill-treatment in the home and negligence by social services, *A* v. *United Kingdom*, No. 25599/94, 23 September 1998, 27 *EHRR* 611 (1999), *Z and Others* v. *United Kingdom*, No. 29392/95, 10 May 2001, 34 *EHRR* 3 (2002), *TP and KM* v. *United Kingdom*, No. 28945/95, 10 May 2001, 34 *EHRR* 2 (2002), *Eccleston* v. *United Kingdom*, inadmissibility decision 18 May 2004; for judicial supervision of implementation of care orders, *S and others* v. *United Kingdom*, admissibility decision 31 August 2004; for immigration, *Gul* v. *Switzerland*, No. 23218/94, 19 February 1996, *Nsona* v. *Netherlands*, No. 23366/94, 28

cial position of children in such situations has not yet been specifically addressed in detail by the European Court, three cases have directly concerned children and conflict: *Aydin* v. *Turkey*,[5] *Isayeva* v. *Russian Federation*[6] and *Behrami* v. *France*.[7] Two other cases (*Osman* v. *United Kingdom* and *Z and Others* v. *United Kingdom*) are also relevant and will be renewed below as well.

Aydin v. Turkey

ECHR Article 3 prohibits torture and inhuman or degrading treatment or punishment.[8] This prohibition is absolute and non-derogable. The ECtHR has always held that, whether or not ill-treatment reaches the 'threshold of severity', to bring it within that prohibition will depend in some instances on the age and sex of the victim.[9] *Aydin* v. *Turkey* concerned a phenomenon that, unfortunately, is all too commonly encountered in armed conflicts: sexual violence committed against young girls. The girls involved are doubly victimised both as females and as children. In the *Aydin* case, in the context of the conflict and state of emergency in south-east Turkey, the applicant was taken away by security forces who interrogated her under torture, stripped her naked and raped her. She was seventeen[10] and had never previously left her village. She was engaged to be married at the time. Despite the rape, the marriage went ahead shortly after the incident and when she later discovered that she was pregnant she feared that the child might not be her husband's but might have resulted from the rape. This caused her additional distress.

The Chamber initially assigned to the case, recognising its importance, relinquished jurisdiction in favour of a Grand Chamber.[11] The Grand Chamber found violations of Articles 3 (torture) and 13 (the right to an effective remedy). The finding of a violation of Article 3 was important not just because it formally and legally recognised that the rape of a young girl captured by security forces was an 'especially grave and abhorrent form of ill-treatment', but also because the Court

---

November 1996, *Sen* v. *Netherlands*, No. 31465/96, 21 December 2001, 36 *EHRR* 7 (2003); for adoption, *P, C and S* v. *United Kingdom*, No. 56547/00, 35 *EHRR* 31 (2002), *Pini and Bertani and Manera and Atripaldi* v. *Romania*, Nos. 78028/01 and 78030/01, 22 June 2004; for contact including contact with the implacably hostile parent, *Gorgulu* v. *Germany*, No. 74969/01, 26 February 2004, *Volesky* v. *Czech Republic*, No. 63627/00, 29 June 2004; *Kosmopoulou* v. *Greece*, No. 60457/00, 5 February 2004.

[5] *Aydin* v. *Turkey*, No. 23178/94, 28 June 1997, 25 *EHRR* 251 (1998).

[6] *Isayeva, Yusupova and Bazayeva* v. *Russia*, No. 57947,48 and 49/00, 24 February 2005.

[7] *Behrami* v. *France*, No. 71412/01.

[8] According to ECHR Article 3: 'no one shall be subjected to torture or to inhuman or degrading treatment or punishment.'

[9] *Ireland* v. *United Kingdom*, Series A, No. 25, 18 January 1978, 2 *EHRR* 25 (1979-1980).

[10] CRC Article 1 defines a child as 'every human being below the age of eighteen years unless, under the law applicable to the child, majority is attained earlier.'

[11] This was in conformity with ECHR Article 30: 'Where a case pending before a Chamber raises a serious question affecting the interpretation of the Convention or the protocols thereto, or where the resolution of a question before the Chamber might have a result inconsistent with a judgment previously delivered by the Court, the Chamber may, at any time before it has rendered its judgment, relinquish jurisdiction in favour of the Grand Chamber, unless one of the parties to the case objects.'

noted that rape leaves 'deep psychological scars which do not respond to the passage of time as quickly as other forms of physical and mental violence.'[12]

The Court also found that Article 13 had been violated by the inadequate and inappropriate response of the Turkish authorities to the incidents. No proper investigation had taken place and no prosecutions had been carried out. The victim therefore had no remedy. In other cases involving rape the Court has held that granting compensation is not enough. There must also be a criminal sanction.[13] The decision in *Aydin* predated the Court's judgment in *Assenov* v. *Bulgaria*.[14] The latter case, which concerned the ill-treatment of a 14-year-old boy by the police (which did not occur in a conflict situation) established a more far-reaching principle. The failure to conduct appropriate and effective investigations and prosecutions into allegations of torture or ill-treatment will not only violate Article 13 but such a failure will, of itself, violate the procedural safeguards which the Court holds to be inherent in Article 3. The mere failure to conduct an effective investigation capable of leading to an effective prosecution thus violates the prohibition on torture and inhuman and degrading treatment, even where the facts which would be evidence of the ill-treatment itself cannot be proved. Following *Aydin* and *Assenov* it is now clear that, in order to comply with the prohibition on torture and ill-treatment in Article 3, there is a duty to investigate and, if possible, to prosecute either of two allegations: sexual violence by security forces or paramilitaries against young girls,[15] or the ill-treatment of any young person by police or security forces.[16]

Isayeva v. *Russian Federation*[17]

This case arose from the conflict in Chechnya in 1999. Despite the scale of the hostilities, the Russian government had not chosen to declare a state of emergency or martial law in the region and had thus not derogated from its obligations under the ECHR.[18] European Convention Article 2, on the right to life, states that:

---

[12] *Aydin* v. *Turkey, supra* n. 5, para. 83.

[13] *X and Y* v. *Netherlands*, No. 8978/80, Series A, No. 91, 26 March 1985, 8 *EHRR* 235 (1986), *MC* v. *Bulgaria*, No. 39272/98, 4 December 2003.

[14] *Assenov* v. *Bulgaria*, No. 24760/94, 28 October 1998, 28 *EHRR* 652 (1999).

[15] Cf., corresponding provisions of Article 12 of the UN Convention Against Torture: 'each State Party shall ensure that its competent authorities proceed to a prompt and impartial investigation, wherever there is reasonable ground that an act of torture has been committed in any territory under its jurisdiction.'

[16] The same principle has been frequently applied, *mutatis mutandis*, to disappearances which raise issues under ECHR Article 2 (right to life).

[17] *Isayeva* v. *Russia*, No. 57950/00, 24 February 2005.

[18] ECHR Article 15 states: 'In time of war or other public emergency threatening the life of the nation any High Contracting Party may take measures derogating from its obligations under this Convention to the extent strictly required by the exigencies of the situation, provided that such measures are not inconsistent with its other obligations under international law. No derogation from Article 2, except in respect of deaths resulting from lawful acts of war, or from Articles 3, 4 (paragraph 1) and 7 shall be made under this provision. Any High Contracting Party availing itself of this right of deroga-

'1. Everyone's right to life shall be protected by law. No one shall be deprived of his life intentionally save in the execution of a sentence of a court following his conviction of a crime for which this penalty is provided by law.' And,

'2. Deprivation of life shall not be regarded as inflicted in contravention of this article when it results from the use of force which is no more than absolutely necessary:

a. in defence of any person from unlawful violence;

b. in order to effect a lawful arrest or to prevent the escape of a person lawfully detained;

c. in action lawfully taken for the purpose of quelling a riot or insurrection.'

A group of civilians, including the two Isayev children, aged sixteen and nine, were part of a convoy leaving their village in Chechnya when the convoy, travelling in a supposedly safe corridor, was bombed by Russian military aircraft. Twelve S-24 non-guided ground-to-air missiles were fired, each creating several thousand pieces of shrapnel with an impact radius in excess of 300 metres. The casualties were manifold. Several adults were seriously injured or killed, the two Isayev children were killed, and many other children were injured. The mother of the two children (and a number of other applicants) complained that the Russian Federation was in violation of Article 2 both for the attacks themselves and for their failure to carry out an effective and adequate investigation into the incidents.

The Court accepted[19] that the situation which existed in Chechnya at the relevant time called for exceptional measures to regain control of the territory and suppress the illegal armed insurgency. However, it found that, even if the attack were a legitimate response to an insurgency attack (which it did not expressly accept), indiscriminately bombing a road along which a large number of civilians – including children – were known to be travelling violated Article 2. The Court also condemned the failure of the Russian authorities to conduct a proper investigation into the incidents. The investigation had been neither timely nor effective and appeared to have been dependent for its progress on the initiative of the survivors or the next of kin. The Russian authorities had failed to identify any individuals, military or civilian, who were responsible for either the declaration of the safe corridor or for the safety of those using it.

Both *Aydin* and *Isayeva* concerned acts of the state authorities which violated negative obligations; the state was supposed to refrain from actions infringing the rights of children under ECHR Articles 2 and 3. States are additionally under a positive obligation to take reasonably necessary steps to protect the rights guaranteed under the Convention, as addressed in the next case presented.

---

tion shall keep the Secretary General of the Council of Europe fully informed of the measures which it has taken and the reasons therefor. It shall also inform the Secretary General of the Council of Europe when such measures have ceased to operate and the provisions of the Convention are again being fully executed.'

[19] *Isayev* v. *Russia*, judgment para. 178.

Behrami v. France[20]

Once the actual fighting ends, the presence of unexploded mines and other ordnance is a major danger that remains in many conflict zones. Children are particularly at risk because they are often unaware of the threat posed by apparently harmless objects they come across even if the mines or bombs are not actually concealed. Many tragic and avoidable deaths and mutilations occur each year.[21]

The case of *Behrami* concerned injuries, and one death, suffered in Kosovo by children aged between ten and fifteen. They were out playing when they came across a number of unexploded cluster bombs which had been dropped by NATO in 1999. Oblivious to the danger, they began playing with the bombs. One of the bombs detonated and caused severe injuries to the children, and the death of one of them. An international military presence (the NATO-led Kosovo Force 'KFOR') had been in Kosovo since 1999 and the area where the incident took place in 2000 had been under the command and control of the French military since the arrival of KFOR in the province. The complaint against France was brought to Strasbourg by the father of the dead boy. The complaint has been 'communicated' to the French government[22] and there have been lengthy exchanges between the applicant and the government. With the permission of the Court, the United Kingdom has also intervened in the case. No decision as to admissibility has been taken by the Chamber.[23]

The case raises complex preliminary questions about jurisdiction in relation to the extraterritorial activities of the armed forces of a state party to the ECHR. Whilst the European Court can only deal with the specific complaint which comes before it, it is clear that the decision in this case will have much wider implications for the extraterritorial activities of the armed forces of European states.[24] Both the French and British governments in the *Behrami* case deny that the events in Kosovo lie within French jurisdiction.

Under Article 1 of the European Convention, 'The High Contracting Parties shall secure to everyone within their jurisdiction the rights and freedoms defined in Section I of this Convention.' Previously, a Grand Chamber of the Court considered jurisdictional issues in *Bankovic* v. *Belgium and Others*.[25] It found that the civilian victims of the bombing of the Belgrade TV station by NATO were not 'within the jurisdiction' of the Contracting Parties for the purposes of Article 1. Jurisdiction, it

---

[20] The author is a member of the legal team representing the applicants in *Behrami*.

[21] The Landmine Monitor, a leading NGO dedicated to the removal of landmines, estimated there were 6,521 landmine-related casualties in 2004, 19% of which harmed children. See <http://www.icbl.org/lm/2005/intro/survivor.html#fn4>.

[22] The case was communicated in September 2003, under Rule 54(2)(b) of the ECtHR's Rules.

[23] Under ECHR Article 35 of the Convention, the Court determines the admissibility of a complaint before it proceeds to examine it on the merits.

[24] For a thorough analysis of extraterritorial jurisdiction, see F. Coomans and M.T. Kamminga, *Extraterritorial Application of Human Rights Treaties* (Antwerp, Intersentia 2004).

[25] *Bankovic* v. *Belgium and others*, No. 52207/99, admissibility decision 12 December 2001.

held, was primarily territorial. The NATO troops did not have command and control on the ground and Serbia was not within the 'espace juridique' of the Convention.[26]

However, two other important cases on jurisdiction and extraterritorial military operations have been decided since *Bankovic*. In the case of *Ilaşçu and Others* v. *Moldova and Russia*,[27] a Grand Chamber of the Court found that the activities of the Russian Army in the breakaway Transdniestrian province of Moldova were within the jurisdiction of Russia for Convention purposes. In the case of *Issa and others* v. *Turkey*[28] the Court found that the actions of Turkish troops in the course of various incursions into Iraq would, in principle, have been within the jurisdiction of Turkey if it had been established, as a finding of fact, that the troops had actually been in the specific area at the time at which the incidents were alleged to have occurred. As these facts had not been established, no violation was found. The applicants in *Issa* asked for the case to be referred to a Grand Chamber, but their request was rejected and the judgment is now final. Another similar case against Turkey,[29] involving deaths resulting from incursions by Turkish forces into Iran, has been communicated to the Turkish Government and is pending. Where the acts or omissions of a multinational presence are concerned, attributing jurisdiction to a single or several individual states may also be problematic.

The application of Article 1 is not confined to issues of jurisdiction. The Court also relies on it to determine the existence of positive as well as negative obligations under the Convention. States are responsible for their omissions as well as for their actions. The *Behrami* case does not concern an act by the French military but a failure to act, which the applicants allege engaged the government's positive obligations under the Convention. Even if the jurisdiction issue discussed above is resolved, the French government's liability will depend on the Court's application of the principle of 'positive obligation' enunciated in two additional cases which are discussed below.

Osman v. United Kingdom

In *Osman*,[30] a 13-year-old boy was persistently harassed and threatened by a schoolteacher with a serious mental disorder. The teacher later developed an obsession with the boy. After multiple incidents had been reported to the police – with no tangible effect – the teacher took a sawn-off shotgun to the child's house and attacked, killing the father and inflicting terrible injuries on the child. The refusal of the United Kingdom authorities to hold the police accountable for their failure to

---

[26] The Federal Republic of Yugoslavia was not at the time a party to the ECHR.

[27] *Ilaşçu and Others* v. *Moldova and Russia*, No. 48787/99, 8 July 2004.

[28] *Issa and Others* v. *Turkey*, No. 31821/96, 16 November 2004.

[29] *Pad and Others* v. *Turkey*, communicated to the government, awaiting admissibility decision.

[30] *Osman* v. *United Kingdom*, No. 23452/94, 28 February 1998, 29 *EHRR* 245 (2000). The author was the representative of the applicants in this case.

respond to the earlier incidents and the child's requests for protection led the Court to hold that ECHR Article 2 (the right to life)[31] could impose, in certain well-defined circumstances, a positive obligation on the authorities to take preventative measures to protect an individual whose life was at risk. The Court pointed out, however, that this obligation could not place a disproportionate burden on the authorities to prevent all harm.

The Court further held that states violate their positive obligation to protect the right to life if they 'knew or ought to have known at the time of the existence of a real and immediate risk to the life of an identified individual or individuals from the criminal acts of a third party and that they failed to take measures within the scope of their powers which, judged reasonably, might have been expected to avoid that risk.'[32] This judgment represented a step forward in the protection of children under the European Convention on Human Rights. The Court particularly emphasised the national authorities' failure to protect the life of a vulnerable child. Therefore, the obligation on the state under Article 2 was all the more important because the life involved was that of a child.[33]

Applying these principles to the *Behrami* case, the Court will have to decide a number of issues. First, whether the French military authorities knew or ought to have known about the risk the cluster bombs posed. Secondly, whether the unexploded ordnance constituted a real and immediate risk to the life of an identifiable child or group of children. Thirdly, to what extent the principle in *Osman* applies when the threat did not emanate from the criminal acts of a third party. Finally, the Court will have to decide whether measures that the authorities failed to take were within their powers, and whether it was reasonable to expect the authorities to have taken them. In the context of all these questions, it is undisputed that French KFOR had been aware of the presence of the unexploded cluster bombs and their location for some 4 or 5 months prior to the incident. They had taken no steps to neutralise them. More importantly, given the reasonableness requirement in *Osman*, nothing had been done to mark or fence off the area as the French military stated that it was not considered 'a high priority'.

---

[31] ECHR Article 2 states 'Everyone's right to life shall be protected by law. No one shall be deprived of his life intentionally save in the execution of a sentence of a court following his conviction of a crime for which this penalty is provided by law. ... Deprivation of life shall not be regarded as inflicted in contravention of this article when it results from the use of force which is no more than absolutely necessary: in defence of any persons from unlawful violence; in order to effect a lawful arrest or to prevent the escape of a person lawfully detained; in action lawfully taken for the purpose of quelling a riot or insurrection.'

[32] *Osman* v. *United Kingdom*, para. 116.

[33] For a particularly in-depth analysis of the ECHR in relation to children's rights, see U. Kilkelly, *The Child and the European Convention on Human Rights* (Dartmouth, Ashgate 2002).

Z and Others v. United Kingdom

While *Osman* concerned an alleged violation of the right to life,[34] *Z and Others*[35] illustrates how positive obligations under Article 3[36] apply to post-conflict situations. As noted above, ECHR Article 1 requires states to secure everyone within their jurisdiction the rights and freedoms in the Convention. When taken in conjunction with Article 3, this positive obligation requires states to take reasonable measures designed to ensure that individuals within their jurisdiction are not subjected to torture or inhuman or degrading treatment, including such ill-treatment administered by private individuals.[37] These measures should provide effective protection, in particular, of children and other vulnerable persons and include reasonable steps to prevent ill-treatment of which the authorities had or ought to have had knowledge.[38] The Court found in Z that the state had a positive obligation to protect vulnerable children from torture or inhuman or degrading treatment. It found that the degree of neglect and abuse meted out to the children by the parents, and the failure by the state to intervene, violated Article 3.

For *Z and Others* v. *United Kingdom* to apply to children in post-conflict situations, the state must have jurisdiction over the individuals concerned. The question of jurisdiction was discussed above in the context of the *Behrami* case. The treatment (or neglect) of the children concerned must reach the threshold of severity prohibited by Article 3. And the state must have failed in its positive obligation to protect the children from the prohibited treatment. Since the age of the victim is an important factor in determining whether that threshold has been crossed, as can be seen from the cases of *Aydin* and *Z and Others* v. *United Kingdom,* compliance with the positive duty on the state to protect children must therefore be subjected to a more rigorous examination.

It is important to note, from *Osman and Z*, that the perpetrator of prohibited treatment need not be state authorities, as in *Aydin* or *Isayeva*. The state is under an obligation to protect an individual from ill-treatment at the hands of private individuals. It is also under an obligation to protect individuals from continuing situations which pose a risk to life or safety.[39] The cases of *Oneryildiz* v. *Turkey* and *Fadeyeva* v. *Russian Federation* are illustrative. Both cases concerned situations in which families, including minor children, were living in a highly dangerous situation which the authorities had failed to take the necessary steps to make safe. The case law of the European Court points to the assumption that, in conflict, but par-

---

[34] The Court found no violation of Article 2 in *Osman,* but found violations of the procedural requirements in Article 6.

[35] The author was a member of the legal team representing the applicants in this case.

[36] See *supra* n. 8.

[37] *Z and Others* v. *United Kingdom*, No. 29392/95, 10 May 2001.

[38] *Osman* v. *United Kingdom*, para. 116.

[39] See, e.g., *Oneryildiz* v. *Turkey*, No. 48939/99, 18 June 2002, *Fadeyeva* v. *Russian Federation* 55723/00, 9 June 2005.

ticularly in post-conflict situations, states are under a specific obligation to protect children not only from prohibited treatment but also from ongoing life or health-threatening situations.

3. DISPLACEMENT FOLLOWING CONFLICT

Unexploded ordnance is a source of serious risk to life and physical integrity, but the displacement that follows conflict can often be damaging to children as well, leaving them without adequate homes or education. The Court's recent decision in the case of *Dogan* v. *Turkey*[40] considered the positive duty on states to ensure that those who have been displaced by violence are not abandoned in situations which leave families in avoidable and unacceptable living conditions (see *Oneryildiz* and *Fadeyeva* above) and in particular leave children without adequate education. Although the plight of the children was not specifically raised in *Dogan*, the difficulties which they encountered were implicitly considered as the core of the Turkish government's failure to take adequate steps to secure the families' return to their villages and to some semblance of normal life. The Court found Turkey to be in violation of Article 1 of ECHR Protocol 1 (the right to peaceful enjoyment of possessions) and did not therefore find it necessary to examine the complaint under Article 8 (the right to respect for private and family life, home and correspondence).

4. REMEDIES

Ubi ius ibi remedium is a maxim of utmost importance when considering the violation of children's rights.[41] However, all too often such violations go unchecked because there is no one able or willing to litigate on behalf of the child victim. Article 34 of the ECHR does not permit the bringing of cases which are *actio popularis*, that is, complaints brought in the general interest rather than by (or on behalf of) named individuals who are personally the victims of violations. In order to ensure that children's rights do not thereby go unvindicated, the European Court has adopted broad and flexible rules governing cases on behalf of children. The approach of the Court in *Scozzari and Giunta* v. *Italy* and other cases[42] suggests that where violations of children's ECHR rights are concerned – and their cases would not otherwise be able to come before the Court – complaints can be brought on their behalf by individuals with a relevant link to the children.[43] This is so even

---

[40] *Dogan and Others* v. *Turkey*, Nos. 8803-8811/02, 8813/02 and 8819/02, 29 June 2004.

[41] See *Aydin* and *Isayeva* above. The phrase means 'Where there is a right, there is a remedy'.

[42] *Scozzari and Giunta* v. *Italy*, Nos. 39221/98 and 41963/98, 13 July 2000, 35 *EHRR* 12 (2002), and *P, C and S* v. *United Kingdom*, No. 56547/00, 16 July 2002, 35 *EHRR* 31 (2002), *Covezzi and Morselli* v. *Italy*, No. 52763/99, 9 May 2003, 38 *EHRR* 28 (2004).

[43] *SP, DP and AT* v. *United Kingdom*, admissibility decision 20 May 1996.

if those individuals would not normally have standing to bring a complaint on their behalf.

The European Convention also requires effective remedies before national authorities. The need to investigate, and where appropriate prosecute, allegations of serious violations of human rights has been discussed above in relation to *Aydin* and *Isayeva*, both as an inherent procedural safeguard (Articles 2 and 3) and a requirement of Article 13. In *Osman* the Court found that the exclusion of the claims brought against the police for a failure to act violated the right of access to court guaranteed in Article 6(1). It held that the case should have been considered on its merits and should not have been automatically excluded by a rule which amounted to immunity from suit for the police. The rule constituted an unjustifiable restriction on the right of access to a court guaranteed under Article 6. However, when considering a similar exclusionary rule in *Z*, the Court granted the children the relief they sought by holding state authorities responsible for their negligence. It found a violation of Article 13 because the absence of a civil remedy in English law meant that the children could not access a judicial process which could lead to the award of the financial compensation which the Court held had to be available in the circumstances. It should be noted that the right to financial compensation will not always suffice. In the *Isayeva* case discussed above the Court expressly found that the obligations under Article 2 could not be satisfied merely by awarding damages. In this context it should also be noted that in the case of *Kutic* v. *Croatia*,[44] the Court found that it was acceptable for a state in a post-conflict situation to postpone the judicial examination of certain civil claims relating to the conflict period but that Article 6 would be violated if the state failed to take urgent measures to amend this situation as time passed.

5. CHILDREN ACCUSED OF SERIOUS CRIMES

The recruitment of child soldiers is expressly prohibited in international law[45] but remains widespread and is addressed in several chapters in this book. This phenomenon and the total breakdown of family and social mores that frequently accompy conflicts lead all too often to situations where children caught up in war are not only victims of crimes, but also commit terrible acts of violence. Significant challenges are posed in dealing with the ensuing investigations and prosecutions whilst paying heed to the special considerations that are due when the alleged perpetrators of appalling crimes were, or still are, children. Whilst the most tragic cases are of very young accused, the most problematic cases are often of older teenagers who, whilst still technically children, are nearing the cusp of adulthood.

---

[44] *Kutic* v. *Croatia*, No. 48778/99, 1 March 2002.

[45] See the CRC Optional Protocol on the Involvement of Children in Armed Conflict. The recent decision in *Kilinc* v. *Turkey*, No. 40145/98, 7 June 2005, highlights the duty owed by military authorities to young and vulnerable conscripts, even if they are not technically children.

The European Court considered the question of children accused of serious crime in the cases of *T* v. *United Kingdom* and *V* v. *United Kingdom*.[46] The judgment considered whether the trial of two 11-year-old boys accused of murdering a toddler was in accordance with Article 6. The applicants also alleged that the way in which their trial was conducted in an adult court was inhuman treatment in violation of Article 3. One issue for the European Court was that of the age of criminal responsibility. In England and Wales, the age of criminal responsibility is ten years old. The two boys in question were aged ten at the time of the commission of the offence and aged eleven when the case was heard in the domestic courts. The Court held that the attribution of criminal responsibility to children aged ten was not a violation of Article 3, as there is no commonly accepted minimum age for the imposition of criminal responsibility, and 'no clear tendency can be ascertained from examination of the relevant international texts and instruments.'[47] The Court therefore held that the age of ten cannot be said to be so young as to differ disproportionately from the age-limit in the other European states. The Court concluded that the attribution of criminal responsibility to the applicants did not in itself give rise to a breach of Article 3 of the Convention.[48] The Court went on to state that trying a child, even as young as eleven, in a criminal court did not violate the fair trial guarantee under Article 6(1).[49] So, at this stage, the Court did not afford any new protection to children accused of serious crime.

However, the Court went on to hold that such a child must be dealt with in a manner which takes full account of his age, level of maturity, and intellectual and emotional capacities, and that steps should be taken to promote his ability to understand and participate in the proceedings. It was noted that there is an international tendency towards protecting the privacy of child defendants that must be balanced with the argument that public trials serve the general interest in the open administration of justice. The Court observed that this balance could be achieved with the provision of a modified procedure for child defendants (for example, selective at-

---

[46] *T* v. *United Kingdom,* No. 24724/94 and *V* v. *United Kingdom*, No. 24888/94, 30 *EHRR* 121 (2000).

[47] *T* v. *United Kingdom*, ibid., para. 71. Relevant international texts concerning the age of criminal responsibility include the United Nations Standard Minimum Rules for the Administration of Juvenile Justice (The Beijing Rules). Rule 4 states concerning the age of criminal responsibility: 'in those legal systems recognising the concept of the age of criminal responsibility for juveniles, the beginning of that age shall not be fixed at too low an age level, bearing in mind the facts of emotional, mental and intellectual maturity.' CRC Article 40(3) states that 'State Parties shall seek to promote the establishment of laws, procedures, authorities, and institutions, specifically applicable to children alleged as, accused of, or recognised as having infringed the penal law, and, in particular: (a) the establishment of a minimum age below which children shall be presumed not to have the capacity to infringe the penal laws; …'. The Committee on the Rights of the Child Report on the United Kingdom (*UN Doc*. CRC/C/15/add.34), 15 February 1995, recommended that 'serious consideration be given to raising the age of criminal responsibility throughout the areas of the United Kingdom.'

[48] *T* v. *United Kingdom*, *supra* n. 47, para. 72.

[49] Ibid., para. 84. For a more elaborate analysis of issues concerning the age of criminal responsibility, see chapters 5 to 7 of this book by Happold, McDiarmid and Veale.

tendance rights and judicious reporting). In *T* and *V*, the Court noted that special measures were taken to account for the age and level of understanding of the defendants, including an explanation of court procedure, a court visit before the trial started and hearing times shortened to reflect the hours of the school day. Although the dock was raised in an effort to enable the defendants to see what was going on, the Court suggested that this only added to the children's discomfort as they felt even more exposed to media and public scrutiny.[50] The Court held that it was insufficient that the applicants were represented by skilled and experienced lawyers. The applicants would have been unlikely to have felt free to consult with their lawyers inside the tense atmosphere of the courtroom and the children's immaturity and disturbed emotional state meant that they would have been unlikely to have been capable of giving clear instructions outside the court.

It was held that the applicants were unable to participate effectively in the proceedings and therefore the children had not had a fair trial, amounting to a violation of ECHR Article 6(1).[51] The Court emphasized safeguards required for the protection of children accused of serious crime. As mentioned above, children being prosecuted should be subjected to a 'modified procedure', the content of which would of course depend on all the circumstances of the case, including the age of the child, his maturity and his intellectual and emotional capacities.[52]

The Court has also looked at the compatibility with the Convention of the way in which the sentences of young people convicted of serious crimes are managed. The case of *Hussain* v. *United Kingdom*[53] concerned a child who was sentenced to be detained 'at Her Majesty's pleasure' (an indeterminate sentence) because of his young age (sixteen years old) at the time of the commission of murder. The Court held that, after the expiry of the 'tariff' period (that is the obligatory minimum part of the sentence), ECHR Article 5(4)[54] required that he was entitled to take legal proceedings to have the continuing legality of his detention periodically reviewed. The decisive ground for his detention was his dangerousness to society, and this would be subject to change because his personality and attitude would develop as he grew older. A failure to have regard to such developments would mean that young persons could be detained for the rest of their lives. The Court considered that such a prospect could raise questions under Article 3 of the Convention. The case of *Singh* v. *United Kingdom*[55] concerned a boy who was only fifteen years old

---

[50] *T* v. *United Kingdom, supra* n. 47, para. 86.

[51] Article 6(3)(b) requires everyone charged with a criminal offence to have 'adequate time and facilities for the preparation of his defence'.

[52] For further cases involving children in the criminal justice system, see *SC* v. *United Kingdom,* No. 60958/00, 15 June 2004, *Koniarska* v. *United Kingdom,* No. 33670/96, admissibility decision 12 October 2000, *DG* v. *Ireland,* No. 39474/98, 16 May 2002.

[53] *Hussain* v. *United Kingdom,* No. 21928/93, 21 February 1996.

[54] ECHR Article 5(4) states: 'Everyone who is deprived of his liberty by arrest or detention shall be entitled to take proceedings by which the lawfulness of his detention shall be decided speedily by a court and his release ordered if the detention is not lawful.'

[55] *Singh* v. *United Kingdom,* No. 23389/94, 21 February 1996.

when convicted of the murder of a 72-year-old woman. He too was sentenced to be detained at Her Majesty's pleasure. The Court again found a violation of ECHR Article 5(4) for similar reasons as in the *Hussain* case, including the fact that the age of the defendant was such as to warrant periodic review of the continuing legality of his detention as his personality and attitude would be subject to change as he matured.

In *T* and *V*, the Court held that, since the detention of the children at Her Majesty's pleasure was for an indefinite period of time, and since the tariff was set by the Home Secretary as opposed to an independent body, then the supervision required by ECHR Article 5(4) was not incorporated into the sentence.[56] Since the House of Lords had quashed the tariff set by the Home Secretary, no new tariff had been set, thus leaving the applicants without access to periodic review of any tariff at all. The Court therefore found a violation of Article 5(4) of the European Convention.

From the cases of *Singh* and *Hussain*, and the subsequent consideration of the issue in *T* and *V*, it is clear that the young age of defendants and their potential to develop are taken into consideration by the Court when deciding whether there has been a violation of the Convention. Applying this case law to the context of prosecuting a child accused of crimes in times of conflict would obviously require the adjudicating body to take account of the age, maturity and intellectual and emotional capacities of the child, in relation to the investigation of the case, the trial itself, the sentencing and the continuing legality of the detention. In the case of child soldiers, many such children have either been recruited or abducted, some even under the age of ten years old. Although they have often been party to 'unbelievable violence, often against their own families or communities, such children are exposed to the worst dangers and horrible suffering, both psychological and physical.'[57] Amnesty International states that these acts are often a result of manipulation and encouragement, acts that the children are often unable to comprehend themselves.

The children in *T* v. *United Kingdom* and *V* v. *United Kingdom* were neither abducted by adults nor manipulated into committing murder. When prosecuting child soldiers (including older teenagers) therefore, it is essential that such factors are considered. Not only do they affect a child's intellectual and emotional capacities, but also his or her ability to comprehend not only the crimes committed, but also the trial procedure. A modified trial procedure, over and above what is envisaged by the ECtHR in *T* and *V* would be even more necessary. These cases and future proceedings concerning children in criminal proceedings will demonstrate the extent to which the Convention will protect the rights of children accused of serious crime. From these cases it is clear that the protection afforded to children may be extensive, particularly under ECHR Article 6, and further evidenced by the willingness of the Court to refer to other international texts regarding children's rights.

---

[56] *T* v. *United Kingdom*, *supra* n. 47, para. 119.
[57] Amnesty International, <www.amnesty.org/pages/childsoldiers-index-eng>.

6.   Children as Victims of Crime

In most jurisdictions it is possible for the victims of criminal offences to be joined as civil parties to the criminal proceedings. A recent case before the European Court of Justice (the Court of the European Union and not the European Court of Human Rights) examined the provisions of the EU's Framework Decision 2001/220/JHA on the Standing of Victims in Criminal Proceedings. The European Court of Justice, relying on a number of decisions of the ECtHR,[58] held that the relevant articles of the Framework Decision must be interpreted as meaning that the national court must be able to authorise young children who claim to have been victims of maltreatment to give their testimony in accordance with arrangements allowing those children to be guaranteed an appropriate level of protection, for example outside the trial and before it takes place.[59]

7.   Concluding Remarks

This chapter has reviewed cases which have been or are pending before the European Court of Human Rights, and which directly concern children in conflict and post-conflict situations. In so doing it has attempted to point to some of the wider standard-setting decisions of the ECtHR. It is hoped that some of these will be particularly relevant in other jurisdictions looking for international standards to which reference can be made in dealing with conflict and post-conflict situations involving children.

---

[58] The ECtHR cases relied on by the European Court of Justice were: *PS* v. *Germany*, No. 33900/96, 20 December 2001; *SN* v. *Sweden*, No. 34209/96, 2 July 2002; *Rachdad* v. *France*, No. 71846/01, 13 November 2003; *Accardi and Others* v. *Italy*, No. 30598/02, 20 January 2005.

[59] European Court of Justice, Case C- 105/03 Pupino, judgment 16 June 2005.

Chapter 14
CONCLUDING OBSERVATIONS

Hans van Ginkel*

This book is unique and innovative in several aspects. It focuses attention upon different international accountability mechanisms for serious violations of the rights of children, primarily as committed in times of armed conflict and as addressed in post-war situations. This book contributes to the bridging of two concepts: the development of international criminal justice and the protection of the rights of children who are often among the more vulnerable in society. While both fields are developing rapidly, as yet they do not always converge sufficiently to form a coherent and adequate response to the many serious violations of the rights of the child in situations of armed conflict. There are still gaps in specifically regulated norms. For example, the deliberate spreading of HIV/AIDS is not yet generally criminalized. Also, often we do not know too well how to deal with violations of children's rights and/or human rights at large.

International law has developed significantly to reflect the growing concern of the international community with the increase in crimes against children. Especially throughout the last decade, horrific stories of mass murder, rape, torture, abduction, deprivation and other inhuman acts against children have compellingly called for further action. This book has gone beyond just condemning this kind of inhuman acts of violence against children and has discussed some concrete policy-relevant suggestions for addressing such acts and their impacts through various forms of international criminal accountability mechanisms.

In assessing what has been achieved one should realise that international law is a primitive instrument. It usually works slowly, if at all. For example, as early as in the aftermath of the Second World War there were many strong voices in favour of establishing an international criminal court. Provision for such a court was made in the 1948 Genocide Convention. Finally, 50 years later, such a court came into existence. Another illustrative example relates to the abolition of the death penalty for people under the age of eighteen. While the 1989 Convention of the Rights of the Child, in its Article 37(a), had already ruled out capital punishment for 'offences committed by persons below eighteen years of age', as William Schabas reminded us in chapter 2 of this book, it was only a full fifteen years later that the US Consti-

---

* Rector, United Nations University, Tokyo, Japan; Under-Secretary-General, United Nations.

K. Arts & V. Popovski (eds.), International Criminal Accountability and the Rights of Children
© 2006, Hague Academic Coalition, The Hague, The Netherlands and the Authors

tutional Court finally ruled (on 1 March 2005) that capital punishment for juvenile offenders is unconstitutional and must be abolished. This is the end of an era, and now all people in the world under the age of eighteen should enjoy a universal freedom from the death penalty.

1. Freedom from Prosecution at International Criminal Courts

There is an emerging consensus that children should be free from prosecution in international criminal courts, as has been referred to in several chapters of this book. The International Criminal Court (ICC) established the age of criminal accountability as eighteen.[1] On the other hand, the Special Court for Sierra Leone (SCSL) has a mandate to prosecute offenders as young as fifteen. In chapter 9 of this book, the founding SCSL Prosecutor David Crane explained persuasively why he declined to take actions against juvenile perpetrators, although some challenge his position. This is a complex issue indeed, in which several child rights aspects come together and may clash with one another, as was substantiated especially in chapters 8, 9 and 10 of this book. If we regard children as having agency and children as young as twelve to be fully capable participants in peace building and post-conflict reconstruction and development, as Saudamini Siegrist highlighted in her account of field experience in Sierra Leone,[2] then we could, and according to some we should, similarly expect children to be capable of behaving badly, up to the intentional commission of international crimes. The ultimate consequence could then also be to resort to criminal prosecution, even in international procedures when appropriate and possible.

Despite the controversies, the following consensus position seems to be emerging from the above debate. Children and young persons who have committed war crimes should be held accountable, but at the domestic and not at the international level. In most instances, alternatives to courtroom criminal procedures would be preferred, for example in truth and reconciliation forums or in substitute procedures or alternative ceremonies or rituals. International tribunals usually have limited time and money and therefore can only deal with the most serious crimes – such as the planning of genocide or command responsibility for crimes against humanity – and the most responsible perpetrators. Soldiers under the age of eighteen can execute criminal command orders from superior officers, but they are not those who orchestrate wars and atrocities.

2. Prohibition of the Recruitment and Enlisting of Child Soldiers

The necessity to unconditionally prohibit and criminalize the forceful recruitment of boys and girls under the age of eighteen as soldiers is an idea that strongly comes

---

[1] ICC Statute, Article 26.
[2] See chapter 4 of this book.

out of this book. The age for the lawful recruitment of soldiers currently differs from country to country with thresholds of eighteen, sixteen, fifteen and even fourteen. The ICC Statute declares as a war crime the enlistment of soldiers under fifteen, but this age threshold is still seen by many as being (far) too low. Recent conflicts have revealed horrific practices of kidnapping children and transforming them into killing machines, and have led to the idea (supported by the UN Security Council) for universal monitoring and reporting of all organizations that recruit children for war purposes.

3. TRANSITIONAL JUSTICE

On several occasions this book has touched on rehabilitation processes in post-conflict societies, linking the imperatives for justice, truth and peace. Accountability is essential to peace building. Moreover, this is not just an issue of the past. Impunity for past crimes undermines confidence in the rule of law and public life both now and in the future. Such impunity may directly contribute to the continuation or even the rise of, for example, sexual violence in the post-conflict society, as among others the case of Rwanda shows.[3] Impunity is not only a problem for particular societies in isolation from the rest of the world. It can have negative repercussions across borders as well. Impunity breeds grievance and revenge that can prolong or reignite violent conflict. The unstable societies involved can affect the security of neighbouring countries and of whole regions. Thus, in addition to the moral imperative of justice, there is a strong practical motive for investigating and prosecuting crimes of the past: it is in the interest of peace in the future. Indeed, there can be 'No peace, without justice'. The prosecution of the top political and military leaders of Nazi Germany and Japan after World War II helped the people in these countries to disengage from feelings of collective guilt and to reintegrate into peaceful societies. In fact, the different approaches to dealing with the past taken in both countries after the War contribute much to the very different levels to which reconciliation has progressed in respectively Europe and East Asia.

Some argue that the search for truth and accountability can be destabilizing and can prolong, even obstruct, the transition to peace. This argument, however, is becoming weaker and weaker. We are witnessing a global acceptance that accountability and justice are an essential part of peace building in post-conflict societies and also, ultimately, for relationships between societies. Justice and accountability

---

[3] C. Mibenge, 'The Post-Conflict Society and the Rights of the Child: a Case Study of Sexual Violence against Minors in Rwanda', unpublished paper presented at the 2005 Hague Academic Coalition Annual Conference in the Parallel Session *Crimes Against Children: The Gender Factor* at the Institute of Social Studies (The Hague, ISS 18 March 2005). See, e.g., also M.C. Omanyondo Ohambe (et al.), *Women's Bodies as a Battleground: Sexual Violence During the War in the Democratic Republic of Congo – South Kivu (1996-2003)* (Uvira, South Kivu, Democratic Republic of Congo, Réseau des Femmes pour un Développement Associatif (RFDA) 2004). At p. 28, the latter report describes Burundi and Rwanda as examples of situations in which post-conflict sexual violence 'has worsened due to the war'.

are integral to – and not in tension with – sustainable peace and stability. This is even more true when it comes to accountability for atrocities against children. In that context there can be no debate about sacrificing justice in the search for peace. The rights of children are absolutely paramount and there can never ever be impunity for severe abuses which involve children.

4.   ACCOUNTABILITY MECHANISMS: GLOBAL, REGIONAL, LOCAL, JUDICIAL
     AND NON-JUDICIAL, AT PRESENT AND IN THE FUTURE

Should justice be local? Should efforts be directed towards strengthening local, rather than global, capacity? This book has discussed the appropriateness of different accountability mechanisms and the benefits of interaction between them. In chapter 8, ICC Prosecutor Luis Moreno-Ocampo re-emphasized that the ICC is not simply a court to punish perpetrators – the Rome Statute is an international treaty for judicial co-operation. The ICC has established global standards and it also makes efforts to help national courts to deal with international crimes. Although one can agree that these international crimes are universal, the approaches to deal with them could be country-specific. Some relatives of victims may simply be satisfied when the truth is revealed, or by listening to the confessions of the perpetrators and allowing them to reintegrate into society. Somewhere else the demand for a fair judicial process and a proper sentence may prevail. Regardless of the choices made, all of these accountability mechanisms should be(come) more child-oriented and child-friendly. The need for proper protection and support for child victims and witnesses of crimes, in particular when involving sexual violence, has been raised in the large majority of the chapters in this book.

     The material presented in this book clearly establishes the value (actual and potential) of interaction, the sharing of experiences and lesson-learning between different international criminal accountability mechanisms. The Special Court for Sierra Leone learned from the experience of the *ad hoc* tribunals ICTY and ICTR. The International Criminal Court in turn is learning from the experience of the Special Court for Sierra Leone and the *ad hoc* tribunals.

5.   SUBJECTS FOR FURTHER DISCUSSION AND RESEARCH

This book has also generated challenging subjects for further reflection, discussion and research. Firstly, there is the concept of 'epistemic community', which in its substance goes back to the work of Grotius (Hugo de Groot). At present it is international in character, existing across borders and based on common values, shared among people from different continents, ethnicities and religions. Epistemic communities have the strength that they can systematically build their arguments, using arguments and counter-arguments, to come to well-reasoned, shared conclusions. Such communities, however, suffer also from the built-in weakness of becoming an 'in-crowd'. Only when they fight this weakness successfully, can they be effective and come to good results. The 'dialogue among civilizations', initiated by the former president of Iran, His Excellency Mohammad Khatami, has also illustrated that in our globalizing world, it is not easy to come to common values.

Secondly, the concept of human dignity and the preservation or protection thereof as an underlying value shared by all, underlies all the chapters of this book. But what is human dignity? There are many different approaches and the best approach might be to describe human dignity as the capacity of human beings to persist, to continue trying against all odds.[4] As long as there is hope, some light at the end of the tunnel, human beings will persevere. However, when this is taken away from them, when there is no hope, they are no longer motivated, which can be seen in every aspect ranging from clothing to meals, housing, personal hygiene, care for their children and other aspects. As William Schabas has argued: war is not in line with human dignity, as it takes away from so many people the hope of a better future, even the most basic human values.[5] Sheer survival in the most primitive forms becomes the most important driving force in all actions. War crimes loom just around the corner. As there cannot exist any so-called 'clean' wars, the beginning of a war must be regarded as the ultimate crime.

Thirdly, in post-conflict situations the priority must go to all strategies and actions that can contribute to a better common future for all. Efforts to establish who was (more) right, or (more) wrong, are much less important than efforts to open up a joint future, in particular for the younger generation. In doing this, we can profit from the remarkable resilience of (young) children in dire circumstances. Too often we stress the vulnerability of children, but it is time to stress their resilience as well. For instance, without such resilience, and maybe some luck, I would not have been in the position to write this chapter, but might instead have been buried in one of the Japanese concentration camps for women and children at Northern Sumatra, more than sixty years ago.

Fourthly and lastly, looking into the future it is crucial to stress the importance of prevention: the need to be prepared to act and to prevent the next case of genocide or crimes against children. There has been a huge gap in the implementation of international criminal law from Nuremberg and Tokyo in the late 1940s till The Hague (ICTY and ICC) and Arusha (ICTR) in the late 1990s. Now that the International Criminal Court is established and operational, the hope is that it will play a preventive and/or deterrent role. As Jenny Kuper has presented in chapter 12 of this book, the military training of armed forces is also gradually built up so as to avoid the commitment of future crimes. However, it is crucial to develop our thinking

---

[4] H. Van Ginkel, 'Enhancement of Human Dignity: On Alienation, Human Dignity, and Responsibility', in Japan Institute of International Affairs, *In Quest of Human Security*, 40th Anniversary Symposium, 11-12 December 1999 (Tokyo, 2001) pp. 36-43.
[5] B. Schabas, 'International Legal Impunity, Accountability and Children', address delivered at the plenary session of the 2005 Hague Academic Coalition Annual Conference, at the Institute of Social Studies (The Hague, ISS, 17 March 2005).

further and to carry out the research needed to inform our thinking adequately. Such research must help feed our creativity and imagination so as to prevent ourselves from being taken hostage by 'business-as-usual' approaches and an incremental development of thinking. Our future-oriented explorative reflections must have the courage to think the unthinkable and to imagine the unimaginable. This is the only way out of the vicious and perpetual spiral of unanticipated violence, inadequate responses thereto, further violence and so on.

INDEX